THE POETRY OF EDWIN MUIR

The Poetry of
Edwin Muir

The Field of Good and Ill

Elizabeth Huberman

New York OXFORD UNIVERSITY PRESS 1971

For one EH and five JH's

Acknowledgments

In preparing this study of Edwin Muir, I have of course taken advantage of the work of previous critics, and I am deeply grateful for the insights and the clues many of them have provided. I am particularly grateful, as all students of Muir must be, to Professor Peter Butter, whose *Edwin Muir: Man and Poet* is an invaluable source of information about aspects of the poet's life which do not appear in his own *An Autobiography*. Still another invaluable key to Muir's outer and inner life is Mrs. Willa Muir's book about their years together, *Belonging;* and I am further indebted to Mrs. Muir for an afternoon of her time when her wit and her gift for story-telling made those years come alive again for me. Through Mrs. Muir, I was led on to George Mackay Brown, a former student as well as a friend of Muir's, and he too was kind enough to share his understanding of the poet with me.

I want also to thank my friend, Laura Capling, for her patience and skill in typing an illegible manuscript. But most of all, I thank my husband, Professor Edward Huberman, for his unfailing assistance and encouragement, and Professor M. L. Rosenthal for his kind but never less than exacting guidance. Where this book falls short, the fault is not that of any of my mentors, but mine alone.

E.H.

Contents

THE POETRY OF EDWIN MUIR

Introduction

My purpose in this study of the poetry of Edwin Muir is to explore, through analysis of the most important poems in each of Muir's volumes, the major themes of his poetry, the directions in which these themes have developed, and the technical resources through which they have been patterned and expressed. Since Muir himself defined the province of poetry as that "vast area of life which science leaves in its original mystery," [1] and since this is the area which his own poetry, at its best, naturally inhabits, it is not possible—nor would it be desirable—to pinpoint the place of every poem on any clear chart. But it is possible, and this is what I have attempted, to find in his work many motifs which were implicit from the very beginning and which continue over the years. Often shifting in form, often joining together and reinforcing each other, they finally result, in his last volume, *One Foot in Eden*, in a coherent whole.

In this process still other significant conclusions about Muir as a poet necessarily emerge: the particular poetic tradition in which he belongs; those poets of the past and of the present with whom his relationship is closest; and above all, his own stature as a poet, both as contemporary critics have measured it and as his own poems reveal it. But since many of these conclusions are scattered, or subordinated to the discussion of individual poems, I shall try to summarize some of them here.

For a just estimate of Muir's stature as a poet, as it happens, there is no better formula than Muir's own assessment of the medieval poet, Robert Henryson. In his *Essays on Literature and Society* Muir said of Henryson that in him were embodied "the fundamental seriousness, humanity, and strength of the Scottish imagination"; [2] and this is a judgment that may equally well be applied to Muir as a poet of the twentieth century. But that is not all. There is present in his work another quality which equally claims attention, which even more emphatically asserts his title to "remain," as T. S. Eliot said, "among those poets who have added glory to the English language"; [3] a quality found indeed in Henryson's work and in that of every true poet, but found in exceptional degree in Muir's; and that is the element of mystery. For as we have seen, the true domain of poetry according to Muir was that "vast area of life" which retains its mystery despite the invasions of science; and in Muir's work the seriousness, the strength, the humanity, are all irradiated by the presence of this mystery, intangible but unmistakable, deriving from the very nature of poetry as he understood it.

How essentially serious Muir's poetry has always been, the themes he consistently made his own sufficiently prove. They are the traditional themes of the great poets, from Homer's time to the present: the struggle between good and evil in the individual, in society, in the universe; the loss of innocence and the quest for its recovery; the nature of human destiny; the destructiveness of time; the enduring joy and power of love. At the same time, Muir has had the strength to handle this traditional material in his own way, on his own terms. Whether he borrows the figures and myths in which he dramatizes his themes from Homer and Sophocles, the Bible and Milton, or finds them in contemporary events and in his own dreams, he always recasts both borrowings and findings to fit his particular vision, to carry his particular signature. And he has had the still greater strength to bear the consequences of his vision. When it reveals, as so often in his earlier volumes, nothing but futility and frustration, madness and despair, he never looks for a simple escape, nor evades the reality which his own experience so painfully proved, that life is ruled by an "iron law," that cruelty and betrayal undermine all hope of safety and negate all faith. He simply grapples with this undeniable reality until, like Lawrence, he "comes through," and on the "far side of despair" finds the possibility of rebirth.

In the theme of rebirth, as Muir slowly discovers it, develops it, and acts it out, moreover, he finds the full scope of his humanity. For although most of *First Poems* are self-centered and subjective; although the "Lost Land" of childhood he mourns there is strictly his own childhood, and the regeneration he experiences in "Ballad of Rebirth" and "Ballad of Eternal Life" is so intimately connected with the obscure imagery of his own dreams that its meaning was not fully clear even to him, Muir gradually turns outward, in succeeding volumes, to a greater objectivity and to a concern with all men. The lost wanderers in *Variations on a Time Theme* are contemporary man as well as Muir; in *Journeys and Places*, Tristram and Hölderlin, as well as the mad old man in "Troy" and the sleeping figure in "The Enchanted Knight" are objective characters who represent Muir only as they represent every man; and when in *The Narrow Place* Muir descends into the deepening sadness of "The Wayside Station," the horror of "Then," and the very nadir of darkness and betrayal in "The Gate," it is again as representative man, not Muir, that he descends. Muir's own experience is discernible still in "The Gate," to be sure, but it is crystallized, objectified, into a universal metaphor. The fortress of adult life that briefly guards childhood security opens for all of us, in the course of time, the very door that we would prefer not to enter: the door to the insecurity, the disillusion, the corruption of adulthood. But having taken us with him to this bottom of the pit, this extremity of depression, Muir takes us with him too when he climbs upward again. The restoration of original harmony which he imagines in "The Ring" is, like the initiation into disenchantment of "The Gate," an objective as well as subjective image.

The question is, on what is this restoration of harmony based? How, in spite of his previous insistence on the prevalence of evil, and his continuing recognition of that prevalence in the twentieth century world with its barbaric violence and cruelty, can Muir imagine even the possibility of any kind of reconciliation? Muir's answer indicates the breadth of his humanity. For Muir's ultimate faith in an abiding, inextinguishable principle of good, underlying and including all violence and cruelty, is basically an acceptance of paradox. In the divided world of time, that is, the interaction of opposites is itself a principle of unity. Good and evil, light and dark, the king on his throne and the rebel in the streets, all work together in involuntary cooperation, for Muir, to form a single whole, "in deep confederacy far from the air"; and in this meeting and merging of contraries, this "Peace of the humming looms/ Weaving from east to west," nothing is excluded. Eve, the world's first sinner, sleeps there in "love and grief," with Adam in her protecting arms. Flowers never known in Eden, "Blossoms of grief and charity," bloom in and bless "these darkened fields" of earth. Even Judas, the archetype of all betrayers, in "The Transfiguration" is finally forgiven. Evil still persists; Muir never overlooks it, nor ceases to struggle against it. But the struggle itself makes the harmony, and in this struggle everything that exists plays a part. Everything, if only by functioning as opposition, contributes to the final resolution and shares in Muir's compassion.

For anyone who would demand a rational explanation of such a reconciliation of irreconcilables, there is of course no answer. This is a vision that can be affirmed or denied, but not explained. It is a manifestation of that element of mystery which, as we have said, pervades Muir's work and is at once a difficulty for the critic and a source of power for the poems. Rooted in dreams and ancestral memories as so many of them are, or in moments of waking insight when the invisible is visible for a moment, the timeless caught for a perceptible instant in time, these poems often baffle our clumsy methods of analysis, yield little to investigation of sources and influences. The visions they present, like those in Blake's poems, must be taken as given; and although the critic may discuss the relationship of one vision to another, or the technical success with which this or that motif is rendered, he cannot quarrel with the essential *donnée*, the vision itself. That springs from the "vast area of life" where the "original mystery" remains intact; and the critic can only rejoice that he is witnessing fresh evidence of the persistence, even today, of this ancient heritage of magic and wonder.

If on the one hand, however, this visionary quality in Muir's poetry makes explication difficult, on the other it helps to determine his place in the company of Scottish, English, and European poets—he was a European as much as a Scottish poet, and perhaps more European than English—and to identify those poets with whom he had the closest affinities. The poetry that he was schooled in as a child, for example, the poetry that stamped its uncompromising seriousness on his view of life and made a short, compressed line and direct, terse speech instinctive for his tongue, was of course the poetry of the Scottish ballad makers; and many of the Scottish ballads are simply, naturally visionary. They are infused with an awareness of some other world, where the birch grows fair on the banks of Paradise. The poetry that he schooled himself in, furthermore, once he realized that poetry was his vocation, and once he gained the leisure to read widely, inevitably covered a much wider range. But again those poets who were closest to him had a similar sense of some other dimension of existence. The medieval and early Renaissance Scottish poets whom he so much admired because their work fused passion with reflection had this sense—had it almost unconsciously, as the ballad-makers had it. It was this sense, more self-consciously re-created, in such English poets as Wordsworth, Traherne, and Vaughan, that first drew Muir to them. They corroborated his own spontaneous perception of the "clouds of glory" attending childhood, the "bright shoots of everlastingness" still discernible in mortal flesh and in everyday life, just as still later Donne, Milton, Blake, Keats, Hopkins, Yeats, and Eliot—when Muir at last came to appreciate Eliot—all reinforced his original intuition that in some way the timeless intersects with time,

7

that behind the trivialities which crowd our lives there is a "shadow of a magnitude."

But because Muir was living more abroad than at home in the early years of his life as a poet, it was writers in other languages than English, writers then little known to the English-speaking public, whose influence he undoubtedly felt most strongly at this critical period. It was writers like Hölderlin, Rilke, and Kafka, whose awareness of the irreducible mystery of life most immediately coincided with and accentuated his own. For in Hölderlin's work, above all in the great poem of his madness, *Patmos*, Muir found the same mystery he himself recognized, a "mystery" which was "not a thing to be explained, but an indefeasible presence." [4] In Rilke, although he did not fully agree with the conception of *"einsehen,"* he did find evidence of inward vision that resembled and perhaps sharpened his own. And, of course, in Kafka he found an endless source of insight into what he too acknowledged as the central enigma, the paradox at the core of existence: on the one hand the Castle, the eternal, divine law, and on the other, the roads determined by temporal, human law, which seem to lead to the Castle but which never reach it. How can a man make his way to that Castle, then, when "it is enveloped in a mystery different from the ordinary mystery of human life, and he does not know the law of that mystery"? [5] To discover the answer to this question became one of Muir's purposes as a poet, and his years of translating Kafka's ingenious variations on the question must surely not only have enlarged his understanding of all its dimensions, but must also have helped to point the direction in which the answer, for Muir at least, finally lay.

This relationship between Muir and the visionary tradition, whether British or European, is, of course, one of the points critics of Muir have frequently commented on. John Holloway, for example, likens Muir's work not only to that of Kafka, who presents the two "icons" of Castle and Court as the "two basic realities which underlie every complexity of surface appearance," but also to that of such post-Impressionist painters as Beckmann, who tried to find "the bridge that leads from the visible to the invisible," and Klee, whose slogan was "from the model to the archetype." [6] Thomas Merton, limiting the range of his comparisons to poets only, claims that Muir is not merely a "metaphysical poet," as he has so often been called, but something much greater, a "poet of metaphysics," like Blake, Wordsworth, Coleridge, and Rilke, [7] while Kimon Friar, in a review of Muir's first *Collected Poems*, strikes a still higher note of praise. "Only Eliot in *Four Quartets* and Yeats in his later poems have touched upon similar resolutions of time in ultimate peace and joy," Friar maintains; and Muir, "who echoes both his masters at times, must take his place among those to whom total vision has been granted, to whom tragedy has been wrought to its uttermost and purified by exaltation and joy." [8]

Without going as far as Friar, most of those critics who admire Muir's work are in general agreement that it is his imaginative power which above all distinguishes his poetry. For J. C. Hall, the editor of that first *Collected Poems*, for instance, the "transfiguring power" of Muir's imagination "gives his poetry its unique significance." [9] Peter H. Butter, author of the single full-length study of Muir's life and poetry, *Edwin Muir: Man and Poet*, and of the shorter Evergreen Pilot Book survey, *Edwin Muir*, says in the latter that his confidence in Muir's position as a "poet of major importance" is based on "the depth and comprehensiveness of the vision which his poems collectively contain"; [10] and Kathleen Raine, in one of her many warm appreciations of Muir, asserts that a "thrice-distilled imaginative quality distinguishes nearly all his poems." [11] Even those critics, furthermore, who have preferred to study some particular aspect of Muir's poetry, as Daniel Hoffman in *Barbarous Knowledge* studies Muir's use of myth, or as J. R. Watson, in an article in the *Critical Quarterly* discusses his treatment of the problem of evil—even these have generally conceded the visionary force of his imagination. "Muir plumbs the unconscious life," remarks Hoffman, for example, "to bring up archetypes and symbols" in the "nets of his language." [12]

Not all critics agree, however, in admiring Muir's poetry.

9

For them the insight into the unconscious and the transfiguring vision are simply not there. They complain instead, in a number of cases, of monotony in Muir's themes from volume to volume; but the major dissenters concentrate on what they claim is a monotony of voice. Jon Silkin, reviewing *One Foot in Eden* in *Poetry*, demurs at the "rather narrow" tonal range of this volume of verse, and the "unadventurous" metrical forms. [13] Graham Hough, although sympathetic to Muir's "sincere following of his own inner direction," feels that he lacks a poet's necessary measure of "the assertive and the histrionic." [14] In the *Pelican Guide to English Literature, 7: The Modern Age*, Charles Tomlinson too sees a "lack" in Muir; his poems "lack . . . that linguistic vigour without which true poetry cannot exist"; [15] while in the *Yale Review* Reed Whittemore reaches the extreme of denunciation in his review of the *Collected Poems, 1921-1951*. Muir's verse, according to Whittemore, "has a nineteenth century iambic (mostly) thud to it. His manner is high and fulsome, being engendered by the big adjectives and corny figures of old pages." [16]

Thus the question is, where between these two poles of praise and condemnation, between Friar's claim that Muir was one to whom "total vision" had been granted, and Whittemore's refusal to see anything but "corny figures of old pages" or to hear anything but an "iambic thud," does the truth lie? What is a reasonable judgment about Muir's accomplishment as a poet and his place in the hierarchy of contemporary poetry? As I indicated earlier in this introduction, it is my contention, which I hope to support in the following chapters, that Muir's accomplishment is a major one, that his work is serious, strong, humane, and above all informed with that mysterious quality of imaginative vision which is the final and essential mark of true poetry. But to make good my claims, to strike the right balance between opposing critical views, it will be necessary to take a closer look at his poems than has perhaps been involved in some of these previous judgments.

As Robin Fulton very wisely comments in an essay on "The Reputation of Edwin Muir" in the *Glasgow Review*, the large majority of these judgments, particularly those published in various periodicals immediately after Muir's death in 1959, are "all very much alike." Because Muir's work was really very little known at that time, these articles "had the air of introducing a new poet rather than paying tribute to a master. Almost to a man the writers confined themselves to summarizing the events of Muir's early life (admirably told by Muir himself twenty years previously) and to giving a cursory glance at those aspects of his verse which must be quite obvious to anyone merely dipping into it." No one, Fulton continues, except for Peter Butter in his short 1962 study of Muir (and, we can now add, his 1967 combined biography and critique, *Edwin Muir: Man and Poet*), has done what clearly must be done to make even a beginning of an assessment of Muir. No one has "seemed able or willing to look at his work steadily and intelligently"; and yet only through such close study of his poems is there any possibility of true evaluation. The task, as we have said, is not easy; "commenting on a Muir poem," indeed, Fulton admits, is "notoriously difficult";[17] even so, this is the method which must be employed and by which I have tried to proceed. By going directly to the poetry itself, by subjecting the major poems in Muir's work, viewed in chronological order, to close analysis and detailed explication, I have hoped to uncover at least some of the richness which more general surveys may have overlooked, and to suggest some of the patterns which have developed in his themes and in his treatment of them over the years.

As I have done this, I have been well aware that Muir's own ghost might be frowning over my shoulder. Speaking of precisely this method of close analysis, Muir wrote in *The Estate of Poetry*, "I confess that this kind of criticism, so thorough and so mistaken, seems to me of very little use to any reader, and that for myself it gives me a faint touch of claustrophobia, the feeling that I am being confined in a narrow place with the poem and the critic, and that I shall not get away until all three of us are exhausted." [18] To this I can only answer that what I am attempting is undertaken in full recognition both of my own limitations and of the limitations of this particular method. But if in more general surveys of his work something is lacking, if his poems are of the kind that will not yield their full meaning except to close scrutiny—and perhaps not even then—what remains except to make the attempt and to ask the ghost for forgiveness?

Furthermore, in spite of all disadvantages and all disapprobation, it seems to me that this close concentration on individual poems, this effort to make the poems unlock themselves, has indeed resulted in certain significant conclusions about Muir's work as a whole. Its strength, its seriousness, its humanity emerge beyond question from the cumulative weight of these successive explications; and even the visionary power, the quality of ultimate mystery, although I may sometimes, inadvertently, have violated its sanctity, not only survives my prying but appears more unmistakably than ever in the miraculous organization, the enormous resonance, that detailed analysis of the poems often reveals. In these analyses, too, the progressive development of Muir's technical skill becomes clear: the change from an initial awkwardness to a final mastery, not indeed of a dazzling repertory of verbal styles and tricks, but of a simple, powerful speech and a quiet music. And clearest of all, perhaps, there develops from volume to volume a design into which all his various themes at last converge: the generation of light from darkness—rebirth. And thus finally Muir is able, like Yeats, to hold "reality and justice," time and eternity, good and evil, in a "single thought"; in the simultaneous opposition and attraction of paradox.

I

*"My childhood all a myth
Enacted in a distant isle."*

On the red stone wall of St. Magnus Cathedral in the far Orkney Islands is a simple plaque which reads: "Edwin Muir, Poet: 1887-1959." Orkney was Edwin Muir's home. He was born there and lived there for the first fourteen years of his life; and however far he later traveled, however long he remained away, he was always drawn back there. Here were, for him, the "waters" and the "watering place" where Robert Frost says a man must come to "Drink and be whole again beyond confusion." The landscape, the history, the social and economic structure of this "distant isle," where what Muir himself called the "myth" of his childhood was "enacted," stamped indelibly on his mind certain patterns against which all his experiences of succeeding years were measured. From those patterns, furthermore, came much of the special vision and many of the special themes which give Muir's poetry its distinctive character: at once simple and complex; strange and haunting, yet familiar and contemporary.

No poet born and raised in such a place could fail to show the mark of his origin in his poetry; and Muir's *Autobiography*—a marvelously sensitive, inward-directed account of his life, which all readers of his poetry should be familiar with—

establishes beyond doubt how deeply the stamp of the Orkneys is set on all his work. For although the chapters which
describe his early childhood on the little green island of Wyre
only occasionally indicate any express connection between his
life and his poems, it is impossible to follow this simple story of
growing up in a tiny agricultural community, isolated from
the mainstream of world events yet rich in its own culture and
history, without realizing that here is the source of many of
those poems, the measure of many others. Here, in the flesh, is
the archetypal fable of human life which Muir in later years
continually tried to recover, to find beneath the confused hap-
penings of history that ordinarily hide it from our sight. For
history, Muir came to believe, is merely the passing, changing
story; it is the underlying fable that endures. Thus he called
the first version of his autobiography, published in 1940, *The
Story and the Fable*; and it was his Orkney boyhood that
taught him to recognize the fable.

Small wonder. In the Orkney Muir remembered, as both
earlier and later versions of the autobiography emphasize, the
fable was visible and vital to everyone. Everyone accepted the
supernatural as natural; everyone as a matter of course believed
in witches and fairies, and mermaids were known to have held
conversations with local farmers. "The Orkney I was born into
was a place where there was no great distinction between the
ordinary and the fabulous," Muir wrote; "the lives of living
men turned into legend." [1] But it was not merely this merging
of life with legend that made Orkney fabulous. Much more,
Muir's recollections suggest, it was the essential harmony and
unity of the whole island world; and above all, for Muir at
least, it was the essential harmony and unity of his own family
life.

For the various members of Muir's immediate family: his
gentle father James, his mother, their four sons and two
daughters, a rather odd Aunt Maggie and an engaging, scan-
dalous cousin Sutherland, were all bound together in a
spontaneous system of co-operation, a natural accord, that not
only provided Edwin, the youngest child, with an ideally
warm and stable environment to grow up in, but also furnished

him with a lasting image of an ideal human society. It was this image, for instance, which was the focal point of the Edenic "original vision of the world" that he had as a child, when "the earth, the houses on the earth, and the life of every human being" seemed "related to the sky overarching them; as if the sky fitted the earth and the earth the sky" (33). And it was this image, years later, which together with Lear's and Bruce's still unbroken kingdoms, unquestionably served as the prototype of that idyllic Golden Age society he imagined in "The Ring," [2] since the people of that society, the poem states specifically, were "a family," and the "old kind-hearted king" was their "foster-father." Here, clearly, were the Muirs transmuted into myth, and their "life" in the poem was, significantly, "a fable."

Not that the Muirs were at all aware of acting out a fable. Far from it. They simply shared as a matter of course in the work of running the Bu, the ninety-five-acre farm that James Muir rented on Wyre. It was a hard life, much harder than the lives of most Orkney farmers today; the landlord was exacting; and meeting his terms each year meant a constant struggle which finally defeated the Muirs. They had to give up the Bu and move to a far less comfortable and productive farm on Mainland island, near Kirkwall. But while they were on Wyre, even though their life was hard, it was also good. If they labored, they labored side by side in love and trust, and there were perhaps as many pleasures as chores for them to share.

Some of the most essential rituals of the farm, for example— planting and harvesting, letting the cows out of the barn in the spring, bringing in the bull to serve the cows, even slaughtering the pig—were exciting in a way that was sometimes terrifying but more often delightful. Then there were quieter, more comfortable pleasures in the rituals of the household: the meals of porridge and milk, or of herring and potatoes, when everyone took turns helping himself from the central dish; or the long winter evenings in the kitchen, when the whole family played draughts (Sutherland shamelessly cheating), or listened to each other playing the fiddle or the melodeon, or sang songs ranging from traditional ballads to revivalist hymns and relatively recent Cockney airs. But happiest of all, for Edwin at least, were the Sunday nights when his father prayed or read from the Bible while the rest of the group knelt around him on the floor. For then, more than at any other time, as Muir remembered, "there was . . . that feeling of complete security and union among us" (26), which would come to signify for him the presence of the fable. And although the listening child could have no understanding of the meaning this ceremony would hold for him in the future, he nevertheless derived a special joy from hearing his father repeat, week after week, certain words of St. Paul's which the grown man would later come to comprehend: "an house not made with hands, eternal in the heavens."

Nor was this sense of security and union limited to those within Muir's family group. Among all the neighbors on Wyre, a similar instinctive, friendly co-operation prevailed. Whenever a man needed help with a special job, such as rebuilding his barn, or putting a ring in a bull's nose, the other farmers and their sons were always on hand to do what had to be done. These men, Muir commented, "did not know ambition and the petty torments of ambition; they did not know what competition was, though they lived at the end of Queen Victoria's reign; they helped one another with their work when help was required, following the old usage; they had a culture made up of legend, folk-song, and the poetry and prose of the Bible; they had customs which sanctioned their instinctive feelings for the earth; their life was an order, and a good order" (63), and it reinforced the sense of order already present among the Muirs. The whole world lay beyond Wyre, but Wyre was a sufficient world for those who lived on it, and it was a harmonious world. "The sky fitted the earth" there, and "the earth the sky."

Even the animals were included in this universal harmony, since they lived in intimate relationship with the men whom they helped with their labor and fed with their flesh. In taking their guiltless lives, as Muir recognized in his *Autobiography*, the men, of course, became guilty; but that guilt had long ago, before history, been absolved through the ritual by which those lives were taken, a ritual "in which were united the ideas of necessity and guilt, turning the killing into a mystery" (48). The farmers of Orkney still evoked that mystery in the ceremonial gravity which attended the occasional slaughter of pig or sheep; and in the long intervals between, they tended pigs and sheep, cattle, horses, and hens with a concern that recognized the natural human dependence on the animal world. "For at the heart of human civilization," Muir recognized as well, "is the byre, the barn, and the midden" (36); and although the connection is obscured today, in a society of supermarkets and frozen beef dinners, mechanized farms, and chemical fertilizers, it nevertheless remains, vital and essential as ever. When we overlook it, we overlook a part of our history and our selves, and we do it at our peril, as we are at last learning. When we are aware of it, we are more fully ourselves for the simple reason that we understand our place. We are not isolated; we belong in a context; and this Muir instinctively realized, by virtue of his growing up on a small farm in a small community, where the original inter-relationships between man and man, man and animal, and man and the earth, the sea, and the seasons, were still plain.

Abiding and important as this sense of order and harmony in the universe was to Muir, however, it remained flawless for only a very short time. Even for a child fortunate enough to possess such an "original vision of the world," as Muir acknowledged, there "comes a moment (the moment at which childhood passes into boyhood or girlhood) when this image is broken and contradiction enters life. It is a phase of emotional and mental strain, and it brings with it a sense of guilt" (33). The death of a neighbor who had been kind to him, a period of sickness he suffered himself, these perhaps prompted in Muir that sense of guilt, of dissonance in the primal harmony which he began to feel at about the age of seven, but eventually the mere passage of time, which changes child into boy and boy into man, would have acquainted him as distressingly with the existence of evil. For evil, Muir came to know, lies in wait from the beginning, so that before the child experiences it, he divines it. "In a child's mind," Muir wrote, "there is at moments a divination of a hidden tragedy taking place around him, that tragedy being the life which he will not live for some years still, though it is there, invisible to him, already" (33). And soon enough he lives what he has foreseen, whatever the actual event that breaks the early Edenic image.

But significantly, for Muir as a child, this normal transition from innocence to experience was abnormally unsettling. Possibly because the innocence he had enjoyed was closer than usual to perfection, the guilt he suddenly inherited was more than usually acute and terrifying. Trying to account for the extraordinary intensity of his feelings at that time, Muir himself suggested that "perhaps at the root . . . was the obsession which all young children have with sex, their brooding curiosity, natural in itself, but coloured with guilt by the thoughts of their elders" (35); and the discovery of sex must of course have contributed to his new sense of sin. Where all children discover sex and sin however, very few react as Muir did, who suffered such agonies of guilt because of a purely imaginary transgression against his father's command not to touch a bag of poisonous sheep dip, that at last he found himself shut off from everyone else, in a private world of fear: "a sort of parallel world divided by an endless, unbreakable sheet of glass from the actual world" (34). Eventually, within a few months, the barrier dissolved; the "actual world appeared again in twisted gleams, as through running glass"; the "frenzied" fear went away; but the world his eyes now saw "was a different world from . . . his first childish one, which never returned again" (35), nor did his extreme sensitivity to evidence that we live on a fallen planet ever completely leave him.

That the world he now lived in was different from his childish one, his father's move from Wyre to a farm called Garth on Mainland, near Kirkwall, unhappily persuaded him. For this was a farm that mercilessly absorbed all of the family's labor and gave little in return but exhaustion, sickness, and the breaching of family unity. He was persuaded, too, by his miserable experience at school, both on Wyre and in Kirkwall. School for him was an airless prison; and although he found some classes at the Kirkwall Burgh School that he enjoyed, the idea of school remained terrifying. He could never, even years later, see "with an untroubled eye" (70) the red towers of St. Magnus Cathedral, which now contains that plaque in his memory, but which he remembered as a landmark on his daily journey from Garth to school. At the same time, there were other disturbing symptoms of a change from the serenity and order he had first known. Puberty brought confusion, fears, and a diffuse sense of guilt. Friendships with other boys resulted in rough play that turned friendship into shame and hatred. Searching for relief from these guilt feelings, the young Edwin underwent a "conversion" during one of the island's periodic religious revivals; but even at the moment of intensest exaltation, he was obscurely aware of the spurious quality of the experience. Such a salvation could not restore his original vision.

It was when he was fourteen and his father decided to leave Orkney for Glasgow, however, that Muir's childhood world was totally shattered. For Glasgow proved to be the exact antithesis of Wyre. Where Wyre had offered, at least to Edwin's eyes, a far more idyllic life pattern than modern society customarily provides, Glasgow presented no pattern at all, but a squalid, brutal chaos. On Wyre, James Muir and his children had a place in a whole. They were respected. Their labor and their friendship counted. In Glasgow, they had no place, no value, no dignity. The sons, even fourteen-year-old Edwin, managed to find jobs and support their parents on the edge of respectability. But the meaning had gone out of existence for all of them, and in the background was always the threat of Glasgow's particularly sordid slums, into which the loss of steady income could quickly catapult the entire family. More dangerous still, because this was a menace that materialized, as the drop into the slums did not, was the constant threat of illness and death. Within five years after the Muirs' arrival in Glasgow, father and mother and two sons were dead. The others, since they were grown by now, went their separate ways, spun off from the vital family center that in Wyre had held them together. The unity and security of those Orkney years were destroyed, and there seemed no possibility, in industrial Glasgow, which to Muir seemed hopelessly mean-spirited and ugly, of finding any new source of security. In fact, Edwin concluded, there was no security, anywhere. What had happened to his family, what he saw every day around him as he walked through the slum streets on his way to work as a clerk in one office or another, proved to him "that life was ruled by an iron law" (103). Not only was his childhood in Orkney irretrievably gone; he denied now all that it had meant.

He denied it, of course, because only by denying it could he survive its loss. His childhood predisposition to acute reaction in the presence of evil remained with him still and threatened, now that his acquaintance with evil was so much more intimate and immediate, to affect him more harmfully than before. Thus when he now suffered a series of physical ailments, these ailments were clearly a phase of that tendency to acute reaction. Just as clearly, on the other hand, they were a defense mechanism against a still greater danger posed by that same tendency—the danger of mental illness. And when his physical health returned, because he was still young—not yet twenty—and essentially tough, if not robust, the only way he could continue to defend his mental health was by refusing to contemplate the agony he had just endured; by deliberately "turning away from death." He "climbed out of those years" of disillusion and bereavement at a terrible cost. "For a long time," as he later confessed, he "did not dare to look back into them" (110). Nor did he dare to look back at Wyre. To maintain what proved to be a highly precarious mental balance, in other words, he canceled as completely as he could both the order and security he had known in Orkney and the later disorder and sorrow that had destroyed them. Because his entire past was unbearable, he tried to throw it all away.

Instead, he looked to the future. He became an even more ardent convert to Socialism that he had ever been, in Orkney, to Jesus. He read "nothing but books pointing towards the future: Shaw, Ibsen, Whitman, Edward Carpenter" (116). When he became enchanted with Heine, it was the "lyrical faith in the future" which he detected behind the "wit and irreverence and charm" that satisfied him most. When Heine no longer

of his enclosure; before he could escape from what, in a poem written years later he called "The Labyrinth," an endless maze that shut him off from the green and living world.

Yet at the same time that his alienation was intensifying so alarmingly, some of the factors that would eventually restore his emotional stability were already at work. For one thing, despite his sense of estrangement, Muir was actually acquiring more and more friends with whom he had political, literary, and intellectual interests in common. Stimulated by this companionship, and driven by his own need for knowledge, he was reading more and more widely, in every field from political theory to French literature (he had taught himself French). What is more, he was beginning to write for *The New Age*. At twenty-six he had sent some Heine-like "lonely, ironic, slightly corpse-like poems" (146) to Orage, who had printed them. Then several years later, still in his Nietzsche phase, he produced what he himself later described as "a series of short notes or aphorisms" in which he "generalized in excited ignorance on creative love and the difference between it and pity," which he "unhesitatingly condemned" (151); and these aphorisms, too, were printed in *The New Age* as a weekly column under the title, "We Moderns." Later published as a book, they excited some of *The New Age* readers because they communicated Muir's own excitement with the world of ideas and words; and they generated considerable romantic interest among some of his lady admirers, as Mrs. Willa Muir tells us in *Belonging*, the memoir of her life with Edwin. But their chief virtue lay in the fact that they drained away most of Muir's Nietzschean pretensions. "The perpetration of the book left . . . [him] naked," he acknowledged later, and he "was the better for it" (151). "After being unhappy for a long time without realizing it, . . .[he] was now genuinely unhappy"; and although he "did not know it," there was now "a possibility of amendment."

Another event of incalculable importance to his lifelong well-being may be linked to the publication of *We Moderns*. One of the ladies impressed by the book invited Muir to a social gathering to which she had also invited a brilliant young graduate of St. Andrews University, Willa Anderson. Willa and Edwin, she thought, would provide entertaining literary conversation by discussing the book. But instead, Willa and Edwin discovered that they both came from the Northern Isles—Willa was a Shetlander—, and they had a delightful non-literary evening exchanging bits of folklore and folk speech and beginning to fall in love. In the spring of 1919, less than a year after they first met, they were married; and thirty-five years later, in *An Autobiography*, Muir still spoke of that marriage as "the most fortunate event" (154) in his life. Willa's unfailing vitality and wit and her unshakable stability helped to restore for him, little by little, that sense of order and equilibrium, of security and love, which the years in Glasgow had destroyed. She gave him back, as he wrote in one of his love poems, written over twenty years after their marriage, "the first good world, the blossom, the blowing seed." She was "a fountain in a waste,/ A well of water in a country dry," [3] and the water he drew from that well was the water of new life.

It must be recognized, however, that Willa did not perform this miracle altogether unaided. Two further developments concurred in working the wonder. Edwin, as well as Willa, had a certain reckless courage; and relying on little else, the two of them, after their marriage, "went down to London without a job between . . . [them], with very little money, and with hopes over which . . . [their] sensible friends shook their heads" (154). Without Willa's encouragement, Muir admitted, he would never "have taken the plunge," he was "still paralysed" by his "inward conflict." But the important point is that he did take this enormous risk; he cut all the ties with the old Glasgow life, where he was doomed forever to be an underpaid clerk with a taste for writing, but where he was sure at least of his daily bread; and at the rather advanced age of thirty-two he set out to seek his fortune in the strange world of literary London. He might, and he did, have to resort to clerking again just to stay alive—his first job in London was wrapping parcels from morning to night—but he was no longer primarily an office worker. He had shifted the emphasis of his life, at least in his own mind. He had chosen at last the career to which his instincts had all along been leading him. He was a writer.

As a writer who had already published in *The New Age*, moreover, Muir naturally visited *The New Age* offices in London, and before long Orage offered to take him on as an assistant. Additional writing assignments followed fast: he became drama critic for *The Scotsman*, did occasional reviewing for *The Athenaeum*, which John Middleton Murry was then editing, until it seemed indeed that the choice he had made was the right one. Yet despite the joy of doing the work for which he was fitted, and despite the happiness of his life with Willa, the deep emotional trouble which dated from his first disastrous years in Glasgow still remained. His sense of alienation was only slightly diminished; that strange mingling of dread and longing with which he had regarded the world around him for so long was hardly abated. Although he would not admit it, he was a neurotic needing help, and so he might have continued had not Orage again come to his assistance in the one way now needed to complete his cure.

Orage spoke of his case to a psychoanalyst, a "brilliant and charming man," who invited Muir round to see him one evening and then proposed a course of analysis "for the mere interest of the thing, and without asking for any payment." Since Muir was interested, too, in the whole "conception of the unconscious" (157) and in the process of psychoanalysis, he agreed to the proposition readily enough. He did not concede, of course, that his condition demanded any treatment; the whole thing was simply an experiment, gratuitously undertaken for the amusement of both parties. Yet on this experiment, so lightly entered into by Muir, the remaining course of his life was to turn. From this analysis came at last the full recovery of mental health toward which his marriage had already begun to lead him. And from this analysis came something more—the astonishing realization that he was not only a writer but a poet.

Not that the realization came in an apocalyptic flash. The first sessions with the analyst were painful ventures into self-knowledge, until Muir "reached a state which resembled conviction of sin, though formulated in different terms." He understood then, as he wrote in *An Autobiography*, "the elementary fact that every one, like myself, was troubled by sensual desires and thoughts, by unacknowledged failures and frustrations causing self-hatred and hatred of others, by dead memories of shame and grief which had been shovelled underground long since because they could not be borne." He saw too "that my lot was the human lot, that when I faced my own unvarnished likeness I was one among all men and women, all of whom had the same desires and thoughts, the same failures and frustrations, the same hidden shames and griefs, and that if they confronted these things they could win a certain liberation from them." What is more, although this recognition was "really a conviction of sin," it was even more a "realization of Original Sin. It took a long time to crystallize. It was not a welcome realization, for nothing is harder than to look at yourself." But slowly Muir learned to look, and as he did so, his "whole world of ideas invisibly changed." The Nietzschean superman, who had so long persuaded him that he must live beyond good and evil, "took himself off without a word" (158); and Muir was left where he had to be, if he was to be a poet: in the fallen world where he could see and accept the good and evil contending daily in his own and in every heart.

While Muir was growing in self-knowledge, however, another development took place which the analyst could not satisfactorily explain. After a period of years in which he had not dreamed at all, Muir suddenly began to have dreams in crowds, which he duly reported to his analyst. But then the character of his dreams began to change. No longer simply images of repressed desires and fears, they began to assume a legendary aspect. They began to occur, as trances and daydreams, during Muir's waking hours as well as in his sleep, until the analyst grew concerned and advised Muir to try to stop them if he could. Before he stopped them, though, Muir went through a curious state, when his "unconscious mind, having unloaded itself, seemed to have become transparent, so that myths and legends entered it without resistance and passed into . . . [his] dreams and daydreams" (159). Thus, what appeared in these visions, aside from certain easily identified motifs of sexual symbolism, was a series of marvelously brilliant fantastic scenes, often completely unearthly in content, which seemed to project fables of the creation, of human destiny, and of immortality. That it was not his own unconscious which invented such dreams, but rather the "something else which the psychologists call the racial unconscious, and for which there are other names" (164), Muir strongly believed at the time and continued to believe, despite the analyst's refusal to commit himself that far. But whatever the source of the visions, they were important for Muir in that they confirmed again that sense of mystery and meaning in the universe he had experienced as a child in Orkney, and they provided a storehouse of archetypal images which he would use over and over, with increasing effectiveness, in his poetry.

As it happened, Muir never completed the full term of his analysis. In the summer of 1921, he and Willa gave up their London jobs, scraped together what little money they had, and took off for Europe, and it was not until Muir had been for several months in Prague that he "knew how much good the analyst had done" him; that his "vague fears," he realized, "were quite gone" (159); and that finally, now he was midway in his life, his imagination was awakening and he could begin to write poetry.

But why Prague? What reason did the two Muirs have for going there? No reason; they simply decided, according to Willa, that "it was high time" they should "see a bit of the world." As to where in the world they should go, they consulted a Czech friend, Janko Lavrin, for advice, and his response was, "Why not go to Prague to begin with?" Prague, he pointed out, "was in the very middle of Europe; it had the best ham in Europe and the best beer." Since "these arguments seemed compelling,"[4] it was to Prague that Willa and Edwin decided to make their way. Thus as casually as Edwin had engaged in the psychoanalysis which was to have so momentous an effect on his life, he and Willa embarked on a journey which was also to prove momentous, since it took them into the heart of a Europe still torn by the effects of one World War and already tormented with premonitions of another; a Europe far more saturated with that sense of original sin which Muir himself had so lately come to feel, than England with its stubborn remnants of Victorian optimism, or even Calvinist Scotland, could ever possibly be.

For although the two Muirs lived what was, on the whole, a gay, lighthearted life in Prague, and later in Dresden and Hellerau, in Italy and Austria; and although here Edwin, released at last from the Glasgow-imposed compulsion *not* to look at his surroundings, could "begin to learn the visible world all over again," could spend "weeks in an orgy of looking" (189) and enjoying it, nevertheless both Willa and Edwin also encountered disturbing signs of something their earlier lives had not prepared them for. Glasgow, it is true, had convinced Edwin that life was ruled by a pitiless "iron law," but that law had been as inhuman and mechanical as a principle of physics. It simply represented the brutal operation of the universe of chaos which had replaced the universe of order he had known on Wyre. His psychoanalysis, too, had convinced him of the ineradicable presence of evil in the human heart, but this had seemed a problem for each individual to wrestle with. Now, on the other hand, he and Willa at last became aware of evil as more than a mechanical law, more than a personal, private source, however universal, of lust and shame and hate. Evil was an active social principle, a force in history.

In Prague, for example, despite the excitement of the new Czech freedom, there were everywhere, particularly in the ravaged faces of some of their friends, reminders of the "hardships the people . . . had suffered during the War" (189). There was a handsome Austrian doctor, always so "pleasant and distant," who cured Willa of bronchitis. He was so convinced that "life was completely unsatisfactory," Edwin noted, that he seemed to the Muirs "like an amiable damned soul speaking to tyros who were not yet either saved or damned" (192). In Dresden and Hellerau there was the "dry rot" of inflation, of which at first they were hardly aware, yet which slowly spread around them, undermining the apparent prosperity and provoking many normally harmless people to find security in strange and dangerous new cults. Worst of all, in both Germany and Austria there was anti-Semitism, overwhelmingly symbolized in the Jewish ghetto where the Muirs by chance spent their first nights in Vienna. From the fanatic *Der Eiserne Besen* (*The Iron Broom*), which they found on booksellers' shelves in lovely Salzburg to the distaste exhibited by Viennese intellectuals at the mere mention of a Jew, the deep stain of anti-Semitism ran through every sector of the Austrian community. It was a "nightmare," the Muirs theorized, created by the same inflation and public misery—but now far more noticeable—which they had belatedly observed in Dresden. They did not realize, any more than most people of good will at the time, "that the nightmare would end in the slaughter of a people" (218); but they did perceive that something was gravely amiss in Austrian as in much European life, and their understanding of the nature of evil, their awareness of its ramifications and its inescapable, active presence, was correspondingly enlarged.

The fact that it was during these four years abroad that Muir first turned to writing serious poetry is therefore of particular importance. The burden of experience with evil which weighs down so many of his poems is quite clearly the result not only of his own personal loss of Eden when he left Orkney for Glasgow, nor yet of his recognition, during analysis, of his own personal share in the human heritage of sin, but also of the social, historic evil which he met in Europe. When that course of psychoanalysis, a happy marriage, and the decision to follow his vocation and became a writer, all worked together to free him from the neurosis and the repressions that had paralyzed his imagination for so many years, it was naturally his early memories of Orkney, from which he had so long and resolutely looked away, that first came alive for him again. "These distant memories returned" to him in Prague and in Hellerau, and the poetry that he wrote there was, quite spontaneously, "a poetry of symbols drawn from memory" (208). But in the meantime, as he later realized, his "image of the world had changed." Orkney was indelibly a part of that image, but only a part. Glasgow, now that he could bear to contemplate that place, necessarily claimed a share of the image too, and so likewise did those four years of living in central Europe, with their intimations of the evil ingrained in the historic past, and their signs of social disaster still to come.

The fact that Muir's wide reading in that crucial time of regenerated imagination was largely in the field of European literature was significant as well. In Hellerau, for instance, a strangely innocent and unworldly "impoverished Junker, Ivo von Lucken," who "lived with Hölderlin more than with any living man," helped Muir to "begin to understand that great poet" (204). At the same time, together with Willa, Muir was exploring the work of Stefan George, of Rilke, and of Hugo von Hofmannsthal, just as earlier—again together with Willa, although her facility with languages carried her farther here—he had ventured as far as he could into Czech literature. Since it was at this time, too, that both Muirs began the series of translations, chiefly from German, that were to provide them with their living for a number of years, necessarily they also explored together a great number of important European prose writers, until Muir became steeped in a way of thinking and feeling that was far more European than British. His affinities as a poet, when he found his own idiom after his awkward, conventional earliest poems, were thus with Hölderlin, Rilke, and Kafka—whom he and Willa began to translate in 1929—rather than with the currently more fashionable poets of the English-speaking world, such as Eliot.

Not, indeed, that Eliot and Muir were actually as unlike each other as they might seem. A comparison of the two does much to reveal Muir's essential qualities as a poet, once he reached full command of his powers. Where Eliot as a technician was dazzlingly inventive and daring, Muir, it is true, was content for the most part to work within traditional forms that he found congenial to his particular style and matter. But underneath this formal divergence, both poets shared certain fundamental attitudes and characteristics. Muir's sense of the predicament of man, for instance, was certainly as agonizing as Eliot's; it simply had different roots. Far more than Eliot's, it sprang from an experience of personal suffering on the one hand, and on the other from the European experience of the ubiquity of evil as a force in human destiny. At the same time, because Muir possessed, as his dreams attested, some of the same visionary pwer that he responded to in Hölderlin, Rilke, and Kafka, his capacity to perceive the countervailing force of good was necessarily greater than that of Eliot, who seemed more often to long for vision than to possess it. The deep joy, the clear serenity of such later Muir poems as "A Birthday," "In Love for Long," "The Annunciation," "The Transfiguration," "Day and Night," demonstrate a perception of the "unseeable/ One glory of the everlasting world" [5] that is undeniably steadier and more assured than the evanescent glimpses in the *Four Quartets* of the "still point of the turning world." Both poets, however, understood that this is where the meaning of existence lies—at that "still point," at the intersection of the timeless with time. The difference was that Muir understood this earlier and longer and was therefore able to build on that foundation a faith, a vision, that included not only the moments of transcendence, but that "Ridiculous . . . waste sad time/ Stretching before and after" [6] which happens to be most of life, and which Eliot had to exclude.

For what Muir as a poet finally learned was a way of bringing together all the separate, jarring elements of his life—the ridiculous, the significant, the bad, the good—into a single whole, where once again everything fitted with everything else, as in his childish "original vision" of the world. But whereas in that vision there had been no place for evil—evil had in fact destroyed it—in this regained unity evil had not only a place but a function. The chaos and grief of Glasgow, the knowledge of original sin that Muir's psychoanalysis and his years in Europe had given him, now stood as one pole of his experience, opposed to the idea of harmony and order given him by those early years in Orkney; and out of the tension between these two opposites, out of their paradoxically symbiotic relationship, came at last a new order that was necessarily stronger because more inclusive than that simple, innocent sense of a whole had been. The belief in "ingenuous good" he had held then, as he wrote in "A Birthday," he found restored to him again when, past fifty, he looked back over the pattern of his life to "discern/It whole or almost whole";[7] but that belief had in the meantime been confirmed by passage through both a private and a public hell.

II

"Before I took the road
Direction ravished my soul."

This sense of a complex whole, this delicate balance of disparate areas of experience which Muir achieved in his later poetry, however, was scarcely even suggested in his *First Poems*, published in 1925. In a number of other respects, *First Poems* anticipates the course Muir would follow in the future so clearly that the volume proves the uncanny accuracy of the two lines from "A Birthday," which stand as an epigraph for this chapter: here, beyond a doubt, the direction Muir would take as a poet had already ravished his soul. But where in succeeding volumes the contrary poles of his life—of innocence and experience, order and disorder—gradually converge towards one another until they meet in the resolution and tension of paradox, here such a motion is not yet apparent, nor even possible. For these poems are drawn for the most part, as Muir himself noted, from a single period of his life, from his boyhood on Wyre. When in Prague and Dresden he recovered at last from that "long illness" which had seized him at fourteen in Glasgow, it was the image of Wyre that first returned to his awakened imagination, and the poetry that he wrote, without realizing it, was a "poetry of symbols drawn from memory." [1] True, because the past that he remembered was

33

lost, those symbols were necessarily tinged with sadness, and almost all the *First Poems* are filled with that peculiarly keen regret we feel for "the days that are no more." But there is no overt reference here either to the brutal facts of Glasgow life which for Muir brought those days to a close, nor to his later exposure to the more subtle and pervasive evil of Europe. On the surface, at least, there is no principle of darkness and disorder to contrast actively with the remembered light of Wyre.

Precisely because these poems are so closely linked with Muir's own past, moreover, they are unlike most of his later work in another way: the majority are subjective, centered wholly on his own experience. Where the later work tends to be more objective, more concerned with the fate of all men, here in *First Poems* it is Muir himself who most often plays the focal part. The themes of recollected childhood and of loss, the visions of pre-human existence and of birth and rebirth all revolve around him. And naturally so. Muir wrote these poems, as we have seen, when he was already in his midthirties; wrote them because psychoanalysis, a happy marriage, and new leisure had suddenly broken up the repressions that had blocked his view of things past and distorted his native impulses and sensibilities. With his newly released imaginative power, he found he had things to say which could not go "properly into prose," and what he had to say was chiefly this: that his life had a significance he had overlooked as he lived it. When he looked back in time now, indeed, it seemed to him, as he wrote in his *Autobiography*, that he was not seeing his life merely, "but all human life"; and he became "conscious of it as a strange and unique process." [2] But although this sense of identity with the whole of mankind shows in the themes of *First Poems*, it was on his own particular past that his imagination instinctively focused. In feeling, in approach, in imagery, *First Poems* are thus, as they almost had to be, the most personal, the least objective and universal of all Muir's poems.

There is, accordingly, a profound dichotomy in *First Poems* between objective themes and subjective treatment; between an attitude largely limited to this first book and subject matter and insights which remain dominant throughout Muir's work.

Instead of the contrast of opposing principles such as gradually develops in later volumes, the polarity which paradoxically becomes unity, the contrast here is rather between tendencies Muir continues to follow and those he abandons after this one trial. In some of the most successful poems here, such as ".Childhood," which significantly stands at the beginning of the volume, this dichotomy is, in fact, hardly noticeable. The poem is stated in terms which are both subjective and objective, both particular and universal; and the important point about this poem, aside from its effectiveness in recalling the security, the timelessness, and the magic of childhood, is the number of ways in which it prefigures future developments in Muir's work. Precisely the same point gives importance to most of the other poems to be discussed in this chapter: almost all are at least partially successful; almost all fuse particular with universal; and almost all foreshadow the themes, the vision, and the mystery of Muir's mature poems. They make plain the "direction" that had already "ravished" Muir, even before he "took the road." In the background, however, are other poems, such as "The Lost Land," "Remembrance," and "Houses," which also treat the childhood motif but treat it in such a way that the personal nostalgia drowns out the general significance, while the nostalgia itself degenerates into sentimentality. These are the poems which represent the tendency Muir did not follow; and these, with others like them, must be kept in mind as the contrary pole of the opposition which prevails in *First Poems*—an opposition which for once Muir resolved by abandonment rather than by reconciliation.

In the direction Muir did choose to follow, moreover; in the themes which he first stated or implied in this volume and then went on to reshape and elaborate for more than thirty years, there are of course oppositions of a much more fundamental nature, for which abandonment could provide no solution. And although in *First Poems* these are still implicit rather than explicit, they are nevertheless inherent in the very subjects Muir chooses here for his own. If they do not take definite shape until later, until Muir seeks in other volumes to work out some of his subjects to their logical consequences, they are nevertheless there, quietly complicating what often, on the surface, seems simple enough; and they too must be kept in mind.

They must be kept in mind, for instance, even in dealing with a poem like "Childhood," which introduces one of the most persistent themes in Muir's poetry: the theme of childhood remembered:

> Long time he lay upon the sunny hill,
>> To his father's house below securely bound.
> Far off the silent, changing sound was still,
>> With the black islands lying thick around.[3]

For although this stanza, with its simple, emphatic rhymes, evokes the clear serenity of a child's world; although the multiple *l*'s suggest the gentle, untroubled tune of a child's lullaby; and although the archaic inversion, "Long time he lay," at once places the whole poem in the region of a child's imagination—a distant yet timeless past, immune to change, still there are intimations here of depths and complexities far beyond a child's usual experience. There is a tranced stillness here, a lingering light, a harmony and security which are only partly accounted for by the fact that in his own boyhood on Wyre Muir actually experienced something very similar. What he knew there, as the previous chapter indicated, was that "original vision of the world" which he recalled in *An Autobiography* as a "state in which the earth, the houses on the earth, and the life of every human being are related to the sky overarching them; as if the sky fitted the earth and the earth the sky." [4] But what he evokes in this poem is something more. When Muir wrote these lines, he was an adult, looking back at his boyhood, and between him and it lay the years he had spent in the "tenth-rate hell" of industrial Glasgow. What lay on the far side of hell, then, could not be anything less than Eden, and thus it is the light of Eden, the reflection of the "clear unfallen world" that illuminates the childhood of this poem and of others in this volume, very much as it illuminates the childhood poems of another farmer's son, John Clare. It is, moreover, the same light, sometimes dim, sometimes radiant, that continues to touch the childhood motif whenever it recurs in Muir's later poetry, so that childhood and Eden imperceptibly blend into a single theme.

But the "Childhood" of this particular poem is not only transfigured; it is timeless. There is a hushed stillness in the first stanza, as we have seen, and in the fourth stanza the literal statement combines with slow monosyllables and a succession of drowsy *s*'s and *sh*'s to give the effect of a complete suspension of time. Time is "finished":

> Oft o'er the sound a ship so slow would pass
>> That in the black hills' gloom it seemed to lie.
> The evening sound was smooth like sunken glass,
>> And time semed finished ere the ship passed by. (9)

What is at work here is not simply an incidental suggestion of youth's natural unconsciousness of time. Here again there is something beyond the range of ordinary childhood. There is a deliberate manipulation of time, which not only hints at another prevailing theme in Muir's later poetry, the theme of time itself, but also provides some clue to the complex significance of that theme as Muir develops it over the years.

Almost tangible behind the suspension of time in this poem, for instance, is the fear that it will not stay suspended, the pain of its inevitable passage. To this universal pain Muir is always particularly sensitive. "Time wakens," he wrote in *An Autobiography*, "a longing more poignant than all the longings caused by the division of lovers in space . . .";[5] and even in the inadequate form of the three other childhood poems in this volume which we have already mentioned—"The Lost Land," "Remembrance," and "Houses"—where time has not stood still, where youth is irretrievably lost, the terrible poignancy of such a longing comes through. It comes through far more effectively, of course, in later, more skillfully handled poems such as "The Myth" and "The Return"; but even when it is not treated as a separate motif, it frequently adds one deeper note among the many in the chord of intolerable sadness that Muir's poetry so often sounds.

Far more important, the very deliberateness of the time suspension here, together with Muir's later attempts (as in poems like "The Stationary Journey") to create a static Now of the imagination, has a hint of something excessive about it. Or obsessive. "Obsession" is in fact the very word that Muir himself uses in a passage which attributes his special feeling about time to a gap between two periods in his life. "I was born before the Industrial Revolution," he pointed out in the earlier version of his autobiography, *The Story and the Fable,* "and am now about two hundred years old. But I have skipped a hundred and fifty of them. I was really born in 1737, and till I was fourteen no time-accidents happened to me. Then in 1751 I set out from Orkney for Glasgow. When I arrived I found that it was not 1751, but 1901, and that a hundred and fifty years had been burned up in my two days' journey. But I myself was still in 1751, and remained there for a long time. All my life since I have been trying to overhaul that invisible leeway. No wonder I am obsessed with Time." [6]

A close reading of this text, however, added to a knowledge of what happened to Muir in Glasgow, suggests that it was not merely the "invisible leeway" between two periods of his life, the impossibility of synchronizing a childhood in a static communal society with adolescence in a dynamic capitalist one, that caused his obsession with time. The visible presence of the past everywhere in Orkney surely played a part, and what he called "time-accidents" played a part that was still more important. For when Muir moved from the relatively slow-moving time of his Orkney home to the accelerated time rate of Glasgow, that acceleration brought the death of four members of his family—father, mother, and two brothers—within four years, a "meaningless waste of inherited virtue," [7] a betrayal of hope and promise, for which Muir could find no explanation "except that life was ruled by an iron law." Thus to Muir time was indeed, as we have seen, the heartbreaking thief of youth, the implacable divider of present from past. Time was also a bewildering riddle of two systems that could not be synchronized. But most significant of all, time was merciless, treacherous cruelty—another face of evil.

When we recognize that time is a face of evil in these early poems, then two further points become clear. What seemed at first glance a rather extreme response to the passage of time appears instead as a repressed response to the problem of evil. That the response is still repressed in this volume is of course not surprising. Although Muir had by now recovered from his neurosis sufficiently to be able to look at his past, the tragedy he had experienced was still too fresh for him to examine it closely. He preferred to look further back, to Orkney, where he had known only the intimations of tragedy. But that the response is here is proof that Muir's lifelong concern with the problem of evil is also here. On the surface he only hints at this theme in some of the more subjective and less successful poems such as "Maya," "The Enchanted Prince," or "An Ancient Song," or he obscurely symbolizes it in "Ballad of Eternal Life." When he treats it directly, he does so in an uncharacteristic, Calvinist fashion, as in "Ballad of the Flood." Yet in one way or another, nevertheless, this is a concern which underlies almost every one of the twenty-four poems in the book.

The slight but disturbing little poem significantly titled "Betrayal" provides additional proof both of this complexity of what seems simple in *First Poems* and of this early association of time with evil and—because time works its destruction so insidiously from within—with treachery. Essentially a restatement of the eternal protest against time: "How with this rage shall beauty hold a plea,/ Whose action is no stronger than a flower?" the poem begins with a simple image of appropriately helpless beauty trapped in time's snare:

> Sometimes I see, caught in a snare,
>   One with a foolish lovely face,
> Who stands with scattered moon-struck air
>   Alone, in a wild woody place. (30)

But very soon the pathetic contrast between frail beauty and entrapping time is blurred. Pathos darkens into horror, and the impersonal destroyer, time, becomes a traitor, a sadist, and a murderer. The very tree-trunks that stand around the snare all "show/ A front of silent treachery"; it is by "hidden guile" that the gaoler does his work; and the work itself is an exercise in torture that recalls Muir's description, in *An Autobiography*, of the slow, agonizing deaths suffered by his two brothers. In poor beauty's "flesh/ Small joyless teeth fret without rest," while the gaoler, time, not content with the operation of his trap, himself "Scores her fine flesh," "inly wastes her flesh away," "strangles her with stealthy bands," and at last, mercifully, "murders her," just as tuberculosis and a brain tumor cruelly wasted and then murdered Willie and Johnnie Muir. And this inescapable resemblance between poem and life demonstrates beyond any doubt, it seems to me, that in Muir's mind, when he was writing *First Poems*, time and evil were the obverse and the reverse of the same coin, and each side bore the mark of treachery. Further, although this near identity of the two dissolves in Muir's succeeding volumes, so that he can write of them separately, some sense of the one continues to color the other. The close association of time with evil and of both with betrayal remains constant in Muir's treatment of all three themes.

Another recurring theme of Muir's, one peculiarly his own, which he comes to connect with both time and evil, with Eden, and even with politics, is the animal theme, which appears in *First Poems* in "Horses." Of all the various shapes the animal motif would assume, all the meanings it would accumulate, hardly any hint is observable here. Yet again the ultimate direction is implicit in the beginning, for all the underlying complexity and all the later developments are deducible—with the help of hindsight—from the central feeling of the poem, a feeling of fear and wonder so intense that it triumphs over forced phrases like "mute ecstatic monsters of the mould" in the third stanza, or awkwardnesses like "seem as standing still" in the second. This fear and wonder, moreover, are what the speaker himself experiences as he watches plough horses at work in the field. He "wonders":

> . . . why, just now
> They seemed so terrible, so wild and strange,
> Like magic power on the stony grange (15)

and he realizes characteristically that the horses recall "some childish hour," when he watched, "fearful, through the blackening rain," the great hooves of horses on his father's farm. Then those

> . . . conquering hooves which trod the stubble down
> Were ritual which turned the field to brown,
> And their great hulks were seraphim of gold,
> Or mute ecstatic monsters on the mould.

But the recollection fades, as it must, and he "must pine"

> Again for that dread country crystalline,
> Where the blank field and the still standing tree
> Were bright and fearful presences to me. (16)

For here, along with the familiar elements—the vision of childhood remembered, the "pining" that is the "poignant" longing wakened by time—there is something new: mystery and magic and a terror which has nothing to do with the gross cruelty of "Betrayal." Thinking back to his own relationship to horses, when he was a little boy, Muir realized that he was afraid of them, but "my fear turned into something else, for it was infused by a longing to go up to them and touch them and simultaneously checked by the knowledge that their hoofs were dangerous: a combination of emotions which amounted to worship in the Old Testament sense."[8] And it is "worship" in this sense which informs this poem: dread and awe of dangerous power; love and reverence for strength and beauty.

But there is even more involved in the complex of emotions behind the poem. An illustration from a copy of *Gulliver's Travels* which Muir's eldest brother won as a school prize enters into the complex, for example. This picture showed a Houyhnhnm, a "great horse sitting on a throne judging a crowd of naked men with hairy, hangdog faces"; and since Muir "took it to be the record of some actual occurrence,"[9] he kept in his mind a disturbingly real image of a horse sitting in judgment on men. Elaborating on the image in his partly autobiographical novel *Poor Tom*, where a young man called

Mansie is his unbearably priggish counterpart, Muir has
Mansie encounter a horse which calls to his mind the school-
book phrase, "a kingly judge." This horse, moreover, "seemed
to be looking . . . from another world which lay like a hidden
kingdom around it";/ and in its strange, steady gaze Mansie
sees the gaze of similar implacable, other-worldly judges of
men: long-faced John Knox, as Mansie remembers him from a
page in *The Scots Worthies*; Michaelangelo's horned Moses,
seen in plaster in a Glasgow shop window; even the Pharaohs
and the Sphinx, recalled from church sermons and somehow
merged into one. [11] Small wonder if, with these images in his
mind, Muir added to his first spontaneous "worship" of horses
several new dimensions of dread and wonder. Nor if the animals themselves put on new characteristics, distinguishable in
this poem, of a sort of alien royalty; of princes and emissaries
from a world beyond human knowledge.

Still more powerful, however, in shaping Muir's feeling for
animals, than either these later impressions or his earliest encounters with the beasts themselves, was the fact that, again
like John Clare, who similarly had a special sensitivity for animals, he was born into the "carnival of birth and death" [12]
which is, or used to be, a farm. And on a farm, birth, copulation,
and death—lambing time, mating time, and slaughtering time
—are all ritual acts. All are ceremonial procedures, sanctified by
performance since the time of Adam, which bind man and animal together in a mysterious union of "necessity and guilt."
About the nature of "this connexion between men and animals," Muir points out, "we know far less than our remote
ancestors did." But both our "unconscious life" and the traditional rites of the farm go back into that remote period, when
"everything was legendary"[13]; when man, beast, and bird lived
close together, and when, if bird and beast were hunted that
man might live, they were also worshipped, that man might be
forgiven. It is from that remote and legendary time, perpetu-
ated still in the pattern of life on the Orkney farm where Muir
grew up, and spoken of still in "our dreams and ancestral memories," [14] that Muir derived his very special conception of the
animal world and our relation to it: "a relation involving," as

we have just seen, "a predestined guilt," and as we shall see in later chapters, "our immortality." [15] Small wonder once more, then, if the complex of emotions involved in "Horses," prefiguring so much to come, is what we have described: love and dread, reverence and mystery.

In this discussion another continuing concern of Muir's has been introduced: "dreams and ancestral memories." These dreams and memories, according to Muir, are one source of our knowledge of those fabulous ages when the nature of the bond between beast and man was originally determined. But that is not all. "Sleep tells us things both about ourselves and the world," Muir believed, "which we could not discover otherwise. Our dreams are a part of experience," as "earlier ages acknowledged," but they are not the "miscellaneous dross of experience" represented by so much of our everyday lives. Together with our memories and waking visions, they are the few "glints of immortality" [16] which shine through the dross. They are the outlines of the eternal "fable" which can sometimes be recognized beneath the dates and incidents of our outward story. And as signals and symbols of this enduring reality beneath the flux of appearances, they were naturally for Muir the stuff of poetry. They were original matter, already half formed in images, awaiting the final shaping Word. What is more, because he had an extraordinary gift for dreaming, Muir always had this original matter available to him; and out of this matter, from the very beginning, he fashioned many of his poems. There are accordingly a number of poems made from dreams in *First Poems*, and thus, once more, *First Poems* indicates the way Muir was to go, the direction that had already seized his soul.

Precisely how many of Muir's poems, either in this or in later volumes, are directly derived from dreams, it is impossible to say. Since he believed that dreams were often more meaningful than waking experience; that, indeed, "no autobiography can confine itself to conscious life," he made a point in his own *Autobiography* of recounting deliberately a great number of dreams. From these accounts may be traced the origins sometimes of whole poems, sometimes of fragmentary passages, lines, or images. On the other hand, an equal quantity of poems, passages, and lines may have sprung from dreams Muir never took the trouble of putting into words. There is no way of knowing. What is clear, however, is this: that the whole world of "dreams and ancestral memories" was one to which Muir had particularly easy access, and that his awareness of this mysterious world informs and underlies whatever he wrote, whether any direct connection can be proved or not. This was the ambience in which he moved, in the constant presence of another mode of being behind and beneath the mode of immediate sense perception, and even his most topical poems, the ones most closely keyed to specific events in the contemporary scene, are full of echoes from this further region of human experience.

In *First Poems*, however, the "contemporary scene" does not exist. That was a later development very definitely not predicted here, because the tendency here was, as we have said, in the other direction: away from the objective, the outer world of solid facts and other people, and towards the subjective, the inward, nostalgic recollection of the past. Here, as a consequence, all is "ghost and glance and gleam," and in this rather attenuated atmosphere, significantly, the dream poems which are present do not flourish as they do later, when toughened by some contact at least with the substantial world. They lack, too, except in one instance, to be discussed later in this chapter—the "Ballad of Hector in Hades," which is actually more a transmutation of a childhood trauma than a pure rendering of dream—the final form and hardness which come from passage through the refining fire of the imagination. For what Muir has done here, in most cases, has been simply to accept the dreams as they came to him rather than to work them into any significant shape. And since in most cases they have no intrinsic organic structure, no firm base of thought and action, they cannot sustain the poems built on them. In "The Lost Land," for example, which retells a dream sequence described in *An Autobiography*, the force of the opening image, as the dreamer stands on the prow of a ship, returning to his lost home, succeeds in carrying the poem effectively for a few quietly whispering, mysterious lines:

And like a mist ere morning I am gone;
My whispering prow through silence furrows on,
I fare far in through circles vast and dim,
Till a grey steeple lifts above the rim. (11)

But as soon as the dreamer reaches the town, it turns into an alien place, and the poem crumbles. The note of authentic longing lapses into trite sentimentality, and the dreamer now wanders in "pale moon-charméd valleys" to gather "giant orchids, light and dead/ . . .[to] make a pallid garland for . . . [his] head" (12).

Even when Muir has far more complex and spectacular dreams to deal with, the same problem persists, the inability to give the dream material poetic form. The effort is sometimes apparent, as in "Ballad of Rebirth," where bits of portentous dialogue are inserted to provide some sort of conceptual basis for the fantastic events of the original dream. But the effect of this patchwork is absurd; much more powerful, simply as narrative, is Muir's wry—and coolly objective—report of the dream in *An Autobiography*, where the "great beast" whose role it is to devour the body which seems to be Muir merely looks "sad and kindly" and eats the corpse "in a businesslike way."[17]

Again, in "Ballad of Eternal Life" (reprinted, much revised, in the final *Collected Poems* as "Ballad of the Soul"), there are evident attempts at connecting links. Further, the whole poem is to some extent redeemed, as "Ballad of Rebirth" is not, by the extraordinary beauty which some scattered stanzas reflect from the vision Muir saw and set down in *An Autobiography*. That vision, however, was confused to begin with. It baffled Muir's psychoanalyst, although he pointed out its sexual symbolism, which by this time Muir could read for himself. And for Muir, too, although he could see in the dream a "discernible pattern . . . of man's evolution and ultimate destiny," there were "things in it to which . . . [he could] attach no clear meaning," parts which remained "quite incomprehensible."[18] That they should still remain incomprehensible when translated essentially unchanged into verse is surely no cause for surprise. Muir "did not know at the time what to do with these mythological dreams," he confessed, and at the time of writing *An Autobiography*, almost twenty years later, he "did not know yet." He "used the trance for a poem, but a poem," he sadly decided, "seems a trifling result from such an experience."[19] If the poem was to be of the order of these ballads, he was right.

The poem, of course, did not have to be of this order. Muir did learn, as we shall see, what to do with his dreams. Even from these unsuccessful poems he salvaged stanzas, phrases, images, and above all the "mythological" approach, to use again in poems to which he was able to give imaginative form. Much of "Ballad of Eternal Life," for instance, reappears more effectively, although not yet with complete clarity and conviction, in "The Fall." The "mountain-headed lion" of "Ballad of the Nightingale" is the lion with "mountain head and sunset brow" of that terrifying poem, "The Road"; the doe from the same ballad returns, for one perfect moment, in "In Love for Long," while the worshipping murderers and animals, again from the same ballad, emerge once more, after twenty years, into the radiance of "The Transfiguration." More important yet, however, in one poem in the *First Poems* volume itself, Muir works with "mythological dream" material of a slightly different kind, and handles it well.

This poem is the "Ballad of Hector in Hades"; the difference, noted earlier, lies in the fact that this ballad is more a transformation of a shameful boyhood memory than a record of a spontaneous dream. In any event, that memory had been buried so deep in Muir's mind for thirty years that he never spoke or thought of it. Then suddenly, "quite spontaneously," the image of the whole poem rose in his thoughts, so clear and coherent that he wrote it down "almost complete, at one sitting." [20] The image rose, that is, from his subconscious, as dreams rise; it rose unbidden, as dreams come; it was, in effect, a waking dream. But "somehow, somewhere," the material of this dream, unlike that which went into the other dream poems of this volume, had undergone an imaginative change. Whereas the obscure psychological symbolism of the other dreams remained obscure in the poems, the personal trauma which was the basis of this dream now returned to Muir's conscious mind in the form of a cultural not a personal myth. The schoolboy Edwin Muir running away from his classmate Freddie Sinclair was now Hector fleeing from Achilles, and Hector's "Ballad" accordingly had a form, a built-in structure and solidity, denied to the unchanged, purely personal substance of "The Lost Land" or the "Ballad of Rebirth."

More than any of the other dream poems, therefore, the "Ballad of Hector" marks the way that Muir would increasingly come to follow in his use of both myth and dream. He would not always fuse the two, as they are fused here, but he would seek to give his dreams an objective form, and he would more and more often employ traditional myth to embody and objectify personal experience and contemporary problems. Thus Hector is not alone. He is only the first in a long line of mythical figures, from Adam to Oedipus, in whose legends Muir works out sometimes his own feelings, whether of alienation and frustration or of acceptance, sometimes his questionings of the nature of history or the relationship of good to evil, and sometimes his visions of final reconciliation and love. For in turning from his early, very private "mythological dreams," with their impenetrable symbols that he himself did not comprehend, to the accepted symbolism of Greek and Biblical myth, Muir found for himself a universal language in which even his most personal ideas could achieve expression.

As Hector initiates this universal language, furthermore, he also introduces a universal landscape. The "empty plain" over which Achilles pursues him is the "bare landscape" of Wyre, Muir's island home. And because the island "was not too big for a child to see in it an image of life: land and sea and sky, good and evil, happiness and grief, life and death," it presented itself to Muir as "a symbolical stage on which the drama of human life . . . could play itself out." It became, without his "knowing it, a universal landscape over which Abraham and

Moses and Achilles and Ulysses and Tristram and all sorts of pilgrims"[21] would pass, and the contours of the island accordingly appear time after time in Muir's poetry as the backdrop against which his legendary heroes act. The sea and hills and town of Wyre are "The sea, the hills, the town" of "The Town Betrayed," which "Achilles, Siegfried, Lancelot" have sworn to destroy. They are the "hills that seemed so low/ In the boundless sea and land" of "The Return of the Greeks"; the "hillock/ So small and smooth and green" of "The Gate"; the "little green hills, the sea" which welcome Theseus when he emerges from "The Labyrinth." Sometimes, it is true, the higher hills, the winding roads, the harvest fields of the Sonntagberg which Muir knew in Austria blend with this island scene, but whatever the variations, the essential, archaic simplicity remains. The landscape is universal precisely because it is stripped to the bone.

In the same way, the style of the Hector ballad is stripped. Not so terse and powerful as a true ballad, the Hector poem nevertheless has a taut, bare line and a direct, urgent movement which distinguish it from most of the other poems in this volume. For as some of the lines and stanzas thus far quoted must already have made apparent, the interest of these poems lies almost entirely in their relevance to Muir's later work. A poem like "The Enchanted Prince," for instance, which opens thus:

Here lying on the ancient mount,
   Through days grown stagnant and too rich,
My half-raised eyes keep sleepy count
Of wild weeds springing in the ditch, (21)

would provoke little excitement except for the fact that it contains the germ of a wonderful poem published more than ten years later, "The Enchanted Knight"; and this stanza is typical of many in the volume. Varied as the feet in this tetrameter quatrain may be, there is no memorable music here, nothing to stir the blood. Neither is there any of that quality of hushed stillness or of wonder which triumphs over occasional awkwardness in "Childhood" and "Horses." What is here, instead, is the same sort of inflated "poetic" diction which was so painfully obvious in the lines cited earlier from "The Lost Land," where the dreamer gathers dead orchids in "moon-charméd valleys." If all of *First Poems* were on the level of "The Enchanted Prince," the volume would give little indication that a true poet was here beginning his apprenticeship.

But all is not on this level. Even among the prevailingly rather uninteresting—metrically speaking—poems in pentameter or tetrameter quatrains, "Childhood" and "Horses," as we have seen, are different. They are unashamedly old fashioned, but for the most part they put all the old fashioned devices to good use—effectively varied rhythm, alliteration, careful modulation of vowel sounds within the line and in end-rhymes, selection of precisely accurate word and phrase—to achieve an admirable unity of structure and statement. They are poems which suggest a coming mastery. In addition, there are two free verse poems here, "When the Trees grow bare on the High Hills," and "Autumn in Prague," which reach a high point in technical skill. Reprinted in both the earlier and the final *Collected Poems,* they are sketches in delicate colors and rhythms which catch the breathless quiet of the autumn air, the feel of life quiescent and withdrawn, and even the sense of waiting for a new beginning that is suggested in the equally delicate sketches of late summer at the end of *One Foot in Eden*—"The Late Wasp" and "The Late Swallow."

There is, too, as we have already indicated, the "Ballad of Hector in Hades," which is the first of a section of six ballads. It is likewise the best of the six, not merely because the myth of Hector and Achilles gives it form—the myth of Noah gives form to the "Ballad of the Flood," as well, yet it is inferior to the Hector poem—nor yet merely because the myth provides a suitable objective correlative for Muir's original childish fear. It is also the best because its style approximates the authentic ballad style, simple, compressed, natural in rhythm, which had been familiar to Muir ever since as a child in the farm kitchen on Wyre on winter evenings he had joined his parents and brothers and sisters in singing the Scottish ballads they all knew by heart. The version of the "Hector" ballad printed in both *Collected Poems* has been cut and revised considerably, yet even in the original in *First Poems* the diction lapses only occasionally into forced phrasing; the action moves rapidly without deviation to its point; and the point, the passage beyond fear, is both dramatically right and psychologically sound. Once more, consequently, *First Poems* prefigures Muir's ultimate direction: the packed simplicity, the natural speech rhythms, the dramatic movement of the best of his later poems.

There are two ballads here, however, "Ballad of the Flood" and "Ballad of the Monk," which mark a style Muir was later to reject; and this instance of rejection, like the rejection of the subjective and the shadowy past, has particular meaning for Muir's whole development and achievement as a poet. For the two ballads are written in Scots, and Muir, of course, was a Scotsman. Was Scots, then, his native language? Was he denying his birthright when he wrote in English? Was he forfeiting the instinctive colloquial rhythms of his childhood speech, the distinctive turns of phrase, the strong syntactical feeling, the earthy metaphor of the Orkney folk, for a castrated English learned in school? And if so, could he ever hope, in this alien, neutralized tongue, to become a real poet?

In the controversy which eventually arose over this problem between Muir and Hugh MacDiarmid, the leader of the Scottish Renaissance movement, it was MacDiarmid's opinion that the answer to every one of these questions but the last was yes, and to that, a resounding no. "No recent Scottish poet writing in English has written poetry of the slightest consequence," [22] MacDiarmid emphatically stated in 1941, in a generalization obviously aimed at Muir. English was not only alien and neutralized, half dead indeed, according to MacDiarmid, but worse, an instrument of exploitation, one more means of keeping the Scots in subjection to England. How could any Scot write a syllable of living poetry in a language against which both his intellect and his feelings must revolt?

How indeed? Muir might well have echoed, for the strange part of this disagreement between the two poets was that Muir partly agreed with MacDiarmid and was altogether as concerned as MacDiarmid over the national disintegration which he saw everywhere around him in Scotland. Writing in "A Note on Scottish Ballads," published in *Latitudes* in 1924, Muir actually anticipated MacDiarmid's judgment on the impotence of a Scottish poet trying to write English. "No writer can write great English who is not born an English writer and in England," said Muir. "And because the current of English is even at this day so much younger, poorer, and more artificial in Scotland than it is in England, it is improbable that Scotland will produce any writer of English of the first rank, or at least that she will do so until her tradition of English is as common, as unforced and unschooled as if it were her native tongue." [23] But between 1924 when he wrote this, and 1936, he came to the reluctant conclusion, which touched off MacDiarmid's anger, that "English was the only practicable . . . language at present" for the Scottish writer. In fact, Scottish writers could create a national literature only by writing in English, as Yeats had created a national literature in Ireland.[24] For in the dozen years between these two pronouncements, Muir had studied and observed tendencies he had not been aware of before, both in Scottish history and in the contemporary Scottish scene.

He had, for one thing, written *John Knox: Portrait of a Calvinist* (dedicated, ironically, "To Hugh M'Diarmid In Admiration"), which was not only a penetrating analysis of Knox's strangely ambivalent character, but also an equally penetrating analysis of the beginnings of that fatal division in Scottish life which in Muir's eyes would continue to "betray" and "rend" the nation "through all its history."[25] Furthermore, in his readings in the Scottish poets, from the ballad-makers and Henryson and Dunbar, down through the "kail-yard school" to the present, he had watched the effects of that dissension on language and literature. The union of thought and feeling, of passion and reflection, which he believed had characterized Scottish poetry while Scotland was still a whole nation with a homogeneous language, was now, he felt, forever destroyed. While English had become the language of maturity and thought, the Scottish dialects had been relegated to a subordinate status, as the language of childhood and feeling, and it was highly unlikely that the twain would ever meet.[26] Finally, in the course of a rambling motor trip which he took through Scotland during the depression and later reported on in *Scottish Journey*, Muir had observed the present results of that same centuries-old division. It was so ingrained and deep-rooted by now, in the intellectual, political, and economic life of the country, that no measure, he was convinced, short of complete economic and social revolution in both England and Scotland could eradicate it and heal the wound.[27] Yet the proposals of the Scottish Nationalists, and MacDiarmid's gallant attempt to restore the Scottish tongue as a vehicle of *both* thought and feeling, seemed to him at that time to fall far short of this radical solution. He therefore had to confess at last, in sadness and in honesty: "I do not believe in the programme of the Scottish Nationalists, for it goes against my reading of history, and seems to me a trivial response to a serious problem."[28] Only four years later, in *The Story and the Fable*, he was to change his mind once more on the question of the Scottish Nationalists. "I believe" in their program, he now wrote, because he had also come to believe that men could organize themselves more satisfactorily, more humanely, in smaller communities. He would "like to see Scotland a self-governing nation."[29] But on the question of language he never changed his mind. He never went back to Scots.

When Muir decided to abandon Scots, consequently, and to write in a language which would never have for him the profound unconscious roots of the "mixture of Norse, Scots and Irish"[30] that he spoke as a child in Orkney, he did not make the decision lightly or happily. He well knew what he was giving up, but because he also knew why he was giving it up, he could not do otherwise. Although the Scots that he uses in "Ballad of the Monk" and "Ballad of the Flood" is lively and graceful, as in the following stanza:

> "O what's yon green hill in the wast
>   Set round wi' mony a tree?"
> "I wat it is Mount Ararat
>   New risen frae the sea," [31]

it is also limited and derivative. "The Twa Corbies," "The Demon Lover," and innumerable other familiar ballads sound through the rhythms and phrases of both these poems, so that the total effect in both cases is one of moderately successful imitation. The vigor of original experience, of mature experience, is not there. There is no trace of the individual voice which can be heard in the Hector ballad. Of the two languages between which Muir had to choose, therefore, because his country was so sadly divided, the one clearly offered him more ease, the other more range and power. In the one he could speak as a child, unconsciously adopting what he heard around him; in the other, as a man, consciously shaping his thought; and it was inevitably the latter that he chose. As he continued to write and think and live in English year after year, he naturally acquired more ease in this second language. But he never completely overcame the original handicap. An occasional stilted phrase, an oddly chosen word, a strange flatness, creeps into some of his poems to the very last, just as the theme of Scotland divided and betrayed by division continues to preoccupy him.

In sum, then, in what they accept and in what they reject, in outright statement and implication, in feeling, vision, and even, at times, in style and form, Muir's *First Poems* indicate what was to come in his later poems for a period of thirty years. Many new elements of course are added, elements of enormous importance which make the difference betwen a hesitant beginning and a sure, craftsman-like, and powerful finish; between amateur poetics and the real thing. Precisely what these elements are will be the subject of the following chapters. But the direction was there originally. In the end, themes, vision, feeling, to quote from "A Birthday" again, "Like travellers return/ And stand where first they stood."

III

"At the dead centre of the boundless plain"

The traveler whose compass points true north may still be far from the Pole; and despite the fact that the direction he was to follow was so clearly indicated, in so many ways, in *First Poems*, Muir was still very far from *One Foot in Eden*. Nor did his next volume, *Chorus of the Newly Dead*, seem, at a cursory glance, to take him much closer.

Yet this small volume, beautifully produced by the Hogarth Press in 1926, was actually an inevitable next step. For the themes with which Muir was concerned in *First Poems*, themes with which he would be concerned all his life, contained, as we have said, inherent oppositions. They were, on a rational level, essentially contradictory. If Eden had come irreparably to grief, if he "must pine/ Again for that dread country crystalline" without any hope of re-entering it, then the millennial visions of "Ballad of the Nightingale," "Ballad of Rebirth," and "Ballad of Eternal Life" were meaningless. If time and evil relentlessly destroyed all hope and promise, if the central principle of the universe could be reduced to a cruel "iron law," then the intimations evoked by "Horses," for instance, of some mysterious dispensation beyond the natural order were pure illusion; and illusion too were the "glints of immortality" that shone in dreams through the "dross of experience." But Muir, as we have seen, was convinced that what his dreams and ancestral memories revealed to him was not illusion. On the one hand, he knew only too well that cruelty and evil were undeniable realities; on the other, he had felt "bright shoots of everlastingness" which he knew were equally real. He was, in fact, firmly committed to both terms of a paradox, and this paradox, which had been only implicit in *First Poems*, but which was to become clearly the determining force and the controlling design of all his later poetry, he openly faces for the first time in *Chorus of the Newly Dead*. How to resolve it, how to reconcile these two irreconcilable aspects of experience, is the question the poem explores, and explores in objective rather than subjective terms. Because *Chorus of the Newly Dead* lacks force, both imaginative and technical, the exploration it makes is hardly penetrating. But it is important, nevertheless, as Muir's earliest attempt to probe an issue that he would return to again and again, and that he would eventually transform from a problem into the solution of that problem.

Eventually, too, he would deal with the problem more subtly, more indirectly, as well as more successfully. Here he attacks it head on. For when he originally conceived the idea for the poem, according to *An Autobiography*, he thought of it as a "chorus in which the dead were to look back at the life they had left and contemplate it from their new station";[1] and this approach, though it practically demands overt metaphysical speculation, remained the basic plan. A very Yeatsian cast of characters, including an Idiot, a Beggar, a Coward, a Harlot, a Hero, a Poet, and a Mystic, all take part in a drama very reminiscent of Hardy. Newly dead, like "The Souls of the Slain," they turn back to describe their lives on earth, and like the Spirits in *The Dynasts*, they comment on the meaning of these lives. They try, apparently, to bring pain and beauty, good and evil, into a single transcendent whole. The trouble is, they really have nothing new or significant, or even very coherent to say. When those characters, for example—and they are the majority—who have lived unfortunate lives, attempt to explain their mortal miseries, they can only echo Hardy again.

It is some anonymous force, some malevolent "They," the equivalent of Hardy's Immanent Will or Great Face behind, which has willed all their pain. Thus the chorus asks in unison, after the Beggar has related his sad story:

> Did They, all knowing, Who bade the dust
> Spawn him, did They give him in trust
> Ought of Their light to realize . . . ? [2]

When the Poet has his turn to speak, on the other hand, he abandons Hardy for a more cheerful view and a more Tennysonian line. He sees some justification for his earthly life in the beauty he found there, in his "stubborn love for passing things" (11). And the Mystic apparently enjoys a sufficient satisfaction with his personal gift for seeing into the inner workings of the cosmic machine. He alone knows ". . . what grinding levers move/ To change the orbit of an eye/ Towards death, towards hate, or full towards love" (14). He alone sees past, present, future together in:

> That stationary country where
>   Achilles drives and Hector runs,
> Making a movement in the air
>   Forever, under all the suns. (15)

But what his insights amount to, or what relation they have to the Poet's love of beauty or the harsh decrees of the tyrannous "They," he never indicates.

If *Chorus of the Newly Dead* fails as a metaphysical statement, it fails too as a poetic structure. Muir had been moved by the idea, but his "imaginative excitement," he himself realized, "never managed to communicate itself, or at best now and then, to the poem."[3] In spite of the fact that the design calls for a difference in voices, for instance, since long-lined choral passages alternate with shorter-lined lyrics or arias spoken by the individual characters, the total effect is that of a single, generally monotonous voice. There is no dramatic exchange among the characters, no mounting intensity, nor even any climactic point. Instead, characters and chorus follow one another punctually, like clockwork, without any change of pace. Nor, for the most part, does style supply what structure lacks, for the style suffers from the same inherent monotony. Superfluous, cloudy adjectives frequently muffle the sense; forced inversions weaken the syntax; and the meter is often mechanical and lifeless.

Yet the level of competence, as a rule, is far higher here than in *First Poems*. These are no moon-charméd valleys or dead orchids. While the meter may be mechanical, it rarely thuds or limps. What is more, Muir has clearly made an effort to break away from the simple quatrain pattern which dominated *First Poems*. The opening chorus, for example, is in six-line stanzas —iambic pentameter quatrains with final couplets—and the concluding chorus is effectively handled in rhyme royal. Several of the characters too speak in stanzaic forms new in Muir: the Idiot in stanzas of eight strongly stressed two-beat lines, obviously intended to indicate a trance-like, withdrawn condition; and the Hero in an elaborate six-line stanza rhyming *a, a, b, c, c, b*, with the *a* and *c* rhymes feminine, the *b* rhymes masculine. None of these innovations, it is true, is sufficiently successful or startling to counteract the essential tedium of the poem, but they demonstrate a developing skill on Muir's part, and an increasing interest in experimentation with new forms and new approaches.

There is another very different and very significant area where *Chorus of the Newly Dead* shows new growth, and that is in its concern with psychological abnormalities, particularly with various degrees of estrangement. For the Idiot, the Beggar, the Harlot, the Coward, even the Hero, who is threatened more by "lying mists of thought" (13) than by the usual physical danger, are all, in one way or another, estranged, shut off from ordinary life. They all suffer, as Butter notes in *Edwin Muir: Man and Poet*, from a sense of alienation;[4] and in this, of course, they resemble Muir himself, who came to feel, after years of trying "not to see" the Glasgow slums all around him, that he was "insulated" from the outside world altogether, imprisoned in a "crystalline globe or bubble."[5] Yet they are not in any sense masks for Muir. Rather, they objectify not only the alienation Muir himself had suffered, but also the alienation he recognized in modern man and society, and in the history which led to that society. In his treatment of these characters, Muir shows the understanding and the compassion of a fellow sufferer. He has an eye for the telling detail that reveals their loneliness and insecurity: the Coward's realization, for instance, that "The tame town mongrels seemed to know/ My secret fear" (8), or the Hero's seeing the boulders by his path as beasts (13). But in spite of this accuracy in description and in spite of the fact that disturbed, frustrated, neurosis-ridden personalities increasingly occupy Muir's attention in his later poetry, it is not merely the personalities themselves, whether like or unlike his own, which are his primary concern. It is the view which he explores through them that matters more, the view already implied in *First Poems* but now extended in range by this device, that the temporal, physical world is charged with menace, that history is a road gone wrong, that "Time and Space" are "A dusty room, a street to pace" (10), with no exit anywhere.

That such a view should result from a poem apparently framed, as we have seen, to fit the irreconcilables of Muir's beliefs into a larger whole, to suggest the "infinite and incalculable forms behind the visible drama,"[6] is more than a little ironic. For what we have here is clearly no resolution of the paradox, but an extension and a confirmation of the darker side. It is true that the dark does not take over altogether. The Mystic, the Poet, and the concluding chorus make feeble gestures on behalf of the light. And no wonder. For Muir himself at this time in his life, after having recovered from his own neurosis, made a happy marriage, and begun at last to earn his living by writing rather than clerking, was more than ever convinced that the visions of reconciliation he saw in his dreams were ultimately trustworthy. In fact, in the very special little German community of Hellerau, inhabited by artists, intellectuals, and "faddists," where he and his wife stayed for a while during these years, he seemed to catch a reflection of the "image of Eden and the prophecy of the time when the lion would lie down with the lamb."[7] This particular Eden, he discovered soon enough, was "nonsensical . . . , no doubt," and the lion and the lamb were "sentimental." But the fact is that even before this Teutonic paradise vanished, swept away by inflation, Hitler, and war; even while Muir was enjoying greater good fortune than he had ever known; even while he was still writing to Sydney Schiff of his plans for completing the *Chorus* by a new movement, begun by the Poet, "away from suffering to its transcendence," and by a final chorus which would "sum up everything and convey some of the glory even of those who pass through life apparently deprived of what it can give, the beggar, the harlot, and so on"[8]—even then a very different feeling directly contrary to his announced purpose was working itself out in the poem in its own way, through those same "deprived" and alienated characters, "the beggar, the harlot, and so on." What they bear witness to is not any transcendence of suffering, nor any hint of glory. In its final effect, therefore, *Chorus of the Newly Dead* reconciles no irreconcilables; rather, it demonstrates once more the workings of that "iron law" which Muir had felt at the heart of the universe during his years in Glasgow: the cruelty, the fear, the pain, the injustice.

But what was unconscious, or at least not fully recognized feeling in *Chorus of the Newly Dead*, becomes conscious purpose in Muir's next full volume of verse, *Variations on a Time Theme* (1934). For in the years that had passed between these two volumes, Muir had ceased to be the raw beginner with "no training" and "no technique" that he was, according to his own confession in *An Autobiography*, when he wrote *First Poems* and the *Chorus*. Then, he admitted, he wrote in "baffling ignorance, blundering and perpetually making mistakes."[9] On the one hand were "the rhythms of English poetry"; on the other, the images in his mind; and all he could do at that point was "to force the one, creaking and complaining, into the mould of the other."[10] But by the early 1930's, when he was working on *Variations*, he was no longer so ignorant. He no longer had to rely on whatever "rhythms of English poetry" were lying conveniently at hand. He had gained, by now, sufficient mastery to choose the forms, the images, the measures, that would serve him, or to adjust and adapt them to his needs. To be sure, his mastery was still far from absolute; but it was secure enough to assure him control of his material; secure enough to assure the general agreement, at least, of purpose and effect. What he says in *Variations on a Time Theme*, accordingly, there can be no doubt he intended to say.

Furthermore, what he intended to say had gathered force and fullness over the years. For not only was he still partially persuaded by the teachings of Nietzsche, to which he had been enthusiastically attached during his last years in Glasgow, that an eternal recurrence really was the pattern of existence, that a continually returning past held man in a hopeless trap, but he was inevitably oppressed by contemporary events. These were years when economic depression deepened in Britain, when strange new forms of violence took shape in Italy and Germany, when another world war seemed every moment at the point of explosion, when that insidious evil the Muirs had felt all around them on the Continent seemed to have taken visible shape in Hitler and his followers. However withdrawn from the mainstream of events they now lived, quietly occupied with their writing and their young son, who filled their waking hours with a "daily sufficiency," they could not escape the universal contagion of fear. The poetry Muir wrote then, which was the poetry of *Variations*, was inevitably, as he himself realized, "tinged with apprehension." [11] But that was not all. The themes which more than ever concerned Muir in his prose writings during those same years, partly by chance, partly no doubt as a final working out of his earlier neurosis, were consistently dark themes of estrangement and betrayal, of suffering, loss, and the continual frustration of good; and those themes inevitably tinged his poetry with their coloring. The sense of the universe as a hostile place which pervades his first novel, *The Marionette* (1927); the fragmentation of nation, family, and personality, the repression of natural good, which is the motif of his biography of John Knox (1929) and of his novel, *The Three Brothers* (1931), set in

Knox's Scotland; the grimy Glasgow slums, which are both the physical and the spiritual landscape of his third novel, *Poor Tom* (1932): all these elements are absorbed into the structure, atmosphere, and meaning of *Variations*, which thus almost had to be what it is, a study of contemporary man trapped in the wilderness of time, exiled from the Eden which once was his home.

To this nightmare vision of man trapped and lost, another nightmare world with which Muir had recently become acquainted must certainly have given confirmation, if nothing more. This was the world of Kafka's writings. For after translating German novels, plays, and stories on order for several years; after turning themselves, as Muir ruefully commented, "into a sort of translation factory" [12] both Willa and Edwin now discovered a writer whose books they themselves wished to translate; and in 1929 they "persuaded" the publisher, Secker, "to commission a translation of Kafka's *The Castle*." [13]

In the next few years, with their translations of this novel and of *The Trial, Amerika,* and most of the short stories, they not only introduced Kafka to the English-speaking public; they so saturated themselves in his works that "at one stage," wrote Muir, "Kafka's stories continued themselves in our dreams, unfolding into slow serpentine nightmares, immovably reasonable." [14]

Yet the Muirs never fully identified with these dreams. They "troubled us," Muir continued, "but not as real dreams would have done, for they did not seem to come from our own minds but from a workshop at the periphery of consciousness. . . ." [15] They came, in other words, from a mind with whose workings the Muirs had made themselves familiar; a mind Muir found closely akin in many ways to his own; a mind whose perception of the "irreconcilability of the divine and the human law" [16] agreed with and helped to clarify Muir's slowly developing, parallel perception; and yet, of course, a completely different and separate mind, one that corroborated but did not dominate the native bent of Muir's own imagination. For what Muir derived from his work with Kafka, essentially, was not any new way of thinking, but a strengthening of what he already thought: a validation of his original sense of the irreducible mystery of life; a ratification of his instinctive turning to certain archetypal symbols, such as a road or a journey and to certain themes, as of estrangement and frustration. When he wrote *Variations on a Time Theme*, therefore, even though he was in the midst of his Kafka translations, the images of entrapment, of fruitless wandering, of regret for some lost glory that he evoked there were his, not Kafka's. They were Kafka-like to begin with—in this quality lies much of their disturbing power—and Muir's intimacy with Kafka's writings could not but have made them more so. But first and last they were Muir's, rooted in his past, whether in Scotland or in Europe, in his preoccupations, and in his intuitions.

How deep those roots in Muir's peculiar feelings and concerns were may be seen from the epigraph he chose for *Variations*, a verse from the seventh chapter of the Book of Daniel: "And another king shall rise after them . . . and think that he may change times and laws, and they shall be given into his hands, until a time, and times, and dividing of times." Aside from the references to "time" and "dividing of times," which make this text appropriate to a sequence of ten separate poems called *Variations on a Time Theme*, the epigraph has no discernible meaning; Muir himself, in fact, when he first referred to it in *John Knox: Portrait of a Calvinist*, called it "inexplicably obscure." [17] But as the text Knox chose for his first sermon as a Protestant preacher in Scotland, it is full of meaning. In his mouth it was an awesomely accurate portent of the strife and division he would bring to Scotland. For Muir, whose antipathy to Calvinism, although more restrained, resembled that of his fellow Scot, John Davidson, it was charged and overcharged with the weight of all the consequences he saw resulting from Knox's career down the centuries: the betrayal of Scotland to England, the splitting of the Scottish nation, the withering of Scottish humanism, the perversion of Scotland's healthy natural instincts. When Muir took this text for *Variations*, accordingly, it could only have been because he wished to add to those images of fragmentation and desolation already in the poem a further perspective: the fragmentation and desolation of Scotland's sad history. Although neither Scotland nor Knox is named in *Variations*, nor is the epigraph identified, it is the dreary, broken country Knox's influence made of Scotland, in Muir's eyes, that provides the environment, the very air of *Variations*: a land of a lost heritage and civilization, a land of aimless, frustrated people, a land scarred and wasted by the "peculiarly brutal form" [18] of industrialism which its history imposed on it.

The industrial wasteland surrounding Glasgow, in fact, appears physically, although namelessly, in the opening section of *Variations*. The "Splintered stumps, flapping bark, ring-wormed boles" of ruined trees, the "Soft milk-white water prisoned in jagged holes/ Like gaps where tusks have been," [19] which the speaking "We" of the poem, representative man, sees all about him, are the same "tattered, worm-ringed trees," the same "filthy pool where yellow-faced children splashed" [20] which Muir encountered when he walked out into the so-called country on Sunday to escape the Glasgow slums. Once this wasteland motif has been announced, its character alters in succeeding sections; it becomes an endless plain, a dead land of dead stones, the wilderness in which the Jews wandered for forty years. But until the seventh section, which marks a climax in the movement of the poem as a whole, as well as a shift in method from various approximations of narrative to metaphysical questioning, it is some type of wasteland, whether Scottish or Biblical, that remains the constant setting.

Since even to speak of a "wasteland," however, is to invoke the ghost of Eliot, perhaps it is best at this point to consider the inevitable question: how closely does this wasteland resemble Eliot's? In certain ways, the answer must be, there is considerable resemblance. Like Eliot's *The Waste Land*, Muir's *Variations* is a sequence: a gathering of fragments, rather than a sustained whole. Like Eliot's, Muir's poem mirrors in this fragmented form, as well as in underlying myth, metaphor, diction and rhythm, the image of a broken world. In Muir's broken world, moreover, there are undeniable echoes of Eliot's voice. It is Eliot's tone of spiritual inanition, for example, his manner of disjointed introspection, which Muir's "We" assumes in Sections One and Five of *Variations*. It is Gerontion and J. Alfred Prufrock, Tiresias and Ferdinand, who speak through lines like these:

> Did we choose idly, following the fawning way,
> Or after years of obstinate dubitation,
> Night sweats, rehearsed refusals, choose at last
> For only the choice was left? (39)

And surely, behind the extravagance of these lines from Section Five:

> Or clinical fantasy begotten by
> The knife of demon Time the vivisector
> Incising nightmares, (44)

must lurk the cool competence of Prufrock's famous invitation:

> Let us go then, you and I,
> When the evening is spread out against the sky
> Like a patient etherised upon a table. . . .

But teasing echoes like these, when actually counted, do not add up to much. Nor does the fact that a profounder similarity between the two poems clearly does exist, in form and in basic image, necessarily mean that *Variations* is an imitation *Waste Land*. In reaching out for a more contemporary statement, Muir naturally experimented with some of the techniques provided by a great innovator. But he had no natural affinity for Eliot's style or approach, as he had for Kafka's. In fact, at the time when he was writing *First Poems*, he did not "even like Eliot's poetry: it took . . . [him] several years to recognize its great virtues." [21] Even now, when he was clearly accommodating some of its virtues to his own purposes, his individual vision remained independent of Eliot's, as it had of Kafka's. After all, he had lived shut in a trap himself, in that "crystalline globe"; his own country, despite its tourist attractions, was still a wasteland; he had no need to take theme or image from Eliot.

Far more, instead, he borrowed from the Bible. The identifiable blighted suburbs of Glasgow which are the landscape of *Variations* in Section One quickly dissolve, as we have seen, into a plain and then into a stony desert where the displaced tribes of Israel wander. For just as Muir universalized and objectified his boyhood fear by giving it the shape of the myth of Hector and Achilles, so he has here given the shape of the Biblical story of the forty years in the wilderness to the fears and frustrations of his manhood, his times, and his nation. The last four sections of *Variations*, it is true, do not depend on this story; rather, they comment on the human condition it exemplifies. In the first six sections the myth sometimes merges with other fables, such as the loss of Eden, or it is almost obscured by the strange settings in which it appears. Yet, whether this was Muir's original intention or not, this myth does underlie all six of these sections as they are now printed, holding them together, however loosely, and directing them towards a climactic point in Section Seven.

Thus in Section One the myth appears in a contemporary setting. The "we," the spokesman for Man, is lost in a twentieth century wilderness, the ravaged Glasgow wasteland. Significantly it is a modern wasteland, for in this section, which announces the theme for the entire sequence, the emphasis is strictly on the predicament of modern man, on his exhaustion, his confusion, his purposelessness. Somehow, he does not know how or where, he has strayed from the right road and now finds himself among "mangled stumps/ And splintered stones," forced to build his house, if he can, in "nameless fields" (40). Using Eliot's hesitant, broken rhythms, he questions insistently: "How did we come here . . . ?" "Where did the road branch?" Or, borrowing Eliot's over-intellectualized vocabulary to indicate intellectual sterility, he wonders, was it those years of "obstinate dubitation,/ Night sweats, rehearsed refusals" (39) which finally resulted in his making the wrong choice? In any event, to all these questions there is no answer.

But despite the absence of answers, and despite the over-all effect this section gives, of a complete dead end, the presence of the ancient myth is still clear. He has come, as the Israelites came into Egypt and then into the desert, from a better land. "We have seen Heaven opening,/ And fields and souls in radiance." He has a tradition to maintain, as the Israelites strove to maintain the rituals of their religion. "Can we sing our songs here?" (40). Although there is no suggestion of eventual deliverance into Canaan, there is definitely the Kafka-like suggestion of a road, a right road, that might have been traveled. For if this stray pilgrim chose the wrong turning, as he clearly did, then there must have been another path he should have chosen. In this road not taken lies the promise that completes the myth, that verifies the presence of exiled Israel behind this modern exile.

Behind the riders on the "boundless plain" in Section Two, as well, the same shadowy exiles stand. They are not visible in the powerful opening lines, with their magnificent, and again Kafka-like image of straining, fruitless effort:

> At the dead centre of the boundless plain
> Does our way end? Our horses pace and pace
> Like steeds for ever labouring on a shield. (40)

But these lines came to Muir, as he wrote to Miss Gwendolen Murphy, editor of *The Modern Poet* (1938), "spontaneously," without his "being conscious of the possible development they implied." Then that "development grew from a variety of associations that would have remained isolated and disconnected but for this image, which acted as a sort of magnet, and drew them into a rough pattern around it," [22] and among the associations thus drawn into the pattern was the Biblical wandering in the wilderness. Instead of a wilderness, the place of exile is now a "boundless plain" where the pacing horses cannot advance beyond "dead centre." Yet even here there is a memory of a day before the horizons were sealed, a lost Eden, a "golden country," now "razed as bare" as another devastated kingdom, Troy. The lines, "We cannot return/ And shall not see the kingdom of our heirs," while admitting imprisonment in the present, at the same time point to some freedom beyond the present, which "our heirs" shall enjoy. Here, clearly, are the children of Abraham in the desert, remembering their forfeited inheritance, and hoping for the promised land which some of them will never see.

Yet so far the Biblical myth has been intimated only. It is not until Section Three that the pattern is at last fully revealed in the final phrase of the final couplet:

> Set free, or outlawed, now I walk the sand
> And search this rubble for the promised land. (43)

For this phrase, "the promised land," simultaneously identifies the underlying myth, evokes a specific, though distant hope, and, because Section Three is not a simple retelling of the story of exile in the desert, defines man's present fate. Beginning in Eden, where Adam, Man, and Muir himself, integrated into a single "I," "dreamed away/ My one eternity and hourless day" (42), this section proceeds in rapid, indeed too brisk couplets, through the familiar steps recorded in the Bible—the slaying of Abel, the building of the Ark, the selling of the birthright, bondage in Egypt—straight to man's destined end, the "sand" and "rubble" of the wilderness. These are the sands and the rubble, the movement of the poem indicates, to which the original lapse from eternity, the primal fall from Eden, inevitably led. These are the sterile and the broken hopes in which man perennially walks, by the very nature of temporal existence.

On the other hand, there is that still unbroken hope, certainly too easily introduced here, contained in the words, "the promised land." What of that? Strategically placed as they are, at the conclusion of the section, these words necessarily function dramatically in the structure of the whole sequence. They reinforce the implications of promise in the two earlier sections. They signal some continuation of the theme in succeeding sections. They provide sudden and therefore startling contrast to the otherwise suffocating gloom all about them. But like the forces of light in *Chorus of the Newly*

Dead, they are too few and too weak really to relieve the gloom. They are one more of Muir's gestures on behalf of his stubborn faith that "All shall be well, and/ All manner of thing shall be well," but this faith has not yet found the way to contradict or even to counterpoise the evidence of his senses to the contrary. Perhaps, too, these words ring particularly hollow in the light of what history was already making of them, and of what Muir himself would make of them in his later, bitter "Moses."

In any event, after this climactic point, the movement of *Variations* slackens, possibly in compliance with a well conceived design; certainly because Sections Four and Five are the weakest of the ten which make up the sequence. Yet even here the basic myth is not forgotten. We are still with the wandering tribes of Israel; in Section Five, the "infidel congregation of mankind," more "wraiths" than human, condemned to a sort of Inferno half Dante's and half Eliot's, still recognize around them the Biblical landscape of their traditional exile: "Once there were ancient cities here, and shrines/ That branched from Adam's world" (44). Only that questionable promise is missing.

When it is restored in Section Six, it is still questionable, even though this section, the last of those built on the wilderness myth, is also the one which follows the original story most faithfully and dwells most on that ambiguous promise. For the sixth section tells again in detail the story of the desert exile to which the events as progressively described in the couplets of Section Three precipitated mankind. But here that impetuous movement has ended. The irregular, confused rhythms of Section One have subsided too, and the ponderous straining of Section Two has relaxed. Instead, a very effectively managed, dazed, dream-walking measure has become the pattern to describe the children of Abraham, circling monotonously in the sand for forty years:

> Forty years this burning
> Circuitous path, feet spurning
> The sliding sand and turning

> The wheel, turning again
> Sharp rock, soft dust, a land
>   Choked in sand. (45)

In memory, now become dream, they recall the coming of
Jehovah "To Sinai's hill one day"; they recall the breaking of
the law that made the wilderness their home; they recall, "In a
separate dream" (46), passing by great kingdoms and distant
towers. But the dream itself has become their reality. Their
nostalgia for home: "Where is our land?" (47) is part of the
dream, and they can not distinguish the promise that once was
given them from the dream which has engulfed it:

> There is a stream
> We have been told of. Where it is
> We do not know. But it is not a dream,
> Though like a dream. (47)

To that stream the same "Fate" that keeps them in the wilderness will eventually lead them, in its own good time. Their
own will, however, is powerless to aid them, for they have lost
their will. Trapped in the "soft dust" so long, they seem now
to belong there; and it is no wonder if, although they long for
the promised land, they also fear it. It represents a reality outside their dream, from which they have been so completely estranged that they dread its contact. They have lived, like
Muir, imprisoned in a "crystalline globe or bubble," from
which they have come to regard the outside world with "min-
gled longing and dread." [23]
   They have reached, indeed, a point of extremest alienation
from the living, green, and fertile world, the world where
willing has meaning and objects are solid. And Muir, who has
led them there through a sequence of six variations on the Biblical fable of exile, now abandons that fable and turns to contemplate their predicament as exemplary of the human condition. It is Time, he concludes very characteristically in the last
lines of Section Seven, Time which has brought man to this
impasse, Time which has imprisoned man in his own frustra-

tions, Time which keeps him from Eternity, where alone he can be free:

> If there's no crack or chink, no escape from Time,
> No spasm, no murderous knife to rape from Time
> The pure and trackless day of liberty;
> . . . .
> Imprisonment's for ever; we're the mock of Time,
> While lost and empty lies Eternity. (48)

But what he seems to say in these final lines is not the whole of what he actually says, nor is what he actually says so simple. For in the first seven lines of this fifteen-line poem, Time is not a destroyer only. Time is savior as well as villain, giver as well as taker. Man is both:

> Ransomed from darkness and released in Time,
> Caught, pinioned, blinded, sealed and cased in
> Time;
> Summoned, elected, armed and crowned by Time,
> Tried and condemned, stripped and disowned by
> Time. (47)

Time is, in other words, the very condition of being at all. Only in time, therefore, can its works be redeemed; only in time can time itself be transcended; "only in time can the moment in the rose-garden" be experienced.

Thus here is the first hint of the kind of reconciliation, of acceptance Muir will finally, even if precariously, achieve: he will find reconciliation in that paradox he had thought, in *Chorus of the Newly Dead*, to resolve. Even earlier in *Variations*, there are hints of an attraction to paradox, in the riddling questions of Section One: "Did we come here/ Through darkness or inexplicable light. . . . ?" (39); in the "stationary journey" of Section Two; and in the central image of that section, the horses pacing without progress. It does not become a unifying principle, however, a foundation for a faith, until this seventh section; and even here it is not maintained. It slips, slides, and perishes into the easier wish, expressed in the second

70

stanza, to escape time altogether. But that it was more than a passing perception, the structure of the section proves, for it is a structure built on paradox. Each of the seven lines in the first stanza and five of the eight lines in the second end with the one word, "Time." The rhyming words are those immediately preceding "Time," as in the pair, ". . . crowned by Time,/ . . . disowned by Time"; and it is notable that in almost every case it is opposites that are paired. Contradictory terms are thus brought together in each couplet; in each couplet, that is, a paradox is stated and then solved, its irreconcilable poles joined in "Time." Contrasted with these couplets of locked opposites are three free lines, appropriately ending in "liberty," "free," and "Eternity," where "Time" has no power. But the over-all pattern of the poem attests that it is in time that opposites are united, and thus only time itself can provide the "crack or chink," the "escape from Time" which the human spirit seeks.

From this perception of paradox as a reconciling principle, Muir retreats in Section Eight to the more conventional view, stated in rather unconvincing imagery and mechanical pentameter couplets, that the true home of the human spirit lies beyond time, in that "fireless kingdom in the sky" (50) arching above the "fire-wheel" of the seasons, where "we, Time's slow martyrs, burn" (49). But with the startling first couplet of Section Nine the paradox returns, and returns, moreover, in a highly complex image involving not only the psychological fragmentation reflected in earlier sections of *Variations*, together with the time-eternity antitheses of Sections Seven and Eight, but also the related dualities of good and evil, man and animal, suggested in *First Poems*. For the image is that of a split personality, a single individual who is two, deftly introduced in a tetrameter couplet where the two halves of the second line oppose each other like the two halves of the one person:

> Packed in my skin from head to toe
> Is one I know and do not know. (50)

The speaker, characteristically, is alienated by this interloper from his true self, his "Soul," who comes only as a "Visitor," and so "seldom" that "I cannot tell/ If he's myself or one that loves me well" (51). But just as the wanderings of Israel in the wilderness, cut off from both its heritage and its hope, were also the wanderings of contemporary man in the wasteland of contemporary society, so this peculiarly twentieth-century case study is also the case of mankind, on a cosmic scale. The interloper here is more than the worser half of a modern psyche, more than Muir's own defense, as Willa Muir suggests in *Belonging*, "against the doctrine of Original Sin" (249) that he had absorbed from the very air of Calvinist Scotland; the interloper is the source of original sin; he is the ancient adversary who brought death—and time—into the world, and all our woe:

> If I could drive this demon out
> I'd put all Time's display to rout.
> Its wounds would turn to flowers and nothing be
> But the first Garden. The one Tree
> Would stand for ever safe and fair
> And Adam's hand stop in the air. (51)

Yet—and this is more and more often the case as Muir speaks more often in a truly individual voice—there is more here than what so readily meets the eye. Demon and originator of sin and mortality that he is, this interloper is not Milton's heroic Satan, essentially distinct from the Adam and Eve he tempted. He is, as Muir knew well enough from his own experience, an inseparable and altogether unheroic part of the human soul; and in another couplet where again the second line is neatly bisected into opposing halves, Muir gives his name and some clue to his identity:

> His name's Indifference,
> Nothing offending, he is all offence. (50)

For increasingly in Muir's eyes it is in such indifference, in unfeeling, unthinking insensivity to the needs of others and to the claims of society, that the root of the world's suffering lies. That "iron law" of life which Muir had learned to recognize in Glasgow, which was the other face of time in *First Poems*, and which dictated the final effect of *Chorus of the Newly Dead*, was indeed a remorseless, indifferent law, insensate in its operation, but it operated, Muir's psychoanalysis and his European sojourn told him, within as well as upon the human spirit. Thus in Muir's novel, *The Three Brothers*, where the basic situation, as he originally planned the book, was a counterpart of that here in Section Nine of *Variations*, the story of twin brothers, "one good, one bad," was to be "a perfectly simple allegory of the soul." [24] Moreover, the "bad" brother, Archie Blackadder, who corresponds to the Interloper, demonstrates his wickedness precisely as the Interloper does. He is utterly indifferent to the wrongs he commits. He lies, cheats, fornicates, betrays his twin, the "good" brother, David, who of course corresponds to "my Soul, my Visitor," then breathes in his sleep at David's side with a "callous and impenetrable rhythm" that David realizes is "stronger than anything else in the world." [25] Naturally more than deliberately evil, "nothing offending," but "all offence," Archie is the "brute insensibility of life" [26] which is at once an inseparable element of the human soul, the root of original sin, and perhaps, as well, a defense against the Calvinist interpretation of that sin.

But "brute insensibility" belongs by definition to animals, not men, and this is the crux of the matter. For Archie—Indifference—is in fact an animal. Speaking of him to David, the twins' elder brother, Sandy, says: "He's a pleasant enough wee beast himself." [27] Despite Muir's reverence for animals as animals, in their own place in the hierarchy of creation, for animals in the human world, for men sunk back into the condition of animals, all appetite and no memory, he has only horror. The "animal with human faculties," as he describes Edmund in his essay, "The Politics of *King Lear*," [28] is for him a primary symbol of evil; the instinctive, heedless malevolence of that animal is the primal fault. Yet—and here is the paradox towards which this reasoning has been leading—that animal is also, necessarily and intrinsically, a part of man. The bad part,

it is true, in a "simple allegory of the soul"; the odious interloper who "can stare at beauty's bosom coldly/ And at
Christ's crucifixion boldly" (50), but still a part without which
man would have no peace. For when the better half of the soul
appears "in pity, for he pities all," to banish Indifference, to re-
dress time's wrongs, to "end all passion, flaw, offence," he
thereby cancels what he "feeds upon." He must "cease," his
"office done" (51). Or, in Blake's profounder couplet:

> Pity no more could be
> If all were as happy as we.

Yet without pity, on the other hand, that "homespun fiend Indifference" would at once return and have man "wholly." To
keep pity alive, to save himself from complete surrender to animal insensibility, man must have both:

> On these double horns
> I take my comfort, they're my truckle bed;
> Could Pity change the crown of thorns
> To roses peace would soon be fled
> And I would have no place to lay my head. (51)

From this unequivocal acceptance of paradox, however,
this clear recognition of the necessary coexistence of good and
evil, Muir retreats once again in the remaining lines of the
poem. Although he resurrects dead Pity, "quickened by my
plight," he does not restore the real wrongs Pity had canceled.
Instead, in lines that vary now from tetrameter to pentameter,
as if to show at least a partial healing of the original divided
personality, he has Pity make for his "delight/ A mimic stage"
where pursuit and battle, cunning and treachery are acted out
in fantasy only, until "at such deceitful art," the "Tears, real
and burning" (52) that vanquish Indifference come to his
eyes. But as the art is deceitful, the victory is deceitful. Neither the wrongs of the world nor the Indifference which
causes and tolerates them can be so easily reckoned with.

As if acknowledging that these last lines of Section Nine
offer too easy a solution to all the frustrations and fears of the

earlier sections of the poem, the final section of *Variations on a Time Theme* offers no solution at all. Instead, it asks questions. It is, frankly, a riddle, as time itself was always a riddle to Muir, as well as destroyer and betrayer. Yet at the same time, it is a satisfying riddle, in that it gathers together into its mystery many of the motifs scattered through preceding sections: the heraldic horses of Section Two, the relationship between animal and man hinted at in Section Nine; the loss of Eden or of some original blessed condition, which underlies all the sections; and the continuing opposition of time to timelessness. As a riddle, too, it provides a fitting conclusion for a sequence where the only real approach to resolution has been in acceptance of the irreconcilable, in paradox.

As a riddle, furthermore, it provides a form with which Muir is more at ease than he seems with those of the earlier sections. For riddles, as Mrs. Muir notes in her *Living With Ballads*, are a traditional ballad element; and in the ballad tradition, as he demonstrated in "Ballad of Hector in Hades," Muir was instinctively at home. This was the form in which, as we pointed out earlier, he had experienced poetry as a child in Orkney, where poems in books, aside from those of Burns, were unknown, but where everyone as a matter of course "knew a great number of ballads and songs which had been handed down from generation to generation." [29] And the rhythms of this form, the compression, the directness, the force, came naturally, like native speech, to his tongue. Section Ten of *Variations*, indeed, is not strictly a ballad so far as stanzaic pattern goes; instead of the typical ballad quatrain or quatrain with a refrain, the stanza here consists of six irregularly rhyming tetrameter lines. But these lines are short enough to enforce the compression of a ballad, and for the most part the diction is simple as a ballad's, the statement as concise, the movement as free. Where the diction departs from simplicity, as in the repeated "fabulous" of stanza two, the polysyllabic "irrecognizably" of stanza three, and the final, dramatic "crucified" of stanza four, the effect is not at all a break in the ballad tone, but rather an intensification of the mystery and portentousness appropriate to a riddle. Similarly, although the shifting rhyme scheme is more complicated than the easy alternate rhymes of a ballad, the complication is not emphatic, does not draw attention. It simply adds another degree of perplexity to the total enigma.

That enigma announces itself at once, in the first stanza:

> Who curbed the lion long ago
> And penned him in this towering field
> And reared him wingless in the sky?
> And quenched the dragon's burning eye,
> Chaining him here to make a show,
> The faithful guardian of the shield? (52)

Yet since the riddle, as we have seen, is related to the entire *Variations* sequence, it cannot be totally insoluble. There must be some clues to indicate the meaning of lion and dragon, the identity of their tamer; and there are. In the first three lines, for example, an unmistakable echo from Eliot points to the significance of the wingless lion. ". . . Who clipped the lion's wings/ And flea'd his rump and pared his claws?" asks Eliot in a passage from "Burbank with a Baedeker: Bleistein with a Cigar," which Muir certainly knew, because he quoted it in a discussion of contemporary poetry;[30] and this cropped animal, a symbol of the decayed glory of Venice, suggests that Muir's lion, too, stands for the loss of some former glory. Still another lion with which Muir was naturally familiar was the lion of the Scottish banner, which like Eliot's beast represents a lost heritage, a broken kingdom—the Glasgow wasteland of Section One, in fact; while yet a third beast, similarly connected, through John Knox, to the fate of Scotland, adds another perspective in time, a metaphysical depth, to this complex symbol of loss. For in the same chapter of the Book of Daniel from which the epigraph for *Variations* was taken, the prophet has a dream of four great animals. While the fourth is rather like a dragon, the first is definitely a lion with eagle's wings, which Daniel "beheld," moreover, till "the wings thereof were plucked." Since dreams were for Muir a way of reaching back in time to timelessness, to Eden before the Fall, to the harmony and wholeness which Muir, as exemplar of modern man, knew in his childhood before he entered the wilderness of the present century, this lion of Daniel's dream must undoubtedly have represented for Muir a figure from the far side of that wilderness, an emblem of the original, eternal order. The plucking of the lion's wings, in turn, must have represented the destruction of the original order, the break between that world and this. And this meaning, half derived from Daniel, half imposed on the text by Scotland's history, remains the essential meaning of Muir's plucked lion, "penned" in the "towering field" of a flag.

The theme of loss and exile which runs through the *Variations* sequence of course confirms this interpretation of the lion, as does a passage in Muir's *Autobiography*, which runs almost parallel to the second stanza of Section Ten, with its "fabulous wave." Here is the stanza:

> A fabulous wave far back in Time
> Flung these calm trophies to this shore
> That looks out on a different sea.
> These relics of a buried war,
> Empty as shape and cold as rhyme,
> Gaze now on fabulous wars to be. (52)

And in *An Autobiography*, describing a dream he had of walking in Spain, where he saw a bas-relief of an enormous Herculean figure, half man and half bull, Muir writes again of "relics" and "waves": "It was like an ancient and rich relic which had survived the long, watery wash of time from an age when animal and man and god lived densely together in the same world: the timeless, crowded age of organic heraldry." [31] But although this passage corroborates the derivation of heraldic lion and dragon from the legendary world before the Fall, when man and animal, each in his right place, lived with the gods in a single community, in one respect it does not correspond to the poem. The figure of the bull-man in *An Autobiography* is a "relic" of what seems peaceful coexistence; the lion and dragon of the poem are "relics of a buried war," which "Gaze now on fabulous wars to be." Is there another enigma here?

Partly, yes; and partly a movement of the whole poem, through this enigma, to another level. For that war, buried now and forgotten, was not like our wars. In that age, when the creatures were all legendary, when beasts were worshipped and sacrificed and hunted, "the hunt, like the worship and the sacrifice, was a ritual act." Beasts "were protagonists in the first sylvan war, half human and half pelted and feathered, from which rose the hearth, the community, and the arts." [32] They were protagonists, that is, in a battle which was not simply destructive, but a necessary and therefore sacred mechanism for the survival of life and the possibility of civilization; and it is as protagonists of that battle that they still remain on flag and shield. But although they remain as signs, their meaning and origin have been forgotten. For us, not for themselves, they are now "Empty as shape and cold as rhyme." Because we have forgotten what they were, yet retain their shapes on our insignia of war, they gaze out now—and what a resonance this second "fabulous" commands—on our very different battles, on our "fabulous wars to be."

From this point on, a double point of view controls the poem. To lion and dragon on flag and shield, the new world where Time's fabulous wave has cast them seems "Irrecognizably the same" (52). The road they see is the "self-same road they know" (53) and have always known. They have no need to "cast a look" behind them, because they live, as Muir makes increasingly clear in his later poems about animals, in an eternal present without a past. In our world, the world of man, on the other hand, dreadful things have happened; long years of history have passed which have drained dragon and lion of the significance they had in that legendary age before history began. The dragon, indeed, for us has "died/ Long since" (53), although his counterpart on the shield is not aware of it, and long since, for us, "the mountain shook/ When the great lion was crucified."

With the word "crucified," as with the distinction in the second stanza between "a buried war" and "wars to be," the poem moves again to another level, assumes another dimension. For "crucified" inevitably evokes the image of Christ, momentarily identifies the lion with that image; and the effect of this identification is to magnify immensely the force of the lion figure. From a nostalgic symbol of the lost age of myth and legend, of the friendly Eden of beast and man before the Fall, the lion is suddenly transformed into a symbol of all spiritual value. Yet at the same time that the lion is transformed—in the very same breath, indeed—with a suddenness that generates extraordinary dramatic power, that symbol of spiritual value is cut down. In a single instant, by the single word, "crucified," the lion is at once deified and destroyed; and since his destruction, which by implication took place long ago, the world has been what it is throughout the whole *Variations* sequence, except for a few glimpses of paradox as a reconciling principle—a spiritual desert.

In those few glimpses, however, Muir suggests what sort of way he will eventually find to lead him out of the desert. It will not be a way to any promised land of the future, nor to any literal Canaan of peace and plenty, but to an imaginative perception of the "clear unfallen world" that still underlies even the contemporary blighted earth; the "blossoms of grief and charity" that bloom even in our "darkened fields." This is, of course, not the way he originally proposed in *Chorus of the Newly Dead*, when he first faced the fact that his beliefs were irreconcilably divided between two contrary poles, that he was firmly committed to both terms of a paradox. Then his intention was to solve the problem by leaving one term of the paradox for the other, by moving "away from suffering to its transcendence." But as we have seen, what actually transpired in the poem, in spite of his announced intention, was a turning away from transcendence towards a deeper experience of suffering, so that in its final effect *Chorus of the Newly Dead* is bleak and despairing. What he did as if involuntarily in the *Chorus*, furthermore, he did deliberately in *Variations on a Time Theme*, which is a sequence of images of man trapped and tortured in a temporal world where his heritage has been destroyed, his purpose lost, and his spiritual values "crucified." Precisely in turning to such a hopeless picture of the human condition, however, and in accepting its inescapable reality,

79

Muir took the necessary first step towards the only solution to his dilemma that could be acceptable to him as a man who insisted on holding on to both its horns. Once he had experienced the extreme of hopelessness, and by experience mastered it, he could reach for the other extreme; and those glimpses of paradox as a principle of unity which occur in *Variations* give promise that the other extreme may be sometime within his grasp.

IV

"The Stationary Journey"

That slight progress towards a reconciling vision which begins to be discernible even in the gloom of *Variations on a Time Theme*, however, is less apparent in Muir's next volume, *Journeys and Places* (1937). For the dominant issue here is one of form. The mood is still dark, as if Muir knew that he had farther yet to go to find that extreme limit of despair he must reach before turning again to the light. But as if he also knew that whatever direction he might take, his arrival at the journey's end depended on a final mastery of his craft as a poet, he pauses in this volume to strengthen the skills he has thus far gained and to try his hand at new ones. In *Variations on a Time Theme*—and indeed in *Chorus of the Newly Dead* as well—he was already clearly experimenting with different objective correlatives, different styles and meters, voices and approaches. But except in the powerful opening lines of Section Two of *Variations,* the enigmatic couplets of Section Nine, and the mysterious balladlike Section Ten, he never quite hit on a style or a voice that was authentically his and no one else's. The distinction of *Journeys and Places* is that here, in the course of his experimenting, he does at last find his own individual way of speaking. What is more, in several of the poems here he achieves that perfect fusion of style and subject, that final economy and inevitability which he had much earlier recognized as the criterion of artistic form.

In *Latitudes*, his first collection of essays, published in 1924, Muir had already formulated a definition of artistic form. It was an aphoristic, rather dogmatic definition that showed his continuing attachment to Nietzsche—Muir was in fact in this volume, as Michael Hamburger observes, an *"esprit fort"* [1] quite different from the modest personality of the later prose. But it was also an illuminating definition, succinct and just, which remains a valid standard by which to measure any man's verse. "Form is attained," Muir wrote then, "when a theme is treated with a sort of final economy and inevitability, and as if fate had put its palm upon it. . . ." [2] And because in *Journeys and Places* Muir gives priority to the attainment of form; because he breaks little new thematic ground but concentrates rather on finding new shapes for his familiar subjects and on perfecting his handling of these subjects, he is able to arrive at that "final economy and inevitability" he himself had called for. The hand of fate has rested firmly on several poems in this volume and lightly touched many more.

Not that the development which is so obvious in this volume is a mere advance in technical proficiency. On the contrary, by means of this greater technical proficiency Muir achieves far greater scope and depth. He suggests unexpected associations in his customary themes, uncovers new implications. Nor is that all. Partly liberated by this increasing formal mastery from that tendency to excessive subjectivity we noticed in *First Poems*, and from a related tendency, observable in much of *Variations*, to shadowy abstraction; and partly no doubt simply impelled to the concrete by a growing sharpness of eye and ear, a greater concern for the solid world outside that now broken "crystalline globe," Muir in these poems makes far more use than ever before of the concrete situation, the sharp, specific detail. Whereas in his earlier volumes, aside, of course, from such exceptions as "Childhood," "Horses," "Ballad of Hector in Hades," and a few passages from *Variations*, he often evoked that sense of mystery, which is one of the distinguishing characteristics of his poetry, only to leave it as mystery, in its own cloudy region, he is now increasingly able to "fit that world to this," to give the mystery objective form or else to reveal its presence in the objective world.

In this progression from the abstract to the concrete, moreover, from the disembodied to the embodied mystery, an important step in Muir's development as a poet is involved. He comes into his own. Instinctively from the beginning a poet who spoke in symbols—Muir wrote to Stephen Spender in 1944, after reading Bowra's *The Heritage of Symbolism*, that he realized he "had been writing symbolist poetry very frequently for years without knowing it" [3]—Muir now, for the simple reason that the symbols he uses are more specific, more easily apprehended, speaks that language with a new authority. Although the wanderings and the exile of *Variations on a Time Theme*, for example, were as certainly as any of the poems in *Journeys and Places* symbols of the "movements" and "pauses in time," [4] of the psychological conditions and of the shape of human destiny, that Muir said *Journeys and Places* stood for, the fact that these wanderings were so often vague, so tenuously attached to their underlying myth, kept them from functioning, as symbols, with full effectiveness. In *Journeys and Places*, on the other hand, the journeys are for the most part clearly defined and particular: the mind's journey back in time, or Tristram's "out from Tintagel gate." The places, in the few "place" poems that are successful, are particular too: ravaged Troy or the "bare wood below the blackening hill" where "The Enchanted Knight" lies sleeping. As a result, precisely because both places and journeys are so particular, so clearly defined, immediately recognizable as natural objects, they are immediately and powerfully effective as symbols. For "the proper and perfect symbol," Ezra Pound once wrote, "is the natural object"; its full depths may be beyond reach, but its surface is unmistakably there to touch and grasp; and this is one of the lessons which Muir demonstrates, in *Journeys and Places*, that he has begun to learn.

The opening poem here, "The Stationary Journey," for example, like so many of the other poems in the volume, is essentially a ballad; and by this utilization of a form which not only allowed him easy control, as a form natural to him, but also demanded concreteness, directness, compression, Muir plainly shows that he is seeking a new simplicity of style which would effect a new clarity and permit a new objectivity of symbol. That new objectivity of symbol is plainly present too in the historic or legendary figures Muir uses to carry the narrative, and in the clearly defined, typical ballad pattern of the narrative itself: it is a journey, a quest for a "different way." Yet at the same time, this is obviously no ordinary ballad. There is a depth beneath this immediately apprehensible surface. The journey is mental more than physical: back into time or inward to "Imagination's one long day."

In actual fact, as the title, borrowed from "sad stationary journey" of Section Two in *Variations on a Time Theme*, at once makes plain, there is really no journey, no movement at all. There is no possibility of movement; the first and last stanzas, significantly enclosing the rest, prove by the stars and the seasons that man is as he was in most of *Variations*, hopelessly imprisoned in time:

> Here at my earthly station set,
>   The revolutions of the year
> Bear me bound and only let
>   This astronomic world appear. (57)

Because man forever rebels against this imprisonment, however, forever seeks escape, if only in illusion, it is with the illusion of escape that the major portion of the poem is concerned. No matter that the road that the quester of the ballad seeks to pursue does not, in fact, exist; the pursuit itself is a road, a way of breaking through the barriers imposed by time and space.

In strict accuracy, two imaginary roads are involved here. First comes the road backward, to the point beyond time's beginning:

> Yet if I could reverse my course
>   Through ever-deepening yesterday,

Retrace the path that led me here,
    Could I find a different way? (57)

Nevertheless, despite the effective link, of both rhyme and alliteration, between "ever-*d*eepening yester*day*" and "*dif*ferent
way," as if only in the deepest past could there be any possibility of a different course, this reversal of time in the end offers
no improvement on the historic record. Progressing, or rather
regressing through the years, from age to manhood to infancy,
from Charlemagne to Saint Augustine to the Pharaohs in the
sands of Egypt, the road back leads at last not to any original
Eden but to the frightening inhumanity of an Eternity without "world, life, and soul" (58). And here, where the metaphysical abstraction which Muir has so far avoided, by using
actual historic names to indicate the recession of time, now
seems inescapable, Muir achieves a small triumph. He finds a
concrete image even for this unearthly concept of impersonal,
immortal Being—an image of pure solid geometry:

For there Immortal Being in
    Solidity more pure than stone
Sleeps through the circle, pillar, arch,
    Spiral, cone, and pentagon. (57)

Interesting and illuminating as a footnote to this stanza is a
strikingly parallel passage in Muir's *Scottish Journey*, where he
talks of the strange geological formations of the North Western Highlands. "These older cones and pyramids," he writes,
"seem to have no connection with time at all; they are unearthly not in any vague but in a quite solid sense, like blocks
of an unknown world scattered blindly over a familiar one.
The thoughts they evoke . . . give one the same feeling one
might have if one could have a glimpse of an eternal world,
such as the world of mathematics, which had no relation to our
human feelings, but was composed of certain shapes which existed in complete changeless autonomy." [5] Even without this
suggestion of a possible source for the image, however, the
stanza is sufficient in itself. It is a chilling and dismaying vision

of pure Being without world or time, and from it Muir naturally recoils to the other road of the poem, the inward road of the "mind's eternity," where the "dead world" can "grow green" again. Here once more he uses particular historic or mythic characters, all existing together, to create the illusion of an eternal Now; and here once more, of course, the road leads to no better alternative than time has already granted. The illusion fails. The imaginative reversal or suspension of time which has been the main action of the poem, however, remains its final effect. It abides because, aside from an occasional stilted phrase, or an archaism such as "eld," it is presented in straightforward, easy language and in specific, solid images—solid as Highland rock.

Equally straightforward, so far as language goes; equally objective and concrete on the surface and far more complex beneath, is another balladlike journey poem from this volume, "The Road." For this road too, like that in "The Stationary Journey," is an apparently simple natural object which is a symbol of inner mysteries. According to the first two lines, for instance:

> There is a road that turning always
>   Cuts off the country of Again, (61)

this road is no more than the road of conventional time, which turns away from Again and cuts it off forever. Yet as the poem develops, the path it takes proceeds in exactly the opposite direction: away from a fresh and ever-changing future, where redemption is possible, back into a vision that had haunted Muir since the time, now many years ago in Glasgow, when he first encountered the teachings of Nietzsche—an Eternal Recurrence of the same horrifying past. Furthermore, it is in this change in the direction and nature of the basic road image that the enormous resonance and the very real terror of this poem lie. The firm ground seems to slip out beneath one's feet as the road of the first two lines, the unequivocal road to the future, imperceptibly shifts into a sort of dead-end street, where time stands still, where "The budding and the fading tree" are one, simultaneously growing and decaying in the eternal Now projected earlier in "The Stationary Journey." Then, although time continues to stand still, the character of the road changes again and the ground drops away altogether. For in the last two stanzas, the road becomes a precipitous plunge into the darkness of the original seed, where life and evil were conceived together: ". . . within the womb,/ The cell of doom," and where:

> . . . small is great and great is small,
> And a blind seed all. (62)

To this sense of slowly, inevitably encroaching terror which the shift in the road image creates, every other element in the poem contributes as well, because this at last is one of those poems on which fate has unquestionably rested its palm. Except for the figure of the "great runner" who "never leaves/ The starting and the finishing tree," all the other half-mythical figures who exemplify the simultaneity of past and present here are types of killer or victim: the archers, the deer, the hunter, the mountain-headed lion already encountered in "Ballad of the Nightingale," the sinking ship, and the man reclining on his tomb. There is no escape from the menace. Nor is there any escape from the tightening web of sound, which in this context becomes menacing too: the insistent rhymes of the five-line stanza (*a*, *b*, *c*, *b*, *b*), the frequent alliteration, the hypnotic repetition of the same or similar words. What is more, because the fifth line in almost every case is either an echo of the fourth or a summing up of the sense of the whole preceding stanza, it takes on the eerie effect of an actual echo, disembodied and ghostly. And diminishing in duration. For as the poem descends into darkness, narrows to the primal "cell of doom," the fifth line of each stanza shrinks correspondingly. Whereas in the earlier stanzas this final line contains three or four stresses, with a varying number of unstressed syllables, in the fifth stanza it contains only four, almost equally stressed syllables: "Sunk past all sound"; and in the sixth it is reduced still further, to the two stern stresses of "The cell of doom." In the seventh and last stanza, it is true, one more stress creeps back into the line: "And a blind seed all"; but that "all," which significantly rhymes with "small" and "fall," results in no real enlargement. It simply universalizes the shrunken doom. In this final word, small indeed becomes great, and great, small; a "million Edens" and a "million Adams" sink into the confines of that one "blind seed."

In the dark of this original, and ultimate, germ, moreover, all distinctions must be lost, and this is precisely the very unsettling effect of the constant reiteration of paradox throughout the poem. For these are not the acceptable paradoxes, the intimations of reconciliation, glimpsed in parts of *Variations on a Time Theme*, but the unacceptable paradoxes of the revolving Nietzschean wheel, which obliterates praise and blame, sin and amendment, in a relentless "order which must be/ Itself and still the same" (115). Since this is the country of Again, it is, of course, primarily time distinctions that are lost, as in the following stanza:

> There the beginning finds the end
>   Before beginning ever can be,
> And the great runner never leaves
>   The starting and the finishing tree,
>   The budding and the fading tree. (61)

But even more than the confusion of beginning and end, past and present, is involved here. While the repeated present participles seem to dissolve time boundaries within a timeless continuum, the repeated participial endings set up another continuum of sound. Such lines in other stanzas, moreover, as "All flies and all in flight must tarry," blot out the customary demarcations of motion; and "For small is great and great is small" cancels measure. When, in the fifth stanza, the whispering *s*'s that blur past with present in the first two lines, "There the *s*hip *s*ailing *s*afe in harbor/ Long *s*ince in many a *s*ea was drowned," recur in the final line with an even more pronounced hushing effect: "*S*unk pa*s*t all *s*ound," not only universal darkness but universal silence seems to bury all. The inevitable next step is taken: to the "cell of doom" and the "Blind seed."

From this terrifying drop into darkness, this descent into madness itself, it is a relief to turn to two more "journey" poems that might be called merely studies in derangement: "Tristram's Journey" and "Hölderlin's Journey." Yet here again, as in "The Stationary Journey" and "The Road," a surface simplicity conceals complexity. Here again clarity of form permits inner resonance; the naturalness of the symbols at once defines and deepens the meaning. What Muir does in "Tristram's Journey," indeed, is to repeat the device he used so effectively in "Ballad of Hector in Hades" and less successfully in *Variations on a Time Theme*: he gives to an inner experience, perhaps his own—the retreat into a state of alienation and the recovery from it—the firm outer shape of a familiar legend. He makes the subjective objective.

Just as in the Hector Ballad, however, in order to make the old legend accommodate the new meaning, he had to adjust the story slightly, shift its emphasis and point, so here, as Butter notes in *Edwin Muir: Man and Poet*, he must go beyond the Malory version of the Tristram romance.[6] Where Malory concludes the incident with Iseult's recognition of Tristram after her hound has "leapt up and licked his face," Muir concludes with the next step, with Tristram's rediscovery of himself and of the world around him: "The round walls hardened as he looked,/ And he was in his place" (66). And by this small degree of difference in the end of the tale, Muir corroborates and completes what his choice of imagery and detail throughout the poem have already signaled, that the story he is really telling is only remotely connected with Tristram's fatal love. It is rather a meticulous account of a temporary mental aberration. It is another study, like those in *Chorus of the Newly Dead* and certain sections of *Variations*, of estrangement and alienation.

This meticulousness, this clinical accuracy, is, in fact, the dominating characteristic of the poem. The abrupt violence of the opening stanza, for example, accurately and briefly indicates the shock that drives Tristram into lunacy:

He strode across the room and flung
  The letter down: 'You need not tell
Your treachery, Harlot!' He was gone
  Ere Iseult fainting fell. (64)

With equal precision and economy, the near repetition of this final line in the last line of the penultimate stanza, "Iseult fell in a swoon," indicates that Tristram has journeyed full circle: he is returning to sanity. In the intervening stanzas, on the other hand, the stanzas of Tristram's madness, the same accuracy dictates the braking of the initial impetus, the abandonment of economy for an obsessive accumulation of detail. There is, thus, the effect of a dazed, trance-like state in the slow, repeated monosyllables, the hovering accents, the long vowels ending each line, of the following stanza:

He turned again and slowly rode
  Into the forest's flickering shade,
And now as sunk in waters green
  Were armour, helm, and blade. (64)

The drawn-out enumeration of "Armour, helm, and blade," furthermore, suggests irrationally fixed attention, while the alliteration that ties "slowly" with "sunk," "forest" with "flickering," as if the elements of earth, air, fire, and water were somehow mixed together, suggests the confusions and distortions of a dream. In the succeeding stanzas, too, images of dream confusion pile up: the castle doubled in the lake; the tower, wood, and hill Tristram passes yet returns to, "Now different, now the same"; Tristram himself, lying so still in the field he seems "One of the rocks"; until in the end confusion sinks into apathy. King Mark and Iseult, her maids, and the scarlet knights and ladies on the tapestry, are equally unimportant in Tristram's eyes. When the hound triggers both Iseult's recognition of him and his own recognition of himself, it is not Iseult, his mistress, who first materializes out of the indifference which has divided him from himself, it is—and here again is a touch of singular accuracy—the small spears of the grass where he has been lying:

> There as he leaned the misted grass
>   Cleared blade by blade below his face,
> The round walls hardened as he looked,
>   And he was in his place. (66)

In the companion piece to this study of Tristram's derangement, "Hölderlin's Journey," on the other hand, the interest is less in observation of madness than in its spiritual implications, and the poem has accordingly still more meaning, still richer suggestion. For although the simple ballad form is the same here, and the same, too, the reliance on an already existing story, the story in each case is significantly different in nature and in the material it provided for Muir to work on. Where Tristram's was a well-known romance, with given circumstances as well as a given plot for Muir to manipulate, the story of Hölderlin's journey gave him only the barest facts. So little was known, indeed, either of Hölderlin or his journey, to the English-speaking public at the time Muir wrote the poem, that he felt it necessary to add an explanatory note to *Journeys and Places*. What he could tell of the journey was simply this: that Hölderlin, having come to work in Bordeaux as a tutor after he had been driven from the house of the woman he loved in Germany by her understandably angry husband, suddenly decided, in the hot summer of 1805, to return to Germany on foot. When he arrived, weeks later, "ragged, emaciated, and out of his mind," [7] he found his Diotima was dead. But of all that he saw, heard, and felt on the way, he left no record. Accordingly, all that he sees, hears, and feels in Muir's poem is Muir's invention, a projection of what Muir believed such a mind must have experienced under such conditions.

But in his invention, Muir was not without guidance. He had Hölderlin's poems, especially those written after the onset of his madness; and he had his own dreams, which often spoke to him of the same things that he found in Hölderlin's poems; spoke to him of such "certain truths," for example, as that the "past exists in the present, that the gods (or what Hölderlin meant by them) mingle with human history, that time and timelessness are inextricably bound up." [8] It is by a fusion of these two surprisingly consistent elements, of motifs from Hölderlin's poems and from his own dreams and poems, that Muir fills in the itinerary of that mad journey from Bordeaux and at the same time transforms it into a spiritual quest. Thus the "maze of little hills,/ Head-high and every hill the same" (66) of the second stanza is undoubtedly the "great plain dotted with little conical hills a little higher than a man's head" [9] of the millennial dream which in *First Poems* resulted in "Ballad of the Nightingale." Yet at the same time, because these hills are "hills of lies," concealing the presence of Diotima, who may be far or near, they also bear some relation to the ambiguous hills of these lines, translated by Muir, from Hölderlin's *Patmos*:

> . . . round are piled
> The peaks of Time, and the best beloved
> Dwell near at hand, languishing
> On inaccessible hills.[10]

The paradox of the near yet inaccessible, moreover, together with the enigma of another two lines, again from *Patmos*: "And blinded I sought/ Something I knew," [11] surely echoes in the following stanza from "Hölderlin's Journey":

> Perhaps already she I sought,
> She, sought and seeker, had gone by,
> And each of us in turn was trapped
> By simple treachery. (67)

But just as surely, every word in this stanza is authentic Muir as well. The bafflement and frustration are his; the sense of treachery is his; the perception of paradox, as we have seen in *Variations on a Time Theme* and "The Road," and shall see again and again, is his too. Between him and Hölderlin, as between him and Kafka, it seems, a natural affinity of vision and feeling simply happened to exist.

Out of this affinity, moreover, Muir evokes more than Hölderlin's initial confusion on his journey, his crazed belief that the Diotima he seeks is perhaps seeking him, just on the other side of that "little world of emerald hills." Muir evokes also Hölderlin's final achievement, through and beyond his madness, of a clarity of vision and a humble acceptance, an acceptance that faintly prefigures, for one of the few times in this volume, Muir's own eventual perception of an ultimate reconciliation of opposites. For the poem does not end, as Daniel Hoffman claims, in a "perfect epiphany of despair." [12] There is despair, certainly, when Hölderlin, looking at a living deer beside another carved in stone, is suddenly and intuitively aware that Diotima is dead, "As if a single thought had sprung/ From the cold and the living head" (67). But there is also enlightenment, and from the enlightenment comes a kind of victory. In recognizing the truth of Diotima's death, Hölderlin simultaneously recognizes the fixed pattern, the appropriately Platonic form, as it were, of his search for her. He now knows "Diotima was dead

>Before I left the starting place;
> Empty the course, the garland gone,
>And all that race as motionless
> As these two heads of stone." (68)

But having seen this vision, very similar to the vision in "The Road," and almost as appalling, of a frozen, predetermined fate, Hölderlin now knows, as well, the futility of striving or rebelling. Instead, in a last stanza of singular sweetness and poignancy, he resigns himself to what must be:

>So Hölderlin mused for thirty years
> On a green hill by Tübingen,
>Dragging in pain a broken mind
> And giving thanks to God and men. (68)

For here, clearly, all passion is spent. The extreme simplicity of the language cancels all preceding complexities and confusions in a new serenity. The single "green hill" erases those earlier, lying "emerald hills," to set in their place the traditional hill of peace and holiness, where it is fitting for thanks to be given "to God and men." And although the third line,

"Dragging in pain a broken mind," serves as reminder that this peace and serenity are the aftermath of tragedy, still the particular phrasing of this line, which seems almost on the point of saying "broken wing" instead of "broken mind," suggests a kind of light in the tragic darkness. The bird with a broken wing can still sing, and Hölderlin, when Diotima was dead and he was mad, still wrote some of his greatest and most radiant poetry, as Muir's last line, "giving thanks to God and men," clearly implies.

In still another "journey" poem of this volume, "The Mythical Journey," many of the motifs from "Hölderlin's Journey" reappear, either as thematic elements or as landmarks in a symbolic scene. And a comparison of these two poems, so similar in motif, so different in effect, is highly illuminating. For the comparison emphasizes more clearly than ever the point already made in the beginning of this chapter: that to attain the "final economy and inevitablity" of form he admired, to give to that "original mystery" of life which we have seen he believed to be the proper province of poetry, a local habitation and a name, Muir was seeking at this point both a tight form, whatever its shape, to compress and concentrate his language, and a specific situation, a concrete symbol, whatever its nature, to focus his meaning. In "Hölderlin's Journey," as in "Tristram's Journey," "The Stationary Journey," and "The Road," he had an approximation of the terse, direct ballad stanza. In "Hölderlin's Journey," again, he had the specific situation of a particular poet's ordeal. And in "Hölderlin's Journey," as a consequence, he wrote a poem at once clear and evocative, simple and mysterious, the incoherence of madness in a remarkably coherent whole.

In "The Mythical Journey," on the other hand, these two essential requirements are lacking. The blank verse of the narrative is loose and inconsistent in style, sometimes pure Eliot, sometimes pure Muir, and sometimes very nearly pure prose. The narrative itself is shapeless, abstract, and confused. The anonymous third person, apparently standing for humanity, who is the protagonist of this quest for a meaning in life, encounters the same "little hills,/ Head-high" that bewildered

Hölderlin, and among them, like Hölderlin, he wanders "seeking that which sought him" (63). The tentative acceptance he reaches at the end, moreover, when "He builds in faith and doubt his shaking house" (63), is perhaps a fainter version of Hölderlin's hard-won acceptance, his willingness, even in pain and broken in mind, still to give "thanks to God and men." But none of this really fits together in an integrated structure. Furthermore, in spite of a magnificent opening evocation of a strange, dark Northland; in spite of the fine image of the sun rising in "Rivers of running gold" across the sea—a startling and welcome flash of color in the usual gray landscape of Muir's poetry—the poem as a whole never takes on the sharpness and concreteness of these subsidiary details. In direct contrast to "Hölderlin's Journey," "The Mythical Journey" remains obscure, incoherent, imperfectly realized.

Not so, however, the first of the "place" poems in this volume of *Journeys and Places*, the poem called "Troy." For this restatement of the Trojan disaster, one of those "pauses in time" to which such "movements" in time as the Greeks' pursuit of glory and vengeance at Ilium have led us, is again, like "The Road," a poem on which fate has set its palm. What was missing in "The Mythical Journey," the specific situation, the defined form, is present here; and present too, as a result, are concentrated power and meaning. At one and the same time, within the compass of twenty-nine straightforward blank verse lines, this poem is a first-rate story, another study in madness, a parody of all military adventures, and a devastating comment on history as mere history, unredeemed by any dispensation beyond itself.

These straightforward blank verse lines are notable, to begin with, because they represent something new for Muir. Although he obviously experimented, in *Variations on a Time Theme*, and in "The Mythical Journey," with different styles of blank verse, he never achieved until now the brisk, rapid movement, the directness, the conciseness he manages so easily here. How did this happen? According to K. L. Goodwin, in *The Influence of Ezra Pound*, it was Pound's example that taught Muir this "exciting narrative" manner;[13] from Pound he derived such typical devices as "the plunging *in medias res* at the beginning; the anticipation of the subject with 'He'; the omission of the verb; the staccato movement of 'Troy taken'; and the loose syntactical linkages, especially with the 'Ands.' " And these elements of Pound's story-telling method are undeniably observable here, as is an even more important aspect of Pound's method: "Direct treatment of the thing." But there is more. Eliot was a master narrator too, and such phrases as "Proud history has such sackends" closely echo Eliot. In the following lines, furthermore:

> Mysterious shadows fell
> Affrighting him whenever a cloud offended
> The sun up in the other world (71)

there is a significant echo of these two lines from Wordsworth's "The Afflictions of Margaret":

> The very shadows of the clouds
> Have power to shake me as they pass.

For this poem, Muir believed, was "the greatest" of the "few poems" in which Wordsworth was "content to tell . . . a story simply as a story," with the disinterestedness of "the makers of the ballads";[15] and the similarity of these two passages can only indicate that what Muir had very much in mind here was the telling of a "story simply as a story," as the ballad-makers told their tales. From whatever master could teach him to do this, plainly Muir was willing to learn.

As for the story Muir tells, here once more, as in the "Ballad of Hector" and "Tristram's Journey," he takes a traditional myth and reshapes it. Or rather, not so much reshapes it, as goes beyond it. For, as Edwin Morgan notes in his study, "Edwin Muir," in *Review*, "What Muir felt most deeply and expressed most movingly was the sense of aftermath . . . , the endurance or patience or suffering of survivors."[16] His question is always, what happens after the familiar sequence of events has ended? After Achilles has slain Hector, what does the shade of Hector feel? After the sacking of Troy and the tragedy of the Trojan Women, what then? Madness, is his answer here; madness, degradation, the reduction of humanity to the level of rats in sewers. But he does not say it. He shows it. Because he shows it, moreover, in the actions of a pathetic, demented old man who still retains, even in the Trojan cellars, some of the dignity of the Trojan defenders, he is able to juxtapose past with present, illusions of heroism with sordid reality, so that the one makes a shattering comment on the other. In the "rat-grey" light, among the "scurfy hills and worm-wet valleys" (71) that are the present travesty of those windy plains where gods and heroes fought, the old man takes the "bold rats" for the great Ajax and Achilles, just as Ajax in his madness once mistook a herd of sheep and goats for the Trojans; and the unstated query is clear; were those famous battles really any more glorious? Were those ranks of warriors and princes, in the end, any more important or heroic than the "rat-hordes" which, "moving, were grey dust shifting in grey dust" (71)?

Yet even while present is implicitly commenting on past in this poem, the events of the present proceed with a momentum of their own, and this momentum has a classic rise and fall. From the abrupt first line and a half, "He all that time among the sewers of Troy/ Scouring for scraps," where the nameless old man is introduced, doing just what the rats do, there is a gradual building up of his character as a human being. He is "venerable," as "venerable" as Priam, the king. His "long, white, round beard," emphasized by this succession of evenly accented monosyllables, is a strictly human feature, and it is the only thing in the poem not soiled by the prevailing grayness. Human, too, in his speech, the old man calls to the rats, "Achilles, Ajax, turn and fight!" until his own cries come back to him as if the "wild Greeks yelled round him" still. And at this point, when he is deepest in his distraction, yet most human in his courage and in his resistance to the rats he seemed at first to resemble, he reaches his apotheosis:

> Yet he withstood them, a brave, mad old man,
> And fought the rats for Troy. (71)

But the defiance that sounds in these lines, where another sequence of monosyllables functions to stress each separate, undaunted word, is obviously a mad, sad defiance. It is the terribly pathetic "wasted bravery" of a Lear or a Quixote. Because the adversaries that arouse this patriotic fervor, ironically, are rats, the old man is undercut at the very moment he achieves a certain grandeur. He seems to fade, after this, into the rat-grey dust, where his human personality is lost. The "chance robber seeking treasure/ Under Troy's riven roots" who drags him to the surface gets not a human word from him. When he sees "Troy like a burial ground/ With tumbled walls for tombs," he still says nothing; and when his captors wrench his limbs to make him tell, " 'Where is the treasure,' " he keeps silent, with a final irony, until he dies. For how should such a daft old man know of any treasure? Or how could there be any greater treasure, indeed, than his own indomitable human spirit, already wasted and mocked by the perversities of history?

This theme, of the waste of the human spirit in a history that is only a story, only a succession of dates and dynasties, unrelated to an underlying fable, is of course a theme suggested by Muir's poetry from the beginning and repeated with increasing clarity until the end. But although among the *Journeys and Places* poems it is stated most forcefully in the direct, dramatic form of "Troy," which looks forward to Muir's later work, it is most insisted on in some of the "place" poems at the end of the volume which look back to the obscurer, more involved style of *Variations on a Time Theme*. For most of these final poems of *Journeys and Places*, ironically, represent more a reversal than an advance in Muir's mastery, whether of the effective use of symbolism or of mere mechanics. After the formal perfection, the objectivity, the directness of poems like "Troy" or "The Road," poems like "The Unfamiliar Place," "The Unattained Place," and "The Solitary Place," although studded with striking images, particularly of autumn and harvesting, are nevertheless abstract and cryptic. The central argument is never objectified in the poems themselves. With its reiterated "I and not I" (81), for example, and its sense of terrible isolation, "The Solitary

Place" might almost be Section Nine of *Variations*, which was similarly based on the split-personality motif. But just as the meaning of that section was not fully apparent without reference to external sources, such as Muir's novel, *The Three Brothers*, so the meaning of the "I and not I" concept here cannot be decoded without outside help. In itself it contains no certain clues to the point Muir had in mind, the inadequacy of mere history to the human soul. For this Muir himself had to supply the key, in a note written to Stephen Spender:

> The theme of the poem was, as I consciously saw it, the modern historical view of the world, in which there is no reality except the development of humanity—humanity being in that case merely an I and not I, a sort of long and interminable monologue of many.[17]

Once this interpretation of "I and not I" is clear, once it is evident that what Muir is projecting in this poem is a state of affairs where there is no reality except this "I and not I," no underlying fable, then the overwhelming loneliness suggested by the poem becomes justified. Then the final lines take on the heartbreaking quality of the cry of an abandoned child:

> O then I am alone,
> I, many and many in one,
> A lost player upon a hill
> On a sad evening when the world is still,
> The house empty, brother and sister gone
> Beyond the reach of sight, or sound of any cry,
> Into the bastion of the mind, behind the shutter of the eye. (81)

But the heartbreak is not inherent in the poem. It depends, as Muir admitted to Spender, on an "argument existing outside the poem." [18] The poem itself, therefore, however related in theme to "Troy," falls far short of "Troy" in clarity, objectivity, and self-sufficiency, as well as in resonance. It lacks that "final economy and inevitability" of form which makes "Troy" a landmark in Muir's increasing mastery of his craft.

There is, however, another such landmark among the

"place" poems, and that is "The Enchanted Knight." Like most of the other "place" poems, it has an autumnal setting, which suggests the suspended animation of the seed in winter, or of the knight himself waiting for some mysterious resurrection. Like the other "place" poems too, it is full of echoes and reflections from other sources—the paralysis of the "hero" for instance suggests the "frustration of the hero" which Muir found to be "an intrinsic part of Kafka's theme" [19]—but although these echoes hint at further extensions of meaning, "The Enchanted Knight" requires no explication or clarification from outside. It is complete in itself. It has its own charge: it is one of those poems on which fate has set its hand.

The germ of "The Enchanted Knight" can of course be found in "The Enchanted Prince" of *First Poems*; but in the later version little of the original is left except the central tranced figure, and even he is radically changed. Where in the earlier poem he was in the awkward position of having to tell his own story while "lying" half asleep on some "ancient mount," [20] now he keeps a more appropriate silence. An omniscient narrator tells the tale and keeps the illusion of the trance unbroken. Far more important, where in the original no reason for the trance was given or even intimated, now a single name, La Belle Dame Sans Merci, not only provides the reason but transforms the whole situation, the whole poem, so that it functions on a level altogether different from that of its predecessor.

It functions, that is, in a long tradition stretching back through Keats to ballad, romance, and folklore: the tradition that the love of a mortal for a "faery's child" brings destruction. But when Muir handles traditional material, ballad or myth, as we have seen, he handles it in his own special way. He reshapes it for his own ends. In this poem, accordingly, although he retains the ballad's objectivity and directness, he does not, like Keats or the ballad-makers, dwell on the familiar fatal events. Instead, simply by invoking the name of the enchantress, he implies these events, then goes on to what interests him more: the aftermath of the story, the plight of the lover after the "faery's child" has cast her evil spell and left him forever "On the cold hill side." For in turning from the expected fairy tale plot, however unhappy, to its still more disturbing results, to the image of the impotent, paralyzed knight lying on a darkening hill in a fading landscape, Muir is turning to another, more powerful image of the contemporary world he projected in *Variations*—a world of alienation, of thwarted impulse, of crippled will. When he demonstrates, line by line here, the intolerable pressure of the nightmare weighing on the forsaken knight, therefore, it is clearly the nightmare of our own age that he points to as well.

Not until the last line of the poem, however, does this relationship with the present become unquestionably plain. Until then, although the relationship is there, gathering intensity, it remains an undercurrent. The surface of the poem is concerned with establishing the heavy oppression of the knight's sleep, its long duration, his frustrating dreams, and all of these are marvelously evoked by a multiplicity of fine details. The late, leafless autumn scene so economically implied in the second line, for instance, "In the *b*are wood *b*elow the *b*lackening hill," where the alliterating *b*'s emphasize the dearth and the darkness, reappears in the second stanza in the pattern of rust that time has engraved on the knight's armor:

> Long since the rust its gardens here has planned,
>   Flowering his armour like an autumn field.
> From his sharp breast-plate to his iron hand
>   A spider's web is stretched, a phantom shield. (74)

And here the fading of one season becomes the fading of many. "Long since" all this began; "long since" the soft *a*'s of "gardens," "armour," "autumn," and "sharp," interwoven with echoing *l*'s, *r*'s, and *s*'s, have been making a quiet music that speaks of quiescence and withdrawal, until in token of the absolute immobility that has gripped the knight all this while—and in token too of long neglect and decay—the spider has spun its web unimpeded across his breast. The frail web, in fact, has altogether replaced the knight's own solid shield.

Yet voices penetrate that unmoving sleep. In the fourth

stanza the cry of a single bird within the otherwise "silent grove" not only emphasizes, by its very loneliness, the physical desolation, the abandonment in which the knight now lies. Because it seems to him some "long-lost" human voice which his will longs to follow even though his body cannot, it emphasizes as well his deprivation of love. His unavailing effort to rise in answer even to this most compelling summons provides the final, conclusive proof of the hopelessness of his condition. He is bound beyond any possibility of release.

Still more effective than imagery of autumn or of lonely bird, however, in stressing the force that paralyzes the knight, and more effective too than the sound pattern of any particular stanza, is the total sound pattern of the whole poem. For although in the first two or three lines of the first stanza this pattern seems innocent; although the repeated *l*'s, the carefully varied vowels, the shifting caesuras, seem to combine only to make a music of unusual richness for Muir's poetry up to now, the richness and the innocence rapidly suffer a sea-change. As early as the end of this same stanza, as the stanza itself proves to the ear, it is evident that the richness is far from innocent:

> *L*ul*l*ed by *L*a Be*ll*e Dame Sans Merci,/ he *l*ies
>   In the bare wood be*l*ow the b*l*ackening hi*ll*.
> The p*l*ough drives nearer now,/ the shadow f*l*ies
>   Past him across the p*l*ain,/ but he *l*ies sti*ll*. (74)

Those repeated *l*'s, for example, introduced by the initial "Lulled," which seems to announce a theme of wholesome sleep, become continually less wholesome as they recur so insistently. No longer pleasant, they are hypnotic, and the sleep they suggest is an unnatural, oppressive sleep. In addition, each of the end-rhymes here significantly includes an *l,* as if to draw the bonds of that sleep tighter with each line, while the double *ll*'s in "Hill" and "still," echoing the "Lulled" and "Belle" of the first line, finally enclose the entire stanza in a locked ring. From this sleep, it seems, there is no arising.

Along with this major alliterative grouping, minor groupings of echoing *w*'s, *r*'s, *s*'s and other consonants are also in operation in this stanza, and they continue interweaving throughout the poem, with now one, now another dominant. It is the disturbing *l*'s of the first stanza, however, which return in force in the two concluding stanzas to complete the pattern begun with "Lulled" in the first line. And in the final line of the final stanza, the single word, "insulting," which of course rhymes with "Lulled," does something more:

> But if a withered *l*eaf should drift
> Across his face and rest, the dread drops start
> Chi*ll* on his forehead. Now he tries to *l*ift/
> The insu*l*ting weight that stays and breaks his heart. (74)

For this word brings to the surface at last the undercurrent of relationship with the contemporary which has been gathering force all along beneath the faded pastoral scenery of the poem. It is, as R. P. Blackmur observed in an essay on Muir, a "modern and moody word," [21] altogether different in feeling from the language of the rest of the poem; and although its use here also implies its own ancient history—"as a frequentative form of the verb *insilire*, to leap upon," again according to Blackmur—this history only confirms the contemporary application. Some evil rooted deep in history divides the will of modern man from its purpose, his heart from its love, his story from the fable that alone gives meaning to human life, and leaps in continual insult on his spirit. It weighs him down in impotence, and "breaks his heart."

With this sudden release of the pent-up contemporary meaning within the poem, furthermore, not only does the poem itself stand revealed in a new light, as a powerful statement of man's predicament today, but the measure of Muir's growth as a poet is revealed as well. From the subjective, sometimes almost sentimental nostalgia of parts of *First Poems*, from the Eliot-like rhythms, the indirections, the frequent obscurities of *Variations*, Muir has come in this volume, *Journeys and Places*, to a new clarity, a new precision, a new depth, and a new voice that is at last completely individual, completely his own. The progress is still uneven, as we have seen; "The Mythical Journey" and many of the "place" poems represent the faults rather than the virtues of Muir's earlier style. But in poems like "The Road," "Troy," and "The Enchanted Knight," he uses a simple, balladlike form; compact, direct language; and symbols as clear and concrete as natural objects to present dramatic, haunting images of the shape of human destiny as it was, as it probably will be, and as it certainly is.

V

If the "direction" that Muir was to follow in his poetry had already "ravished" his soul before he "took the road"; if many of the themes he was to reshape and refine all his life were already implicit in his work as early as *First Poems*, it is still not until his fifth volume, *The Narrow Place* of 1943, that direction and themes become unmistakably clear. For now at last, as a number of poems in *Journeys and Places* demonstrated, Muir's long apprenticeship is over. He has arrived at an indisputable technical mastery, and as a result he is free to make explicit those themes which have been latent in his poetry from the beginning; to make plain the direction he has been half blindly following.

At the same time, too, he necessarily defines and strengthens the two opposite terms of the paradox to which, as we have seen, he was so firmly committed. And here is another reason for the greater clarity of both theme and direction in *The Narrow Place*. For in this volume Muir converts this inherent contradiction in all his thoughts and instincts into a source of strength. Instead of narrowing his vision by settling for one or the other pole of the contradiction; instead of wavering unhappily and feebly between the two, he now insists on encompassing both. He "would have them both, would nothing miss." He takes, in other words, the position already predicted in certain sections of *Variations on a Time Theme*: the position that paradox must be accepted, that it is the only possible principle of reconciliation.

This is, of course, the position of Blake, who accepted Innocence and Experience, Reason and Imagination. It is the position intimated by Keats, in the "Ode to a Grecian Urn," when he uses what Kenneth Burke calls the "mystic oxymoron" [1] of unheard melodies to signal the movement of the poem to an ultimate transcendence of contradiction. It is, indeed, the fitting of "that world to this" which every visionary poet who does not abolish this world altogether must somehow manage. Although in taking this position Muir by no means reaches an unshaken stability—one term or another of the paradox keeps insisting on dominance throughout his poetry to the end—still it is in the acceptance of paradox that he finds his "one point of rest," the steady needle marking the direction which so long before had ravished his soul.

Even the arrangement of the poems in *The Narrow Place*, indeed, suggests this commitment to paradox. For the two opposing sides are almost equally represented here. Denial and affirmation, Yea and Nay, confront each other with very nearly impartial symmetry. Where at least half of the first sixteen poems are poems of the darker side, of despair, disillusion, and disgust; and where the seventeenth poem, "The Gate," which happens to stand exactly midway through the volume, represents the nadir of horror and desolation, the last sixteen poems all maintain the contrary side of the paradox. In one way or another, they are all poems of affirmation, of understanding, hope, and love. But the Yea they say is not any light-hearted acquiescence in things as they are. Since Muir's commitment to paradox is finally a commitment to reconciliation rather than division, his Yea must include and transcend his Nay, and this is precisely what these later poems do. They take account of dark as well as light, of evil as well as good; they acknowledge that both are rooted together in some mysterious "deep confederacy far from the air"; and they still find, within this ambiguous alliance, the "saving proof" of some incorruptible good.

To reach this reassuring, although hardly dazzling vision, however, Muir had to come a long way. Uncertain from the beginning in *First Poems* whether to choose the darker or the brighter view, choosing the darker almost in spite of himself in *Chorus of the Newly Dead* and choosing it deliberately in *Variations on a Time Theme*, Muir was still undecided even in *Journeys and Places* as to his final choice. For although there, as we have seen, the question of form was the paramount issue, the question of light or dark, negation or affirmation, still stood in the background. If the three most perfectly formed poems in the volume, "The Road," "Troy," and "The Enchanted Knight," were uncompromising statements of terror and blackness, on the other hand, Tristram returned to sanity, Hölderlin gave thanks even in madness, the harvest poems suggested the resurrection of the seed, and the lovely final poem of the volume, "The Dreamt-Of Place," for a moment canceled Dante's Hell before reason woke to ask, "Where is the knife, the butcher,/ The victim?" (88) Which to believe? The dream of reconciliation or the fact of the knife? In this poem, as in the volume as a whole, "there was no answer"; the question remained. And although it is still to be answered in *The Narrow Place* in the opening poem, "To J. F. H.," the answer that seems to be taking shape in the immediately succeeding poems is surely, "the knife." It is not until "The Gate" is past that the downward plunge of the volume is arrested and the slow movement upwards towards the light, towards that vision of some abiding good beyond both knife and victim is at last begun.

Because "To J. F. H. (1897-1934)" is based on a momentary illusion of the fusion of opposites, of life and death, time and eternity, it is a particularly fitting poem to open this book of opposites which converge towards each other in final union. But for the most part it carries its metaphysical burden lightly. It is a direct address to a dear friend, John Holms, to whom *Variations on a Time Theme* had been dedicated, and whom

Muir characterized in a warm and sensitive portrait in *An Autobiography*, as "the most remarkable man I ever met";[2] and it speaks in the vigorous, colloquial, yet intellectual terms of a friendship that was a rare meeting of minds: "Our minds were completely open to each other."[3] So free, so spontaneous, is the speaking voice, indeed, that the deliberate pauses, the bursts of speed, the swellings and the fallings off of what seems natural speech rhythm almost obscure the underlying iambic pentameter measure; and the scattered alliteration, the irregular rhymes are so understated, so gently insinuated, that at first they are similarly obscured. It is not until very near the end of the first verse paragraph, twelve lines long, that the formal dimensions of rhyme, alliteration, and meter impose themselves so that they cannot be ignored. At this point too something else occurs. What had seemed an address to a living friend proves to be directed to a dead one. For the ominous "narrow valley" of the tenth line, waking the echo of the "bowling alley" so strangely paired with it in the second line, and the "dead," of the twelfth and last line, harking back to "head" of line five, at once complete the identification of the rhyming pattern and disclose the brutal fact that requires some formal pattern to make it bearable: Holms is "seven years dead." "A chance face flying past" had triggered the illusion that Holms was there again in the flesh, and the speaker now, in lines where the repeated *f*'s deepen at last into the *v* of the fatal "seven," simultaneously sees him alive and knows he is buried:

> It was you, yet some
> Soft finger somewhere turned a different day,
> The day I left you in that narrow valley,
> Close to my foot, but already far away;
> And I remembered you were seven years dead. (91)

Dead or not, however, Holms is still present to his friend, "so clearly" present "in the hot still afternoon" that the familiar colloquy—for it seems a colloquy, even though in fact it is a monologue—continues without interruption. It merely shifts to another level. The question now is, what world are they both in together? The world of the living or of the dead? "Had I cracked the shell/ That hides the secret souls, had I fallen through . . . ?" asks the speaker, using here, by the way, a metaphor of a crack between the two worlds remarkably similar to one used by Rilke, with whose work again Muir had both a familiarity and an affinity, in "Todeserfahrung" ("Experience of Death"):

> Doch als du gingst, da brach in diese Bühne
> Ein Streifen Wirklichkeit *durch jenen Spalt*
> Durch den du hingingst . . . .
> (But when you went, there broke on this scene
> A streak of reality *through that crack*
> Through which you went. [Italics and translation mine])[4]

If this is the land of the dead, furthermore, is it simply a "commonplace" facsimile of the land of the living? A country of "Again" like the eternally recurring past of "The Road"? Whatever it is, it is close at hand, on the other side of a dividing wall no thicker than a "shell," no harder to leap than a "low dike"; and this is the piercing, terrifying insight suddenly revealed here. That "chance face flying past" had "made a hole in space,/ The hole you looked through always" (92), the speaker tells Holms; and in lines where the diction is now heightened, the rhyme scheme drawn closer into a quatrain, he confesses that he knows at last:

> The sight you saw there, the terror and mystery
> Of unrepeatable life so plainly given
> To you half wrapped still in eternity
> Who had come by such a simple road from heaven. (92)

The opposites of life and death, time and eternity, are now no longer fused. The "clock-hand" has "moved," life and time have resumed their normal passage. But in the sharp new awareness which the poem has reached, of the proximity of death and eternity, the "terror and mystery" of this passage are enormously magnified.

After the brief convergence of opposites in this poem, however—a convergence which is not really so much a reconciliation as a confusion that ironically leads to increased insight—a profound separation begins in this volume between the two contrary tendencies in Muir's philosophy. The faith in the enduring and redeeming fable grows fainter; a sense of disgust and dismay at the pervasive horror of evil increases, as does a fear of the cruel and treacherous "iron law" at the heart of life; and the next few poems in *The Narrow Place*—"The Wayside Station," "The River," "Then," "The Refugees," and "Scotland 1941"—are all expressions of that disgust and that fear. What is more, "The Wayside Station," "The River," and "The Refugees" are expressions of a particular fear, the terror and burden of life in the disasters and wars of the twentieth century; and they convey this sense of our contemporary nightmare in a way that represents a new departure for Muir— through contemporary images.

Instead of masking the application to the modern world in the form of ancient myth or medieval romance, as in *Variations on a Time Theme* or "The Enchanted Knight," Muir uses, in "The Wayside Station," for instance, the very modern, altogether unromantic view seen from a Scottish railway station at dawn of a cold winter day. His approach, it is true, is still oblique. There are no signs of death or destruction in this rural landscape, with its central interior scene. But a sense of oppression and sorrow pervades the whole and gradually deepens until the last few lines disclose what has been the source of distress all along: "Time and war and history" (93). As Muir recalled later in a radio talk discussing the genesis of the poem, which he said took shape in his mind while he was stopping every morning during the early days of the last World War, at a little town called Leuchars, to change trains on his way to work in the Food Office at Dundee, "over everything hung the thought of war." [5] And this is what he makes happen in the poem, low-keyed and understated as it is: over everything here, the field, the farm, the wood, the engine smoke "Crawling across the field in serpent sorrow" (92), broods the intolerable, the "insulting weight" of the burden imposed on simple, everyday living by the inescapable presence of modern war.

The first stanza, simply a landscape etched in tones of black, white, and grey, conveys at once, in its every detail, the sense of the sadness of the coming day. The blank verse lines, slowed by hovering accents, move wearily; the repeated *s*'s sigh, as in "Crawling across the field in serpent sorrow"; the imagery is all imagery of heaviness and effort: the "struggling day" is "held down," "Flat in the east," by "stolid clouds." Only the "warm hearth" of the breaking day is friendly and restful, and that is "far off." Here the light simply shows the mournful contrast of the white gulls against the "furrows' black unturning waves" (92). In the second stanza, moreover, where the eye of the viewer turns from the fields outside to byre, stall, and room within the farmstead, this feeling of sadness is intensified as the living creatures sheltered here, cattle and farmer, ploughboy and lovers, all wake with the anguish of reluctance in their bones.

For although while the sleepers are waking the rhythm quickens momentarily and the lines break into free verse, the original slow five-stress measure soon resumes, not so much with weariness now as with a steady implacability, the implacability of an irresistible, impersonal force. In addition, those contrasting blacks and whites of the first stanza now reappear with even more poignant, more ominous associations: in the dark bedroom where the lovers part, "the pillows gleam/ Great and mysterious as deep hills of snow,/ An inaccessible land" (93). Then, outside once more, in lines where the *s*'s continue to sigh, the shadowy wood "stands waiting/ While the bright snare slips coil by coil around it,/ Bright silver on every branch" (93), until finally, with the words "snare" and "coil," the whole poem suddenly comes into new focus. What the day is bringing is not merely another twelve hours of the drudgery and ills to which all flesh is heir, but the reactivation of some monstrous infernal machine. With the light, that fatal process of history and war, from which the night had granted a reprieve, is again set in motion:

> The lonely stream
> That rode through darkness leaps the gap of light,
> Its voice grown loud, and starts its winding journey
> Through the day and time and war and history. (93)

This is, of course, the triumph of "The Wayside Station," this tremendous impact, this reverberation through time and the solar system which the otherwise carefully modulated poem delivers, almost unexpectedly, in its last lines. But it is a triumph not repeated in the two following poems which refer even more specifically to contemporary disaster, "The River" and "The Refugees." For though the controlling metaphor of "The River" is the same metaphor of a stream as time and history which so powerfully concludes "The Wayside Station," the effect is not the same. There is not the same sense of history as inevitable, agonizing process. Following some unnamed river of Europe through devastated countryside and city, the speaker in this poem sees a long series of sad partings, wrecked bridges, burning homes, but somehow the series produces no cumulative impression. The individual images of catastrophe, on the other hand, are not sharp enough to be appalling, nor are they as suggestively disturbing as the small, indirect details, the "sad cattle," the groaning farmer, of "The Wayside Station." As for "The Refugees," the open preaching to which Muir resorts here does not really communicate the compassion and concern for the plight of the "homeless,/ Nationless and nameless" (95), which he so obviously feels. For what is lacking, finally, in both the poems, is nothing less than imaginative vision. What is lacking is a formula for the emotion that is there, but unshaped and undirected.

That deficiency is amply supplied, however, in another poem of terror in *The Narrow Place*, "Then," because it is precisely in its strange and original vision of pure and timeless, rather than simply contemporary, terror that the particular power of this poem lies. It is a vision which plants the aggressive instinct so deep in the human psyche that its roots extend back beyond man in time, and even beyond man's animal ancestors, to the limestone of remote geological ages. Then, even then, when the foraminifers were laying down their minute outworn shells in unimaginable numbers; when "There were no men and women . . . at all"; and when "the flesh [was] lying alone" (94) in some amorphous, pre-skeletal, gelatinous state, even then the shadows of human creatures to be were already cast on the limestone wall in fighting attitudes. Even then, before there was speech, there were groans. And before there was milk, there was blood.

The question, "Where was I ere I came to man?" ("The Fall," 69) is, of course, as several critics have noted, one of Muir's constant concerns. In *The Scottish Tradition in Literature*, for example, Kurt Wittig quotes a phrase from Neil Gunn, " 'the monstrous beginnings of life,' " in order to point out how Gunn's awareness "of man's pre-human heredity, and his conception of it as a living force . . . [are] similar to Edwin Muir's." [6] Muir's awareness of life's "monstrous beginnings" is evident as early as *First Poems*, where "Logos" and "Ballad of Eternal Life" are both thronged with dream-derived images and symbols of the origins of life: strange snow-white giants lying in ocean caverns with generations at their breasts, or headless, boneless creatures swimming in the sea. In *Journeys and Places*, in both "The Stationary Journey" and "The Fall," which is largely a more effective retelling of the dream sequence that was the basis of "Ballad of Eternal Life," Muir again explores the question, "What shape had I before the Fall?" (68); and even in his last poems, not published until after his death, he asks the same question. When in "I see the image," he pictures a stone thrown backward towards time's source, he wonders, "What will catch it,/ Hand, or paw, or gullet of sea-monster?" (297).

Yet in none of these instances of Muir's preoccupation with life's beginnings is he heedless of its ends, and certainly not in "Then." "Our minds are possessed by three mysteries," he wrote in *An Autobiography*: "where we come from, where we are going, and, since we are not alone, but members of a countless family, how we should live with one another"; and all three of these mysteries, he went on to add, are really "aspects of one question" [7]; they cannot be separated from each other. If "Then" is a horrifying vision of where we came from, accordingly, of the impulse towards violence ingrained in man even before man existed, it must also be a vision of where we are going, of the repeated warfare that has been our fate so far, and the unending slaughter that seems to be our destiny. Nor is that all. If images of war, past, present, and future coalesce in this poem, as they do, then there must also be telescoped within it—and this is another source of its power—a millennial lapse of time. It seems, as Muir himself wrote of Eliot's *The Waste Land*, in a comment that applies remarkably to his own very different poem, to "roll back [and forward] through time until the contemporary scene finds its original in one that happened long ago, giving the feeling that we are contemplating the prototypes of human conduct. The effect," as Muir concluded of the Eliot poem, "is above all an effect of depth." [8]

But this effect, of extraordinary depth in time, and this insight into a strange, pre-human form of being, do not derive solely from the underlying image in "Then." Effect and insight derive from the structure and the language of the poem as well. For as R. P. Blackmur suggests, in the study of Muir to which we have previously referred, Muir has a way of making "runes." He makes, says Blackmur, "an old script, an older and different alphabet, out of the general mystery and the common intuition, inescapably present, when looked at, in our regular vocabulary of word and myth and attitude"; [9] and it is in something like runes, in a language that evokes older and darker powers than the everyday usages of "our regular vocabulary" can summon, that this poem is written. It is built, quite simply, on a principle of ritual repetition. It insistently reiterates certain words and related sounds as if by this reiteration it could call to our conscious minds the secret formulae, the forgotten meanings, buried deep in our subconscious responses. As symmetry and logic dictate, furthermore, the two key words in this repetitive pattern are none other than the key words of the central vision itself: they are "blood" and "wall."

Thus, in the first of the three stanzas of the poem:

> There were no men and women then at all,
> But the flesh lying alone,
> And angry shadows fighting on a wall
> That now and then sent out a groan
> Buried in lime and stone,
> And sweated now and then like tortured wood
> Big drops that looked yet did not look like blood. (94)

the very first pair of rhymes not only introduces the key
"wall," but introduces it with another word, "all," that is so
close to it in sound as to be almost the same. Throughout the
rest of the poem, furthermore, this pairing of "wall" and "all"
continues: "wall" itself is repeated five times in the course of
the brief twenty lines that make up the poem, while "all" occurs three times, until the recurring chiming actually does
affect the meaning of the word. The final "wall" of the poem,
at the end of the nineteenth line, is no longer merely the solid
mass of primeval limestone, visited by uncanny pre-human
shadows as it is in the third line. Prompted by the deeper note
of the obliquely rhyming "lull" in the second stanza, and by
the peculiar sadness of the assonantal rhymes, "haunted" and
"unwanted," in the third stanza, the underlying phonetic similarity of "wall" to "wail" slowly emerges; and in the last few
lines of the poem:

> The wall was haunted
> By mute maternal presences whose sighing
> Fluttered the fighting shadows and shook the wall
> As if that fury of death itself were dying. (95)

the wall is literally penetrated and shaken by all the maternal
wailing over spilled blood that the coming years must bring.

"Blood" is, of course, the second key word in the repetitive
pattern of the poem. Although the word "shadows," which
also plays a minor part in the pattern, is repeated equally often
—four times—it is "blood" which stands significantly at the
end of the last line of the first stanza, and it is "blood" which
not only rhymes obliquely with "wood" in the preceding line,
but joins the thudding *d*'s of its four separate occurrences to a

long series of stops, varying from *d* to *t* and *pt*, that extends through all three stanzas. To Stephen Spender, in *Poetry Since 1939*, this series seemed less than successful. He found the line, "Until another in its shadow arrayed it," from the second stanza, "awkward, and not strengthened by the fact that 'arrayed it' is supposed to rhyme with 'faded.' ";[10] and it is undeniable that both the inversion and the rhyme here are forced. In the context of the whole series and the whole poem, however, this flaw dwindles into relative insignificance. What is important is the fact that the emphatic stops beat on, unremittingly, like the pulse of human blood, and the blood pulses only to be shed, to leave a "blood-mark on the wall;/ And that [is] all; the blood . . . [is] all."

That any vision of terror could be blacker than this is almost inconceivable, yet in "The Gate," the poem that stands precisely at the center of *The Narrow Place*, the poem that marks at one and the same time the extreme point of Muir's commitment to despair and the highest point of his poetic achievement up to this time, there is a blacker vision. For although both this poem and "Then" are based on essentially the same concept, that evil is inherent in the heart of life; and although "Then," as we have seen, develops this concept with stunning power, still there is a certain remoteness, an alien, almost abstract quality in "Then." After all, the image it presents is the image of a pre-human existence simplified to two things, to shadows and bloodstains on a wall. But the complexities of "The Gate" are entirely, intimately human. The themes it treats: the loss of innocence, the initiation of the child into the mysteries and corruption of the adult world, and the ultimate cruelty and betrayal which lie at the center of that world, are themes each man and woman has experienced in his bones; and this is the difference in the darkness of the two poems. Deep as the darkness of "Then" may be, it remains outside us, something we look at, even though something far inside us recognizes itself in the image. The darkness of "The Gate," however, is something altogether within, something we know by touch. With Hopkins, what we feel here is the very "fell of dark."

The whole structure of the poem, indeed, signals a terrifying downward plunge from light into dark, from safety into loss and fear. A strong caesura in the twelfth line ("And made them strange as gods./ We sat that day" (110)) divides the freely handled blank verse lines of the poem almost exactly in half, and in each half there is a parallel descending movement. Beginning in both cases with the phrase "We sat," and the image of two children huddled securely against a protecting wall, both sections of the poem immediately qualify that security. It is a "stern" security in the first half; and in the second, the children are "outcast" as well as "safe." But whereas in the opening section the threat to the children is only implied in the care their guardians take to mask their "tell-tale faces," and in the "shame" they feel for the "rich food" that seems to make their bodies indecent, in the second section that threat is realized. The children's familiar world shrivels before their eyes, leaving them outside, outcast, as they have been by the adult world. And now, when they have no other refuge, the "huge gate" that they must turn and enter swings open behind them. Like a tolling bell, the four successive heavy stresses of the last line ("And then behind us the *huge gate swung open*") mark the inevitable end of innocence, the beginning of a different, disturbing future.

In *An Autobiography*, as we have seen, Muir wrote that "in a child's mind there is at moments a divination of a hidden tragedy taking place around him, that tragedy being the life he will not live for some years still, though it is there, invisible to him, already";[11] and in these terms the first half of "The Gate" records one of those moments of divination. The second half is the entry into tragedy. But there is still another, a secondary movement in operation here, and this is a movement of passage, an initiation rite, which is as firmly structured into the poem as the descent into tragedy and is perhaps more important in determining the tone, the emotional coloring, of the whole. For while there is fear in "The Gate," there is neither pity nor purgation. Once the two brief glimpses of safety and innocence are past, there is only a confluence of painful feelings: shame, disillusion, loneliness, and dread of some unknown horror beyond the portal.

The initiation theme opens with the word "Outside," strategically placed at the beginning of the second line. The children in the poem are for some reason "outsiders," who do not belong with their fathers inside the fortress, but must remain "outside" the walls. Their entrance into the fortress is in fact explicitly forbidden, tabooed. For the sentence in the fourth line, "We could not enter there," clearly implies prohibition as well as inability, and the idea of prohibition is reinforced by the "frowned" and "stern" of the preceding line. With the fifth and sixth lines, the basis of the interdiction develops: the children are still too immature, their "palates" too "unpracticed" for the "gross and strong" quality of life within the walls; and the note of coarseness, indecency, even corruption, sounded by "gross" strongly suggests that the secrets which the children are not permitted to penetrate are sexual. The fact that the fathers feel forced, in dealing with the children, to assume a lost innocence, to mask their "tell-tale faces" (blushing? leering?) still further confirms the presence of the sexual mystery, while their "shame/ For the rich food that plumped their lusty bodies" establishes that presence beyond a doubt.

For not only is the shame which adults feel before children most often a shame for their more fully developed sexual characteristics, but that full development is plainly indicated here, in "plumped" and "lusty bodies." To be sure, the motive for the "shame" is said to be the "rich food" which fed these bodies, rather than the bodies themselves; but eating and other forms of sensuality are often connected, as the phrase "unpracticed palates," a euphemism for physical immaturity, implies, and as William Empson notes in his essay on *Alice in Wonderland*. By coincidence, Empson even uses Muir's phrase, "rich food," which he says is "the child's symbol for all luxuries reserved for grown-ups." [12] And pre-eminent among those luxuries is of course the imperfectly understood but fearfully attractive sexual act. That this is Muir's symbolism too, his choice of the word "lusty" to modify "bodies" clearly proves. For "lusty" not only speaks its own meaning; it encloses "lust"; and "lust," too, in the Calvinist tradition which Muir seems to be invoking by his allusions to stern prohibitions, of course carries a special weight of condemnation for all sins of the flesh.

At this point, however, the first section of the poem comes to an end, and in the second section the mood and the focus of attention shift away, temporarily, from the fleshly mysteries of the adult world. The children's own world comes into view, a landscape recognizable as another version of that Orkney landscape of Muir's boyhood. The smooth green hillock is the mound he knew as the Castle near his father's farm; the pond is perhaps the sound between the islands that he often watched from the Castle hill, as in those lines from "Childhood" in *First Poems*:

> Long time he lay upon the sunny hill,
>   To his father's house below securely bound.
> Far off the silent, changing sound was still,
>   With the black islands lying thick around.[13]

But a comparison between these two renderings of the same scene immediately shows a vast difference. While the four lines just quoted are touched with Wordsworth's "visionary gleam," the hill and pond of "The Gate" are sunless. The "scene" is "well-worn," not new or bright, and although the hillock is pleasantly "smooth and green," it is also "small," as if outgrown. It is toylike, "intended" indeed for children, "for us alone and childhood," but intended to narrow the view, not expand it to any glimpse of that "imperial palace" of our origins. Even before the shrunken twenty-first line announces the fact, "But suddenly all seemed old," the fact is evident; the childhood world of the poem has already lost its largeness and splendor. It is "old" because the children are "old"; they have grown up. Whereas, as children, they were excluded from the stronghold of adult life, now as adults themselves they are ready for admission. The image of the fortress, with all its suggestions of the sexual mystery, returns; the gates swing open, and the *rite de passage*, the initiation, is on the point of accomplishment.

Thus, viewed as patterned on a ritual of initiation into maturity, "The Gate" takes a forward direction, steps over a threshold. As patterned on the theme of lost innocence, the tragic change from an early Eden to the fallen world we all live in, the poem moves downward. And it is from this doubling of theme and movement that much of the peculiarly ambivalent quality of the poem, its special density of texture, naturally results. Yet underlying even this source of ambivalence and density is still another, implicit in the controlling image itself, in the picture of a fortress outside whose walls two children sit secure until the gates open to receive them. For the fact is that the passage of these children from safety, even a shrinking safety, outside the walls, to some unimaginable, blank horror when the "huge gates" swing open, is contrary to all the usual expectations. The danger is customarily outside; refuge, within. Although this contrary current runs deep, almost unnoticed, under the more obvious details and patterns of the poem, it nevertheless qualifies these details and patterns, however imperceptibly, and helps to account for the sense of oppression, of fear and betrayal, which the poem as a whole conveys.

What is more, this same contrary current reveals a relationship, otherwise easily overlooked, between this poem and a major strain in Muir's work apparently very different from either the initiation or the loss of Eden theme; and this, as Butter notes in his shorter study, *Edwin Muir*, [14] is the apprehension of treachery from within. In its earliest forms this motif was most often involved with time. Time, for instance, was the traitor who caught poor Beauty in a snare in "Betrayal" in *First Poems*, and "inly" wasted her flesh away. Again, in *Variations on a Time Theme*, time was the traitor who trapped mankind in the wilderness and kept him from the promised land. Even in "The Gate," although time is not specifically mentioned, it is still the passage of time which brings the children to maturity and opens for them the gates of a frightening future. But treachery for Muir can wear other and more intimate shapes than that of time. In Section Nine of *Variations*, treachery wears man's own skin. "Packed in my skin from head to toe," lives the root of all evil, indifference, the "brute insensibility of life"; [15] and from within the stronghold of man's own heart, indifference betrays every virtue that heart inclines to. Similarly, in Muir's novel, *The Three Brothers*, this same callous indifference takes the form of one of the twins, Archie Blackadder, who lives side by side with his "good" twin, David, only to frustrate, and of course, betray him. For Archie, "a pleasant enough wee beast himself" is that inseparable animal half of the human soul without which man would not be man, yet with which there can be no permanent peace. Archie is the traitor who thrives in every man, who *is* one aspect of that man; he is the eternal evil at the core of life.

Significantly, to symbolize this existence of evil at the center, which is the basic theme of the novel, Muir uses precisely the same image he uses in "The Gate"—the image of a fortress impregnable without, but open, through the gate, to treachery within. In "The Castle," too, a poem in his next volume, *The Voyage*, he uses very briefly the same image and almost the very words of the novel, to express the same theme:

> There was a little private gate,
> A little wicked wicket gate,
> The wizened warder let them through. (129)

But in *The Three Brothers* he reiterates and elaborates. When David, still a little boy, asks his father to explain how the Calvinists managed to get into the Castle at St. Andrews and kill the Cardinal, the elder Blackadder answers: "Ay, but just listen a wee. If you go round the corner of the castle what should you come to but another gate, a wee thing that ye would hardly notice, a wee, wicked-looking wee gate." [16] Then, David wonders, "A man can be killed in the middle of a castle?" And Blackadder admits, "Aye, it's so." [17] As David grows up, he discovers there are many gates to the middle of the castle, many ways by which danger and destruction can enter the strongest and inmost keep. War, for example, breaks many castles down. His own brother Archie constantly betrays him and brings him trouble. Death insidiously attacks his mother, his other brother, and his sweetheart. Even the trusting animals of the farm are led to slaughter, until David finally sees in everything the sheer naked terror of existence. Nowhere is there any "security, nor any trust that was kept by the powers of the world." He thinks then of "Cardinal Beaton butchered in the inmost chamber of the Castle, and the pig, nourished and petted, and at last dragged out into the sunlit yard, and its throat cut by the hands which had fondled and fed it," and he asks himself, as he had asked his father, "What help was there in this world save in God alone?" [18] But what help was there in God, who if the universe was cruel, "was its burning centre and axle?" And this, the awful cruelty at the heart of the universe, at the center where help and trust ought most to be looked for, this is the deep core of terror which in "The Gate" cancels our expectations of a stronghold and makes the move from outside into "the inmost chamber of the Castle" a descent into the heart of darkness.

From this central, lowest circle of Inferno, inhabited as in Dante by the image of betrayal, Muir like Dante slowly climbs upward towards the open air and the stars of heaven. In all sixteen of the succeeding poems in *The Narrow Place*, he makes some affirmation on behalf of the light. Even on the way down to this pit, in the earlier half of the volume, there had been momentary pauses in the descent, poems in which he had maintained his faith in the light despite the surrounding and increasing darkness. In "Scotland 1941" after a bitter indictment of the divisiveness, the spiritual poverty, the dull materialism, of modern Scotland, he still finds something to praise and to pity in the "wasted bravery" of "Montrose, Mackail, Argyle" (98). In "The Letter," which Butter believes may have been prompted by the wish to heal the rift between him and MacDiarmid,[19] he tries to undo the anger and hurt of a quarrel with a friend. In "The Human Fold" and "The Narrow Place," although he evokes again the sense of captivity in time that was so oppressive in *Variations*, he also evokes some of those "glints of immortality" vouchsafed in dreams. That strange sentence, for example, that twice in "The Human Fold" suddenly generates a new and different current: "I lean my cheek from eternity / For time to slap, for time to slap" (100), he heard spoken in a dream; [20] the image of the profusely foliaged trees, too, which magically shade the sleeper on "The parsimonious ground" of "The Narrow Place," came to him in a dream, a dream "strangely transfigured and transposed," [21] of his childhood home; and both sentence and image suggest a possibility of some ultimate reconciliation, beyond the prevailing gloom.

In "The Recurrence," on the other hand, Muir takes an even more positive stand. Although he makes no declaration of any firm faith, he specifically denies the appalling vision he had once contemplated, in half belief, in "The Road." That the wheel of things will revolve forever, that the past will eternally return, are concepts he now puts into Nietzsche's mouth. But his own heart, like Yeats's, makes a different reply: "What has been can never return" (104). In "The Good Man in Hell," furthermore,—the "most Herbertian poem in modern poetry," according to Joseph H. Summers,[22] he plays with the idea of the illusoriness of evil. If one good man, he conjectures, were accidentally "housed in Hell," not only would he not succumb to the surrounding devils; he would plant the single "doubt of evil" there that would bring redeeming grace and let "all Eden . . . enter in" (104). But this remains, of course, only a conjecture; the whole poem is dependent on the initial "if"; and it is not until "The Gate" is passed and the upward movement of the entire volume begun, that Muir at last reaches the point of making his first fully unconditional affirmation.

That affirmation is contained in "The Ring," and "The Ring" is therefore peculiarly important, not only in itself, simply as a well-made poem of eight stanzas in beautifully managed *terza rima*, but also as a landmark on Muir's journey up from the depths. It is equally important, furthermore, as a guide to the steps in Muir's thinking that led him on this upward journey. For although on the surface the poem seems simple enough, like some familiar folk tale, it actually brings together many different themes that have occupied Muir for years, and for the first time weaves them into a coherent whole. It rounds them, in fact, into a "ring" that heals division and transcends opposition; a "ring" that corresponds to a profounder level of meaning in the title than at first appears and indicates an even greater appropriateness than immediately meets the eye in the *terza rima* stanza with its enclosing rhymes.

The alliterating *f*'s of the opening stanza, for example, by calling attention to the "fable" that ends the third line, immediately indicate the presence here of Muir's lifelong concern with the eternal pattern underlying the changing story, the miscellaneous incidents, of human life:

> Long since we were a family, a people,
> The legends say: an old kind-hearted king
> Was our foster father, and our life a fable. (114)

But these lines suggest more. There is in them both an image of Muir's own family group on Wyre, and a clear echo of the three opening lines of "Scotland 1941":

> We were a tribe, a family, a people.
> Wallace and Bruce guard now a painted field.
> And all may read the folio of our fable. (97)

As a result, it is evident that although "The Ring" is a universal parable, dealing with the fate of mankind in general, it has a particular application as well to the fate of Edwin Muir, and in his fate, to that of Scotland. What is more, this particular application to Scotland illuminates and illustrates the general situation. For the disaster that wrecked Scotland, the spiritual, political, and economic division experienced in that country, is a paradigm of the division that has fragmented both contemporary man and his world. Similarly, the wholeness that Scotland once knew, at least in Muir's eyes—the unity of a nation where people lived together as in a family, with reciprocal rights and responsibilities—is exemplary of society as it was "long since" in the golden age, and as, ideally, it could be again.

Still another echo in both these passages opens up an entirely new area of associations. In a letter to Stephen Spender, Muir once quoted several "intimations of poems" which he claimed he could not get on with, and one of these intimations was as follows:

> We were a tribe, a family, a people.
> King Lear was our father.[23]

That "old kind-hearted king" of "The Ring," therefore, most surprisingly turns out to be the Lear of ancient Britain. But he is not exactly Shakespeare's Lear. Rather, he is a Lear who represents an order of society, an order that like the community on Wyre or the original state of Scotland was bound together by "a sort of piety and human fitness, a natural piety." [24] For in Muir's essay, "The politics of *King Lear*," originally delivered at the University of Glasgow as the W. P. Ker lecture for 1946, it is to the ideas of society represented in the play that he directs his attention; and what he says about the play, accordingly, puts both characters and action in a new perspective, where everything is polarized around two contrary political conceptions. On the one hand is the old, the unified, the traditional, the human, which Lear stands for—imperfectly, Muir admits. On the other is the new, the individualistic, the amoral and impersonal, which Goneril, Regan, Cornwall, Oswald, and above all, Edmund stand for. And it is precisely this polarization that Muir sees in *King Lear* which is also the organizing principle of "The Ring." Just as Lear, even with his too late understood sense of social obligation, is in total opposition to his daughters, who recognize no obligation beyond their own appetites, so the familylike community life of mutual responsibilities represented by the first two stanzas of "The Ring" is in total opposition to the divisive animal forces which break through "the grassy ring" and destroy its treasures.

But here another of Muir's persistent themes enters the poem: the animal-man relationship. To animals such as the "Horses" of *First Poems*, as we have seen, Muir accorded reverence, love, and wonder. These animals were bound to man, he believed, in a mysterious relationship of necessity and guilt as deeply rooted and sanctified in time as that age, "long since," when Lear ruled his people like a father. The "bull and adder and ape,/ Lion and fox" who batter the turf and nose the shrine in "The Ring," however, are different. They acknowledge neither any bonds to man nor any traditional sanctity. They presume, in fact, to be men themselves; they are "all dressed by fancy fine/ In human flesh and armed with arrows and spears." Like Lear's daughters, and Oswald and Edmund, who are their counterparts, they are animals in act and thought, human in face and faculties. Yet because their humanity lies only in their outward form, because as animals they have no memory—they "haughtily put aside the sorrowful years"—and therefore no sense of responsibility, no loyalty, no compassion, they are symbols of evil according to one of Muir's special definitions of the term. "For it may be," he wrote in "The Politics of *King Lear*," in reference to Goneril and Regan, "that evil consists in a hiatus in the soul, a craving blank, a lack of one of the essential threads which bind experience into a coherent whole and give it a consistent meaning"; [25] and this inner blankness, this indifference where there should be memory and heart and understanding, is what makes the half-human animals of "The Ring" so supremely vicious. They are vicious in that brute, insensible way that we have already seen in Archie Blackadder. They are the original diabolical force that, as Indifference, lodged beneath the skin in *Variations*, or within the citadel in "The Gate." They are the insensate terror and cruelty at the "burning centre and axle" of the human soul, of history, and of the universe.

The question is, then, what makes this difference? Why are the animals in "Horses" objects of worship when they too have no memory, no sense of the past? Why in "The Ring" are they creatures to be abhorred? The answer involves a strange experience Muir had in Glasgow in 1919, just before he married Willa Anderson. He was at this point deep in his studies of Nietzsche and had convinced himself, he thought, that "all belief in any other life than the life we live here and now" was "an imputation on the purity of immediate experience, which . . . was guiltless and beyond good and evil." [26] But while he was riding home from work on a crowded tram car one hot summer evening, he suddenly saw all the people around him as animals. At the same time, in his mind's eye, he "saw countless other tram cars where animals sat or got on or off with mechanical dexterity, as if they had been trained in a circus"; and what was still worse, he saw "that in all Glasgow, in all Scotland, in all the world, there was nothing but millions of such creatures living an animal life and moving towards an animal death as towards a great slaughter-house." He realized then that he could not bear such a vision, "could not bear mankind as a swarming race of thinking animals." [27] Somewhere, if life was not to be a "curious, irrelevant desolation," [28] there had to be at least one living, immortal soul. And in that realization of Muir's, that he could not endure to go on living except in the belief "that man has a soul and that it is immortal," [29] lies the answer to the question at issue.

For although man is harmoniously bound to the animal world, as we have seen, when life is lived according to the fable; and although the animal world in itself is good and innocent, nevertheless that bond is broken and that goodness and innocence cease when the fable is forgotten and when, in denial of the immortal spirit that is one half of his being, man lapses back into the beast that is the other half. Then, as Muir wrote of *King Lear* in *An Autobiography*, "when man is swallowed up in nature nature is corrupted and man is corrupted." [30] Then man and animal merge into savage tigers like Lear's daughters, who turn their father out of doors into the storm, or into brute herds, like those of "The Ring," that in sheer ignorance and indifference overturn the shrines of the fable, the old "sacred tradition of human society." Then, in short, man-become-animal is evil, and the animal in man is the emblem of the evil that not only does exist, as Muir had long since acknowledged, but has existed ever since Eden was lost and time and history began.

Furthermore, because evil never ceases to exist, both "The Ring" and *King Lear* have a contemporary application. That opposition between piety and brutality, human society and the anarchy of tooth and claw, represented in the conflict between Lear and his daughters, was not, in Muir's eyes, a temporary phenomenon limited to Shakespeare's age. On the contrary, he saw it as permeating history, becoming continually more acute and complex, until in our own century it affected every aspect of existence. On the side of animal appetite and irresponsibility that Goneril, Regan, and Edmund stood for, new forces were now ranged: capitalism and uncontrolled industrialism, with their concomitant subservience to things, [31] and all the various manifestations of totalitarianism. Even Socialism, which Muir adopted as a creed long before it was fashionable, and to which he always remained loyal in a non-sectarian way, by its emphasis on strictly utilitarian and temporal goals seemed to him to increase the strength of the assault on the old way of life, with its assertion of moral and spiritual values. Yet that old way of life, it seemed equally clear to him, refused to be crushed altogether. Like the elements which perennially opposed it, the traditional way of natural piety assumed more modern shapes, such as the resistance Muir witnessed throughout Europe to Nazi and later, Communist terror, but it remained essentially what Lear, the "old kind-hearted king" and his kingdom symbolized—an order of society based on the characteristics that make man human rather than animal. And it is this persistent struggle of different shapes but intrinsically the same forces that both "The Ring" and *King Lear*, according to Muir, indirectly but unmistakably mirror, just as it is this struggle which many of his later poems, such as "The Interrogation" and "The Usurpers" far more directly mirror again.

But there is still one more aspect of "The Ring," and that the most important, to be accounted for. There is reconciliation here, as there is not in *King Lear*. Those beasts who broke down the "quiet keep" of "The Ring" remained to father sons, and it is these sons whose voices, speaking throughout the poem, in the last lines introduce the hope of restoring the original good. With a Biblical simplicity and dignity, with the quiet of emotion recollected in true tranquillity, these voices recall:

> We are their sons, but long ago we heard
> Our fathers or our fathers' fathers say
> Out of their dreams the long forgotten word

> That rounded again the ring where sleeping lay
> Our treasures, still unrusted and unmarred. (113)

For as easily, as simply as this, like Eurydice in Muir's late, perfect little poem, "Orpheus' Dream," the reconciliation is suddenly "there." Out of dreams, those dreams which bring "glints of immortality," which re-establish connections with the forgotten but never completely lost world where men who were immortal spirits as well as animals lived in harmony with each other and with nature, comes a memory which revives in the sons the kingdom their fathers destroyed, rounds again the ring of security and love their fathers shattered. Yet since the blood of these evil, these bestial fathers still flows in the veins of the sons, the kingdom clearly is not, cannot be, the same. It is greater. It now contains both evil and good, resolves the discord between animal and man, closes a new circle, a new ring, where experience is included with innocence, the story with the fable. And thus at last Muir reaches the point to which he has been tending. He acknowledges at last, in the parable of this poem, what he states explicitly in another, closely related poem of affirmation, "The Trophy," that the only resolution of paradox lies in its acceptance; that opposites which seem irreconcilable "here" in the accidents of time are reconciled "there" in the eternal pattern of the fable:

> Regent and rebel clash in horror and blood
> Here on the blindfold battlefield. But there,
> Motionless in the grove of evil and good
> They grow together and their roots are twined
> In deep confederacy far from the air,
> Sharing the secret trophy each with other;
> And king and rebel are like brother and brother,
> Or father and son, co-princes of one mind,
> Irreconcilables, their treaty signed. (116)

Once Muir has made this affirmation, moreover; once he has recognized and accepted this necessary confederacy of good and evil, he experiences, it seems, a kind of release. No longer so obsessed with the presence of wickedness and betrayal in the world, because he sees the good that grows there too, flourishing "sweet and wild" even in the imprisonment of wrong, he now turns, for the first time in his years of writing poetry, to giving outright and joyful praise to that good. But what he praises now, in the remaining pages of *The Narrow Place*, is, of course, a very different good from the untried innocence of the lost childhood-Eden he had so often looked back to. That was a good which was contaminated by contact with evil, as the children of "The Gate" were contaminated by contact with their elders. That was a good which the intrusion of time and tragedy shattered and spoiled. This, on the other hand, is the good that springs from experience, that absorbs and transmutes into its own substance the ravages of time, of indifference, of active malice, and still remains miraculously unspoiled and whole. This, in other words, is the living proof of the resolution of paradox; and since of all goods on this planet, the most miraculous and the most compact of paradox is love, particularly the enduring love of a man and woman in marriage, it is the love between himself and his wife that Muir praises first of all. "The Annunciation," "The Confirmation," and "The Commemoration," which are the three poems immediately following "The Trophy," are all celebrations of the marriage which Muir called "the most fortunate event in my life."

As celebrations of so essentially paradoxical a relationship, furthermore, all three of these poems not unnaturally bear an affinity to the love poems of that most paradoxical of poets, John Donne. But where in the second, "The Confirmation," this affinity is muted, in "The Annunciation" and "The Commemoration" there is a deliberate play on themes suggested by Donne's "The Extasie." For by one of these strange sea-changes of the mind, this poem, which did not move Muir so much as some passages from Traherne when he first heard it recited, shortly after his marriage, by his friend John Holms, [32] apparently remained in his memory over the years until his own studies of Donne, together with his more intimate understanding of the complexities both of marriage and of poetry, revealed to him that it contained a language for his own deepest love. Thus, as the climax of "The Annunciation," Muir uses both the general theme which runs through all of "The Extasie," the theme of the dualism of body and soul which love makes one, and the particular figure, from lines 53 and 54, of souls as couriers for bodies. As the climax of "The Commemoration," again, he simply reverses Donne's neat paradox, "this dialogue of one" (l.74), into "Our monologue of two." Yet as always when Muir borrows from another poet, he makes what he borrows peculiarly his. Close as the relationship may be here, between his own poems and Donne's, the voice, the style, the imagery, the pattern of development in Muir's poems are Muir's alone.

Where, for example, Donne's alternately rhymed tetrameter quatrains, with their involved syntax and their largely polysyllabic, metaphysical vocabulary, necessarily move with a certain restraint, a formal dignity, however unmistakable the current of passion underneath, Muir's more unconventionally rhymed trimeter lines have a freer, quicker pace, a more lilting rhythm. For although, like "The Extasie," Muir's poems take the multiple paradoxes of love for subject, they do not explore those polarities in such scrupulous detail. Instead, they ride, as it were, the crests of a series of waves. In the four eight-line stanzas of which each is composed, they pass rapidly from image to image of contradictions harmonized, impossibilities made possible by love: liberty in an iron reign, wealth that grows by being squandered, invisible virtue expanding like fruit on the bough, an immaterial chain that "time cannot undo." What is more, as they advance in this way towards the climactic points provided by the themes from Donne, not only do they gather intensity, but the voice in each case gains more and more of a quality hitherto very rare in Muir—the quality of song. "The Annunciation" begins, indeed, with an announcement that song is Muir's intent:

> Now in this iron reign
> I sing the liberty
> Where each asks from each
> What each most wants to give. (117)

For now that he has stepped up from the shadow, now that his purpose is praise, he naturally uses the medium of praise, which is song. In this medium, moreover, although the motifs adapted from Donne are still discernible, they are changed. The thought that Donne re-created into feeling, according to T. S. Eliot, Muir re-creates again into song.

Oddly enough, however, as if despite his purpose he still required some prompting from outside to reach the level of song; as if he were not yet certain enough of his own lyric power, the only other poem of pure singing in this volume, "The Bird," is likewise a variation on a theme by another poet, this time Hopkins. It is likewise a variation that Muir has made his own and not an imitation. For what Muir has done in "The Bird"—which a *TLS* reviewer of *The Narrow Place* in 1943 called one of his best poems,[33] has been to use Hopkins' "The Windhover" as a model, but to so completely change its scale and its point that its nature is transformed as well. Where Hopkins' poem is an organ blast of praise and delight for the falcon that is Christ, Muir's is a delicate single voice, half human and half bird, rejoicing at the flight of a bird that is a human soul.

To deal with the resemblances first: Muir's controlling metaphor in "The Bird" is, like Hopkins', the flight of a bird; his meter is a modified version of Hopkins' sprung rhythm; alliteration, assonance, internal rhyme, are all versions of Hopkins' technique too, as is the reiteration of present participle forms and other -*ing* rhymes. Even the simile comparing the bird's pivoting wing-tip to a heel is almost the same. Where Hopkins has, ". . . then off, off forth on a swing,/ As a skate's heel sweeps smooth on a bow-bend," Muir, who addresses the bird directly, has this: "Pensively pausing, suddenly changing your mind/ To turn at ease on the heel of a wing-tip" (120). Yet in all these likenesses there is, as we have said, such a difference of scale and of point that the two poems, in their inmost meaning, are as unlike as a fall in a mountain brook and Niagara. For whatever Muir takes from Hopkins, he makes more modest. From the very form of the poem, which he diminishes from fourteen to twelve lines, thus avoiding all the associations and expectations involved in the sonnet tradition, to the central metaphor, which Muir reduces on the one hand from a princely falcon to a mere bird, an anonymous citizen of the air, and on the other from Christ to one of His creatures, a human soul, Muir makes each detail that echoes Hopkins quieter, smaller, humble rather than majestic. He makes each detail less sectarian, too, by eliminating Hopkins' specifically Christian references. The voice that speaks—or sings—in "The Bird" is simply the voice of a humanist who has come up from the black terror and disgust of "The Gate" to reach the belief that every man is an immortal spirit; and the "wide-winged soul" that soars and sings like an "adventurous bird" consequently enters its "crystalline world" apparently without benefit of clergy. What could be farther from Hopkins in tone and intent? Yet, at the same time, what could be closer in essential joy and wonder before what Muir called that "vast area of life which science leaves in its original mystery," which both poets recognized and reverenced?

From the depths represented by "The Gate" to these heights is a distance equal to the gap between hell and heaven. But not only has Muir ascended this distance in the last half of this volume, he has, as we have seen, succeeded in reconciling the two extremes. Where "The Gate" is all darkness and loss, and "The Bird" all "airy winging" and singing, most of the other poems in the latter half of the book look to both extremes and then beyond them to their resolution. Soul and body, the material and immaterial, time and the timeless, man and woman, are all gathered together in a "monologue of two," a single "strong and subtle chain" in the love poems. Good and evil, man and animal, the fable and the story are reconciled in "The Ring." In "The Guess," too, as in "The Ring," a dream brings back the forgotten fable, until "there seemed/ Nothing more natural than blessedness"; a "long forgotten guess" shows, "past chaos, the natural shape we take" (121). It is, however, in the last two poems of the volume, "The Question" and above all "The Day," that the resolution of paradox suggested by the arrangement of the volume, figured in the parable of "The Ring," realized in the reality of love, is set forth most clearly in rational discourse. For although "The Question," by its interrogative form—it is a single question of eight lines—avoids making any dogmatic statement, its content implies a statement nevertheless; it is a series of opposites which meet and merge. And although "The Day" likewise avoids positive assertion by basing its conclusions on three parallel conditional clauses, it nevertheless contrives, on the basis of these repeated "ifs," to build a single sentence which in seventeen irregularly rhymed iambic pentameter lines of utmost syntactical clarity threads its way through the contrary poles of free will and necessity, good and evil, acceptance and revolt, time and eternity, and reconciles them all. Or rather, prays that they may be reconciled. For the conclusion that follows the three "if" clauses is introduced by the formula of prayer: "Oh give me":

> Oh give me clarity and love that now
> The way I walk may truly trace again
> The in eternity written and hidden way;
> Make pure my heart and will, and me allow
> The acceptance and revolt, the yea and nay,
> The denial and the blessing that are my own. (122)

And as a prayer of piercing simplicity, humility, and sweetness, it becomes a fitting conclusion for the whole volume, which has been a descent into darkness and a rebirth into the light of acceptance and praise.

VI

Because in the sublunary scheme of things, however, irreconcilables remain stubbornly irreconcilable, that vision of a reconciliation of opposites with which Muir concluded *The Narrow Place* could not possibly be sustained for long. In his next two volumes, *The Voyage* (1946) and *The Labyrinth* (1949), the shadows close in once more. Once more Muir wrestles with the shapes of evil that he finds in "time and war and history," and particularly, by implication at least, in contemporary history. Once more too, in both volumes, he breaks through the shadows to reach the shores of light. But in neither *The Voyage* nor *The Labyrinth* is the division between descent and ascent, between dark and light, so precisely defined as in *The Narrow Place*. In neither volume, furthermore, is there any recurrence of the absolute, unmitigated blackness of "Then" or "The Gate," while in both books there are new degrees of light. For the first time Muir relaxes his hitherto unremitting seriousness, to deal with subjects simply because they are interesting or pleasant or appealingly ironical. For the first time, as well, Muir discovers his own lyric voice, pure and true, and altogether unprompted now by any other poet.

That the blackness of "The Gate" may be approximated but

never quite repeated in these two books, the first poem in *The Voyage,* "The Return of the Greeks," at once suggests. For this poem, which is so typical of Muir and so contemporary at the same time in the jaundiced eye it casts on accepted stereotypes of heroism and success, not only reiterates in a different context—the return of the Greek warriors to their homes after the siege of Troy—the same themes of disillusion and loss which were part of the complex meaning of "The Gate," but it even uses much the same scenery. The "huge heartbreaking wall" of Troy that occupied the attention of the besieging Greeks for "ten years without a change" (125), inevitably recalls the "towering stronghold," the "huge" portal of the fortress in "The Gate." When the Greeks come back to their own land, moreover, they see just what the two children of "The Gate" saw when they looked at the world they had outgrown. That "universal landscape" [1] of Muir's own Orkney boyhood which grew "dull and shrunken" for the children and dwindled to a "well-worn scene, a hillock/ So small and smooth and green it seemed intended/ For us alone and childhood," is likewise a "childish scene" for the Greeks. Around them are the same "hillocks squat and low," and "everything" for them also is "trite and strange." After the "intense employ" of their years of glory, the small domestic tasks to which their lives must now be reduced naturally seem meaningless and repellent. But between these veterans who have lost their occupation and the extremity of despair which awaited the children beyond "The Gate," inside their fathers' fortress, stands a protective power which was not present in the earlier poem. Where in "The Gate" the stronghold which seemed to offer protection in fact harbored betrayal, here, in the last two stanzas, the soldiers' "grey-haired wives" and loyal Penelope, "alone in her tower," (126) who wait for their men and promise nothing, in fact provide the only security that is sure, the only citadel immune to treachery.

For in *The Narrow Place,* as we have seen, after the central, lowest point of "The Gate" was passed, the poems in which Muir first gave outright praise to the firm and unshakeable good he now recognized in the world were the three love poems to his wife. Only two pages earlier, moreover, as if he intended to provide a more impersonal prologue for these personal poems, in "The Return of Odysseus" (114), he had already used the proverbial loyalty of Penelope as a symbol of love's redeeming and enduring power, a power as strong as that of the fate which simultaneously directed Odysseus "on the long/ And winding road of the world" to find his way back to her. And it is this power of love, which he himself had experienced, and which he symbolizes repeatedly in the legend of Penelope, that in "The Return of the Greeks" and in many later poems intervenes for Muir between the awareness of darkness and evil that every man must have, and that sense of an inmost core of betrayal, of a "burning centre and axle" of cruelty at the heart of the universe, which was particularly Muir's, and which he communicated in "The Gate." However appalling the forces of hatred and brute indifference may appear to him still, he no longer loses sight of the grace that grows beside them.

If this grace saves "The Return of the Greeks" from final despair, however, it does not alter the fact that both the prevailing tone and the dominant statement of the poem are expressions of regret, of *ennui*, of downright nausea. Carefully constructed throughout to produce exactly these sensations, the poem begins with a deliberately non-committal line, "The veteran Greeks came home" (125), which in apparent innocence builds on all our associations and expectations of the heroic in connection with the Greeks and their exploits, only to let us down unmercifully in the next lines. Those survivors of Homeric battles do not return in pomp and pride; tired and numb, they come "Sleepwandering from the war." And then a series of let-downs follows: their galleys sail clumsily, "Blundering over the bar"; their bodies are covered with "rags and tatters," until even their "intense employ" before the Trojan walls is seen, in the light of contemporary disillusion, as not really so glorious after all. In an unusual, ironical aside, Muir even notes that the Greek soldiers stayed "Just out of the arrows' range"!

Yet whatever their conduct on the plains of Troy, they had

at least a purpose there, to break down that "huge heartbreaking wall." And now that their purpose is accomplished, they have nothing left to live for. The cliffs and headlands of their own country seem no more than insignificant hills, lost in "the boundless sea and land"; the scenes of their youth are "childish"; the neatly divided, peaceful fields are "Past thinking trite and strange" (126). What have these weary, tattered, aging men to occupy them, without the illusion at least of heroic action, "Reading the walls of Troy"? What was the point of that illusion, even, if it brought them back to this?

Not that Muir uses here any of the noble periods of Ecclesiastes' "Vanity of vanities. . . ." Rather, the predominantly declarative sentence structure and the limited, in fact repetitive vocabulary together suggest a uniformity, a monotony, which corroborates the ancient text, while the sound pattern intensifies the monotony. The brief trimeter lines of the six-line stanzas, which contain only two rhymes, *a*, *b*, *a*, *b*, *b*, *a*, bring back those two lone rhymes too fast. There is no escaping them. They set up a constant, tedious chiming which is made more tedious still by the fact that the first and last lines of each stanza always end in identical rhymes; sometimes, indeed, as in the following stanza, in identical phrases:

> But everything trite and strange,
> The peace, the parcelled ground,
> The vinerows, never a change!
> The past and present bound
> In one oblivious round
> Past thinking trite and strange. (126)

Nor is that all. Precisely the same rhyme sounds recur in several stanzas: the *a* rhyme of this, the sixth stanza, for example, is the *b* rhyme of the second. And even when there is no exact duplication of rhyme, there are assonantal rhymes which link stanza to stanza throughout the whole poem. Thus the [o] and [a] sounds of the rhymes in the first stanza "The veteran Greeks came home/ Sleepwandering from the war") are repeated in the third (Their eyes knew every stone/ In the huge heartbreaking wall"), varied by a slight modulation of the [a] in the fourth ("Now even the hills seemed low/ In the boundless sea and land"), and partially reiterated in the fifth ("And when they arrived at last/ They found a childish scene"). What is more, that repetitive vocabulary mentioned above of course contributes to the sum of insistently recurring sounds: "wall," "past," "years," "strange," "came home," are all repeated at least three times. And finally, within each stanza, patterns of alliteration result in consonantal echoes that interweave with the echoing vowels in a network of reduplicated sound that at last becomes nearly unbearable. The boredom, the disillusion of these Hellenic heroes home from the war, by the end of the sixth stanza is physically present in every syllable.

In the final two stanzas, however, there is that change we have noticed. The "grey-haired wives" introduce a new theme, the theme of loyalty and love which counteracts the set of the rest of the poem towards complete despair, and they introduce a new end-rhyme as well. The [ai] of "wives" represents the most extreme departure in the entire eight stanzas from the prevailing [o] and [a] rhymes, and although the last stanza returns to [o] and a variation thereof, [au], there is enough of a hint of a second syllable in the final r of Penelope's "tower" and "hour" for this stanza to be different. True, like the change in theme, the change in sound is muted. Just as the wives raise no outcry but simply wait, these slight variations in the vowels do not assert themselves; they wait for recognition. But they testify to what the quiet wives and Penelope, alone and steadfast in her tower, testify to likewise: that there is a limit to despair and disgust, however profound, and that limit is set by love.

In a number of succeeding poems in *The Voyage*, too, Muir comes close to the depths of bitterness and blackness of "The Gate," only to avoid that final vision of the betrayal at the center. In "The Castle," for example, as was pointed out in the preceding chapter, he uses precisely the same metaphor which functioned so chillingly in both "The Gate" and *The Three Brothers*, the metaphor of an impregnable fortress betrayed from within. He even uses the very words which conveyed such fear to David Blackadder in that novel:

There was a little private gate,
A little wicked wicket gate.
The wizened warder let them through. (129)

Yet instead of terror, the effect produced in this poem is merely one of irony, and of course the question which immediately demands an answer is, Why? What are the differences in the way Muir has handled the metaphor here, which have led to such different results?

For one thing, the whole structure of the poem is calculated to culminate in an ironic twist, rather than to spiral downward, like "The Gate," into increasing darkness. Where questionable phrases and unsettling, ambiguous images gradually transformed the fortress there from a refuge into a threat, here every detail adds to the picture of ease and security. Danger is unthinkable. There seems "no threat to us at all." And just because danger is unthinkable, it is of course inevitable, as the Greeks discovered long ago. After such hubris, what but disaster? The poem could not end in any way but this:

Oh then our maze of tunnelled stone
Grew thin and treacherous as air.
The cause was lost without a groan,
The famous citadel overthrown,
And all its secret galleries bare. (129)

But by relying so heavily on inevitable, almost mechanical retribution in this poem, Muir forfeits the psychological terrors deriving from uncertainty and ambiguity. He forfeits, too, in the relatively mechanical rhythm of the poem both the subtle cadences of menace and doom of "The Gate" and the equally effective, suffocating tedium of "The Return of the Greeks." Above all, in the final stanza, when he attributes the betrayal of the Castle to a specific cause, to "gold," he forfeits the tremendous power of the undefined symbol. It was precisely because he never specified what lay within the stronghold of "The Gate" that the imagination could catch, through the merest hints and suggestions, some glimpse of the central horror. When those hints are eliminated, when the symbol is reduced to the tritest of all the baits of treachery, gold, then there is little left for the imagination to work on. Instead of the journey to the heart of darkness which was "The Gate," Muir gives us in "The Castle" an O. Henry story in rhyme.

In another poet, so neatly contrived a performance might be cleverly effective. But Muir is not a poet of clever effects. He is a poet of original insight, of vision that penetrates and transforms the accepted surface of things; and when he deals only with outward appearances, however affecting or intriguing, however closely related to his most persistent themes, he is not fully himself. "The Castle" is intriguing, certainly. It is full of characteristic Muir phrases and images. It is an expression of the theme of betrayal which haunted Muir all his life. Yet it is not one of those poems which no one but Muir could have written. The inward depth and mystery are lacking.

It is indeed this lack of depth, this absence of any of Muir's singularly penetrating perceptions, that keeps "The Castle" from even suggesting the horrors of "The Gate." But what of "Moses," another poem of betrayal, and one that bears Muir's signature unmistakably? This too, bitter as it is, does not equal "The Gate" in darkness. Although both the shock of Muir's own discovery of the poison of anti-Semitism in Austria and the smoke of the chimneys at Auschwitz and Buchenwald inevitably color this picture of Moses' dream of the Promised Land and of what history made of that dream, still the poem retains to the end some of the brightness and beatitude of the first vision of Canaan. And again the question is, Why? When Muir used the symbol of the Promised Land in *Variations on a Time Theme*, he already found it questionable; it was a dubious goal towards which the tribes of Israel, lost in the wilderness, seemed to be only halfheartedly heading. Now, in 1946, it was surely more dubious still; and indeed the ambiguities of that promise, the disasters into which it led those who believed in it, are precisely the point of a major portion of this new treatment of the fatal covenant. Yet at the end of the poem, after the disasters have been suggested if not fully recounted, it is the dream that still "stands becalmed in time for ever:/ White robes and sabbath peace, the snow-white emblem" (130). Why?

Just as the last two stanzas of "The Return of the Greeks" quietly set a limit to the disillusion and nausea of the preceding stanzas, so the first fourteen lines of "Moses," which describe the "holiday land, the sabbath land" that Moses saw from Pisgah hill, establish a pattern of peace and order, of life at one with the fable as in the opening lines of "Scotland 1941" or "The Ring," which no succeeding tragedies can obliterate altogether. For these are particularly beautiful blank verse lines, phrased in an English of Biblical purity and dignity, and compact of images derived partly from Muir's millennial dreams, partly from his Orkney childhood, when life was similarly filled with the "homely smell" of farm animals and produce, and civilization centered around "Byre, barn and stall."[2] And those images, as we have seen through the whole course of Muir's life, were stubbornly durable. No matter how devastating the shock of the so-called realities of life—the Glasgow slums, the deaths of brothers, father, and mother, the menial, low-paid jobs, the growth of Nazi and Fascist terror in Europe, the final cataclysm of war—those signs and intimations of some beneficent dispensation beyond the piled-up misfortunes of the moment resisted complete cancellation. For a time indeed they were eclipsed. That time is recorded in *An Autobiography*, in portions of *Poor Tom* and *The Three Brothers*, in poems such as "Troy," "The Enchanted Knight," "Then," and above all, "The Gate." But they returned again, as Muir learned to accept both them and his misfortunes, both innocence and experience, together, until finally, as he acknowledges in "The Myth":

> Unshakeable arise alone
> The reverie and the name. (145)

And it is "the reverie and the name" which are the immortal substance of Moses' dream and of the first movement of the poem.

In music, of course, the memory of a first movement is never lost. It remains as the axis of sound from which subsequent movements take their character as variations or contrasts. Similarly, the memory of Moses' prophetic vision remains here as the axis from which the subsequent events in the history of the Jews—and by extension all mankind—take their definition. It is in contrast with the spacious and tranquil scene, the sweet, grave diction of this initial section that the immediately following lines, the plain practical sense of the common people "who dream/ Such common dreams and see so little" seem so disturbing and petty. What these followers of the great leader realize is the political reality which unfortunately the great leader has overlooked: the tribes already living in Canaan are not going to be happy about the arrival of another tribe to conquer them. But compared with the glamor of the prophet's vision, such political realism seems at first mere quibbling. Mean in the terms employed, abrasive in diction and rhythm, it is a wholly unworthy comment on Moses' larger view.

Or is it? For now, as the level of the people's understanding develops and their voice takes on a different, nobler tone, a new movement begins in which they recognize both Moses' dream and their own criticism of it as inadequate. Neither guessed the full tragedy and irony of the fate determined for the chosen nation that "first great day" when Moses beheld Canaan:

> But we did not see,
> We did not see and Moses did not see,
> The great disaster, exile, diaspora,
> The holy bread of the land crumbled and broken
> In Babylon, Caesarea, Alexandria
> As on a splendid dish, or gnawed as offal.
> Nor did we see, beyond, the ghetto rising,
> Toledo, Cracow, Vienna, Budapesth, . . . (130)

And again it is the contrast with the original bright promise that gives these lines their particular poignancy, that deepens the note of lament for the loss of that brightness and sharpens the disgust for the squalor of ghettos, the terror of pogroms, that must take its place.

There is a further movement yet, a further stage in the growth of the people's understanding, where for the first time in the poem they name the maker of the false promise, the source, even beyond Moses, of the deceiving dream. And although they make no open accusation; although they seem to ask only how they, the dull-witted, could be expected to foresee such things, there is certainly an implied arraignment of the original deceiver in their self-questioning:

> How could we have seen such things? How could we have seen
> That plot of ground pledged by the God of Moses
> Trampled by sequent tribes, seized and forgotten
> As a child seizes and forgets a toy, . . . (130)

For if they could not have predicted the developments which would stem from that pledge of a "plot of ground," the pledger Himself, the God of Moses, surely should have known. As Deity omnipotent and omniscient, He must have known, and this knowledge makes Him guilty of a betrayal beyond human reckoning or conception. He is the "burning centre and axle" of cruelty which Muir saw at the core of life in "The Gate," and the victims of that cruelty are thus not the Jews alone, but all mankind. The indictment, even unspoken, is shattering.

Yet it is not on that note of censure and indignation that the poem concludes. As the opening theme in music returns at the close, after intervening passages seem to have altered its form and meaning altogether, so Moses' original vision returns at the end of the poem to reassert its validity. However reprehensible Jehovah's dealings with His worshippers, however brutal the treatment accorded them by history, that vision of sabbath peace which was once granted, which once had its moment of reality, still remains untarnished and pure, "becalmed in time for ever." Again Muir's faith in his intuitions of a reconciliation beyond all betrayals, whether wrought by time or history or by the arbitrary Old Testament God, restores his sense of the incorruptible good that flourishes at the heart of life beside the evil. And again a plunge like that of "The Gate" into unrelieved blackness is averted.

The blackness is averted too in another poem which takes a broken covenant for subject; and this poem, called "The Covenant," because it is short and because it recapitulates so many of Muir's most recurrent motifs, deserves to be quoted in full:

> The covenant of god and animal,
> The frieze of fabulous creatures winged and crowned,
> And in the midst the woman and the man—
>
> Lost long ago in fields beyond the Fall—
> Keep faith in sleep-walled night and there are found
> On our long journey back where we began.
>
> There the heraldic crest of nature lost
> Shines out again until the weariless wave
> Roofs with its sliding horror all that realm.
>
> What jealousy, what rage could overwhelm
> The golden lion and lamb and vault a grave
> For innocence, innocence past defence or cost? (132)

Here, however, the covenant of the first line is a very different covenant from that established between Moses and his God. It is simply the natural, prelapsarian harmony of that legendary age when, as Muir believed, "animal and man and god lived densely together in the same world: the timeless, crowded age of organic heraldry."[3] It is the age sorrowfully recalled by the wingless lion and the blinded dragon of Section Ten in *Variations on a Time Theme*, mysteriously and not quite successfully evoked in the "sylvan war half human and half feathered,/ Perennial emblem painted on the shield" of "The Little General" (111) and the "sylvan wars in bronze within the shield" of "The Grove." It is, of course, the lost age of innocence, and the woman and the man in the midst of the "creatures winged and crowned" are Eve and Adam, still unacquainted with the apple. Yet, since, as Muir also believed, "our unconscious life goes back into" that time,[4] it is possible even now to return to it in dreams, to satisfy at least a little our urge to know ourselves by discovering where we came from, and to restore in "sleep-walled night" the long disrupted wholeness of that world before the Fall.

But when sleep is over, the "fabulous wave far back in Time" (52) that first overwhelmed this Peaceable Kingdom flows over it once more, "Roofs with its sliding horror all that realm"; and as a result, the "covenant" of the title assumes a more sinister connotation than the agreeable concord of god, animal, and man, depicted in the opening stanza. For what is the source of the "weariless wave"? Clearly not the Peaceable Kingdom itself. Some malign outside power seems to be suggested, and just as the self-questioning of the people in "Moses" implied an accusation of the God whose omniscience could see the betrayal contained in the promise, so the questioning final stanza here implies the responsibility and guilt of whatever force it was that created Eden only to destroy it. To have created innocence, surely, was to have undertaken the obligation to protect it, but this unnamed creator repudiated that obligation, broke his covenant with the "golden lion and lamb" he made, and like the God of Moses stands convicted of perfidy.

Deeply reproving, infinitely sad as this final stanza may be, however, it is still not the very "fell of dark" that "The Gate" was, nor is the whole poem shadowed, like "The Gate," with a sense of doom. The sadness of the latter half of the poem here is balanced by the serenity and wonder of the first half, where the long lost golden age, the Wordsworthian "imperial palace" of our beginnings, is actually recovered for a moment in sleep. And even in the last two stanzas, when the wave of time washes back over the shining "heraldic crest" of the first natural world, the richly varied rhythms of the long pentameter lines, the interwoven rhymes of the tercets, the lapidary simplicity of the diction, the beautifully managed agreement of alliteration with internal consonants, as in "The golden lion and lamb and vault a grave," all combine to make a music too sweet for real bitterness. This is melancholy, almost as seductive in its different, more austere fashion, as the melancholy of Keats's ode. Even injured, innocence here has a charm that soothes indignation and alleviates grief.

After this sequence of poems more or less concerned with instances of betrayal, however, Muir does not go on, as he did in *The Narrow Place,* directly to images of reconciliation and harmony. Instead, in this volume, *The Voyage,* he pauses for a time to experiment with new themes and approaches, or new approaches for old themes; and that contemporary feeling which the spoken disillusion, the unspoken accusations in the poems of betrayal conveyed now finds expression in other ways: in the subjects Muir chooses, in the more nervous rhythms he sometimes uses, in the more colloquial language, and in the ironic attitude, say, of "The Rider Victory."

Thus, although the title poem, based on a story told to Muir by Eric Linklater, as Butter reports,[5] is essentially a strange tale of sailors so long out of sight of "familiar landfall, slender mast" (136) of any other ship, that they almost believe there is no harbor or land left for them to find, it is also far more than a tale. Because Muir characteristically plays with the paradox inherent in the situation, the poem becomes a series of metaphysical speculations on time and timelessness, illusion and reality, word and thing, very much in the twentieth-century mode. The difficulty in this poem is that although Muir develops these speculations out of the narrative smoothly enough; although, too, he keeps the narrative advancing briskly through concise ballad stanzas; and although certain of these stanzas and certain lines have a haunting beauty, still the poem as a whole lacks the singleness of feeling, the tight, organic unity, the driving force, to make it wholly compelling. Either as fantastic story or as reflection on the eternal polarities, or as semantic parable, it is diluted, its power dispersed.

In the next poem in the volume, "The Fathers," too, although Muir turns in a still different direction, to a theme he has often touched on or implied before, but never so clearly articulated, the theme again is one our post-Freudian world finds particularly fascinating: the ancient but now increasingly persuasive idea that our fathers live on in us, that what we are is what they were, and to know ourselves, we must know them. For that urge to learn where we come from, which Muir called in *An Autobiography* one of the three mysteries that possess our minds,[6] and which kept him preoccupied, as we have seen, with life's "monstrous beginnings," with our pre-human heredity, also kept him intensely concerned with our human inheritance. "The life of every man," to quote from the *Autobiography* again, "is an endlessly repeated performance of the life of man," [7] and to find the outlines of that archetypal pattern, that fable from which all our lives take their measure, however far they may deviate, Muir looked again and again not only into his own life and the lives of his contemporaries and immediate ancestors, but also into story, myth, and archeological remnant of the remotest past. Sometimes, as in "The Wheel" in *The Narrow Place*, he rebelled against the impositions of his predecessors:

> Loves and hates are thrust
> Upon me by the acrimonious dead,
> The buried thesis, long since rusted knife,
> Revengeful dust. (105)

Sometimes, as in "Twice-Done, Once-Done" in *The Voyage*, he accepted the design laid down for him:

> I could neither rise nor fall
> But that Adam fell.
> Had he fallen once for all,
> There'd be nothing to tell. (134)

But always the search went on, to understand his own individuality and that of every man through the patterns traced by his forefathers, and it continues in his work until the very end, in such late poems as "The Island" and "Into Thirty Centuries Born."

In this particular poem, "The Fathers," however, the major thrust of feeling is neither rebellion nor acceptance, but actual experience, experience of the fact that our fathers do survive in us, their breath does burden ours, their ancient fears and angers still quicken our blood. Although, it is true, the book-keeping metaphor on which the first stanza is built does not contribute to this effect, the simple combination in the next two stanzas of archaic images with living flesh and blood, of "blackened bone,/ Cellar and choking cave" with "careless brows" and "unhurried veins" functions admirably to superimpose the one on the other, to make both contemporary, alive, and felt. But even more than the imagery, the deftly handled rhyme and metrical patterns of the three-beat lines which compose these stanzas succeed in producing an incantatory effect, a magic spell, which seems capable of summoning the ghosts of the past to inhabit the bodies of the present. The emphatic, irregularly recurring rhymes, the strong alliteration, reminiscent of Anglo-Saxon verse with its mysterious riddles and runes, the delicately modulated vowels that temper that alliteration, as Harvey Gross points out in his *Sound and Form in Modern Poetry*,[8] all impose an irresistible charm on the ear. What is more, the strong, insistent stresses, which vary so dramatically in their fall from line to line, as the accents shift or the number of syllables in a foot differ, not only recall Yeats's style, as Gross notes again (70), but equal his vigor in raising "images and memories" from the dark by the power of musical speech. What is commanded in these accents must be done, what is invoked must appear.

That Yeatsian quality observable in this poem, moreover, is not at all unusual in Muir, particularly in his later work. Since Yeats of course has many qualities, many styles, it is not always the same characteristic that seems to echo in Muir; and since Muir's own voice is always predominant, no matter what other poet may seem to be speaking in the background, the echo is rarely a strong one. It can be heard very clearly, however, in the little poem, "The House," where the situation is an almost exact counterpart of that in Yeats's "The Song of the Old Mother." Muir's old woman, with her bitter knowledge that the young have yet to learn, moreover, clearly belongs in the company of Crazy Jane and Mrs. Mary Moore. Her tough, very contemporary, very colloquial talk, marked with an occasional word from more formal usage, is like theirs too, and one of the formal words she uses, "ignorant," in the first line of the final stanza, " 'For the young and the rich are ignorant' " (144) has an inescapably Yeatsian ring. Lines from Yeats like "I would be ignorant as the dawn" immediately come to mind. Or, closer still, "We loved each other and were ignorant."

In "Suburban Dream"—another strictly contemporary poem in setting, in language, and in feeling—there is likewise an affinity with Yeats. Not in style, certainly. There is no similarity in this poem to any of Yeats's more typical traits in diction, rhythm, or theme; but there is an identity in what might be called anti-masculine insight: a capacity, that is, not only for seeing into the feminine mind, but for understanding at least one of the many instinctive feminine reactions to the masculine character. Yeats in a number of poems shows this quality; it is one of the several kinds of insight woven into "Leda and the Swan"; it is apparent in Crazy Jane, the Woman Young and Old, the Lady and the Chambermaid from the story of "The Three Bushes"; and it is apparent in "Suburban Dream" as well. Could only a native of an historically exploited, colonial country like Ireland or Scotland, sympathize so keenly with the exploited and dominated of every country, the women and their wards? Whatever the answer, that sympathy which Yeats the Irishman so surely had, Muir the Scot has as well, and he senses here with extraordinary delicacy the unexpressed, even unacknowledged, feeling of relief, of lightened heart and delicious peace, that the "women, school girls, children," and even "a schoolboy here and there" all experience while the men are away at work, "the masters gone" (147).

Both "The House" and "Suburban Dream," of course, represent another strain in Muir beside the Yeatsian. They also exemplify those poems in which, as we indicated at the beginning of this chapter, Muir relaxes his seriousness a little, puts the cosmic verities somewhat to the side, and plays with an idea almost, if not quite, simply because of its intrinsic interest. In the marvelous fourteen-line poem, "The Rider Victory," for instance, which surely belongs among this group, many of Muir's familiar concerns are clearly present: paradox is here— the horseman halted in mid-air through no barrier is in his way; the suspension of time is here, the frustration of the hero, the road that does not lead to the "waiting kingdom" after all. But here these motifs do not add up to the usual conclusions. They are simply there, suspended in air like horse and rider, suggesting everything and stating nothing, while Muir, with an unusually edged and ironic, very twentieth-century tone, exploits to the full the enigma they create. He never fully identifies the figure he is talking about, for example. Although it is clear that he is simply describing an equestrian statue in the middle of an empty bridge, he opens up all sorts of other possible interpretations by capitalizing the word "Victory" in the first line:

> The rider Victory reins his horse
> Midway across the empty bridge
> As if head-tall he had met a wall. (142)

Is this thwarted rider a symbol, like the Greeks returned from their wars, of the vanity of worldly ambition? Does he represent the absurdity of all supposed military victories, the emptiness of history, that "stationary storm that cannot bate/ Its neutral violence" ("The Wheel," 105)? Muir does not say. He leaves the problem to the reader.

To reinforce this riddling effect, Muir again, as in "The Fathers," uses a strong alliterative pattern, together with the insistent rhymes that seem to be traditionally associated with mystifying spells: the initial and final *r* of "rider," for example, is not only repeated in "reins," but occurs internally as well in "Victory" and "horse," and again, in the next line, in "across" and "bridge." The internal rhymes of the third line, "tall" and "wall" are immediately echoed in the end-rhyme of the fourth line, "all," and once more in the seventh line, "fall." But the device that most decisively establishes the enigmatic character of the poem is the artfully unsettling combination of simple, colloquial diction with terms from a vocabulary at once more stately and Latinate, more weighted with implications of further meaning; and in the second stanza particularly this more resonant terminology takes over. The precarious position of the horse, for instance, is indicated at the end of the first stanza in altogether colloquial, unceremonious terms; the animal is checked "So suddenly, you'd think he'd fall." But in the first line of the second stanza this scarcely maintained balance becomes an act of levitation; horse and rider are both magically "suspended." They are both transformed, too, into mythical creatures, "Leaping on air and legendary"; the air that both supports and halts them is "implacable" as fate; and in the last line, in a phrase that almost but not quite identifies them, a phrase that wonderfully completes the rhyme with "legendary," they freeze into "motionless statuary." No apter comment could be made on this series of transformations than something Muir himself wrote in *Latitudes* long before: "Except intellectually, the greatest thing is to me the most enigmatical thing; that which is meaning and yet has no meaning; what is called magic." [9]

There are many kinds of magic, however. There is the magic of elusive meaning, such as "The Rider Victory" exemplifies, and there is the greater magic of inexpressible meaning momentarily expressed. This was the kind of magic evoked in the affirmative poems of the preceding volume, "The Annunciation" and "The Commemoration," "The Ring," "The Guess," and "The Day," because they do what rationally cannot be done; they resolve paradox, reconcile opposites. And it is this kind of magic which many of the remaining poems in this volume evoke again, still more irresistibly as Muir returns now to the basic pattern of his poetry, the opposition and the interdependence of light and dark. But just as Muir never descends in *The Voyage* to the extreme of dejection represented in *The Narrow Place* by "The Gate," so in the concluding poems of this volume he ascends higher into the light. He now sees more clearly than ever before where he has been, where he is, and where he hopes to go.

He sees, that is, three different views of life, which he described in an article on "Afterthoughts to an Autobiography" that he wrote for *The Scots Magazine* in 1940. He had been looking back into his past, into what he called "Yesterday's

Mirror," to write the story of his life; and as a result, he realized that whereas once all he could discern in that glass was the "iron law," the "burning centre and axle" of life he had known in Glasgow, now he is able to look further back, beyond Glasgow to his childhood. Now he can make out a scene where there is "an indefeasible rightness beneath the wrongness of things; a struggle between good and evil, and not merely the victory of evil." Nor is that all. There is a third possible view, he realizes, given "only to the greatest poets and mystics at their greatest moments," a view that is "beyond rational description," a view where, as in "The Trophy," the "king on his throne and the rebel raising his standard in the market place" each "plays a part in a supertemporal drama," the issue of which is "glory." And although Muir never claims to be a mystic or a poet of that rank, nevertheless it is manifestly this view, which "reconciles all opposites," [10] that he has perceived at least with the eye of the imagination. It was this view which informed the final poems of *The Narrow Place* and which now informs, with even greater conviction, such poems of *The Voyage* as "The Three Mirrors," "The Myth," "Song," the two sonnets, "The Transmutation" and "Time Held in Time's Despite," and above all, "A Birthday" and "In Love for Long."

These three ways of looking at life, as it happens, are precisely the subject of "The Three Mirrors," which therefore has particular importance as a key both to the changes in Muir's philosophy over the years and to the meaning he attached to a number of his most frequent symbols. In the "first glass," for instance, he sees what he learned to see in his Glasgow years, when "The mountain summits were sealed/ In incomprehensible wrath" (140); and the roots that run wrong here, the paths that are askew, the roads that inevitably lead the victim to his doom, are all symbols of the evil that seemed to him then to dominate the world. When he looks into the "second glass," on the other hand, he sees a vision of good, symbolized by his Orkney childhood: "Father and mother and child,/ The house with its single tree." But the good does not remain secure. It is cracked and bent, significantly, by an "angry law," and the "child at peace in his play," again very significantly, changes as he goes "through a door" (141). For the metaphor here is that of initiation which functioned in "The Gate"; and just as the arrival of maturity there shriveled and blasted the children's world, while the adult world within the fortress menaced them with its own stern laws, so growth and experience here bring the shames and taboos—perhaps the Calvinist taboos that so irked Muir—that spoil original innocence. And although the childhood vision is not obliterated altogether in this "second glass," it has to make way for the intrusions of time: "locked in love and grief," good and evil must embrace together.

When Muir comes to the "third glass," as Butter points out,[11] he changes the syntax of his statement. For the adverbial time clause, "When I looked," which he uses in speaking of the first two mirrors, he substitutes the conditional "If I looked," to indicate that the view to be seen in this mirror is not necessarily within his own experience. Yet if this view does not spring from his experience, it surely springs from what we have seen to be his deepest beliefs, his most persuasive intuitions, inasmuch as he expresses it in imagery which is peculiarly and persistently his own. Here again, as they were in "The Trophy" and as they will be in "One Foot in Eden," are "evil and good/ Standing side by side." Here are the "wise king" and the "rebel," each in his own place. And here are himself and his wife, united in that love which thrives on paradox, defends against the dark, and proves the impossible, the reconciliation in a greater harmony of all the world's wrong:

> If I could look I should see
> The world's house open wide,
> The million million rooms
> And the quick god everywhere
> Glowing at work and at rest,
> Tranquillity in the air,
> Peace of the humming looms
> Weaving from east to west,
> And you and myself there. (141)

Whether Muir has looked into this mirror or not, he knows what is there.

He knows what is there, of course, because in his own life he has been there. He has not, perhaps, experienced the supreme, transcendent vision of a mystic, but he has lived in Eden: and this fact, that Eden is his native land, gives to another poem, "The Myth," one of his loveliest lyrics, its peculiarly heartbreaking quality. For "The Myth" is infused with that longing, already present as we have seen in some of his earliest poems, which Muir said was awakened by the passage of time, a "longing more poignant than all the longings caused by the division of lovers in space";[12] and the object of that longing here is the country of his infancy, which was also, as it happened, the world before the Fall. It is thus not only the regret for lost innocence, shared by all mankind, but the personal nostalgia for his own past, the intense, impossible yearning for the "days that are no more," that sounds in the sweet, sad music of the three common measure quatrains which make up the first stanza. That "distant isle" (144) is the island of Wyre, where his father's farm stood. The universal "myth" of a golden age "enacted" there was his own "childhood." He himself felt how it was for time to stand still, not yet the destroyer. He himself partook of that life that was a fable, lived in natural piety. He himself was guarded at his play by those spiritual presences which stood as "faithful watchers" over all that blessedness; and whether those watchers are possibly the angels posted by Gabriel to guard the walls of Paradise, or perhaps the four Apostles to whom children pray to guard their beds, is of no importance. They are the final proof, the uncontrovertible tokens, of the entire and perfect security which surrounded that "country crystalline" where Muir spent his first years, and for which all the rest of his life, as he said in "Horses," he was to "pine."

For time did not stand still forever, and after Paradise came the Fall. But in the second stanza of "The Myth," which represents this fall from grace, it is not the usual Glasgow inferno, the world of wrath and evil, which appears. Instead it is something new, a "tragi-comedy," a "Ridiculous war of dreams and shames," as if from the vantage point of the age he had reached —he is now "past the prime" (145)—this sojourn in the pit took on a slightly different aspect. No longer so vast in its extent nor so impenetrable in its blackness as it once seemed, the pit in the perspective of so many later years looks after all a little absurd, and the language of the first quatrain reflects this absurdity. The term "tragi-comedy" speaks for itself. It is reinforced by the rhyme with another term, "Pyrrhic victory," which epitomizes the futility and the irony of what once seemed an unrelieved, grim struggle against life's "iron law"; and the masterly "Ridiculous" ties both "tragi-comedy" and "Pyrrhic victory" together even more securely by echoing and emphasizing both meaning and sound. In addition, the abrupt introduction of an anapaestic foot into the second line ("Ridiculous war of dreams and shames"), together with the use of a trochaic foot to begin the third line ("Waged for a Pyrrhic victory"), adds a self-mocking note that not only contrasts with the prevailingly dreamlike movement of the first stanza, but accentuates the ironic quality of this second stanza.

Yet as this stanza advances into its second and third quatrains, as flesh and blood war with reveries and names, and the reverie learns to "play its useful part," the measure of the first stanza returns. By the concluding lines of the third quatrain here, moreover, an image of reconciliation has returned as well. Not the original Eden, but a weaving together of "radiant east and west" which recalls the "Peace of the humming looms/ Weaving from east to west" (141) that the third mirror revealed to those who could look into it. And with the third stanza even the original Eden comes back, although not, alas, as it originally was. It has survived a "deluge." That "long watery wash of Time" [13] which "roofed with its sliding horror" (132) the world's first age of innocence has flooded, too, Muir's "distant isle," and what remains is not "consolidated flesh and bone," not "the dying song/ The flower, the falling wave" (144), the child at play in the wood, but the intangible works of the imagination, "the reverie and the name." The "watchers" are still there, but they have "risen" from the waters that submerged them. They stand "Like monuments a deluge leaves" (145) in a desolate landscape, and the "sheaves" of the harvest they guard are "invisible." Here, surely, is a testament to the triumph of the spirit and to the immortality of Eden in the spirit, but here also is an infinitely sad lament for all that was sweet and fragile in the flesh, all that incarnated Eden in the longed-for past. If this is an affirmation, and it is, it brings tears to the eyes.

The final two poems of *The Voyage*, "A Birthday" and "In Love for Long," however, do not lament. They transmute lamentation into rejoicing. The most concise and most perfect of all Muir's statements of affirmation, they accept everything: flesh and spirit, good and evil, "all sweets and sours that grow" (157), the ravages of time and the gift of love. They accept all equally and with equal delight, in an irrational yet absolutely convincing gladness, that derives as much from their music as from their literal meaning. For the lyrical voice here is at last indisputably and solely Muir's; and although he has already used this voice more quietly in his love poems to his wife and in a few other poems—in "The Myth," for instance, in a minor key—here for the first time he breaks into full, spontaneous song. And as Edwin Morgan observes, Muir's lyrical style, when it is successful, has a "particular sweetness" that is "like the sudden scent of some wild flower." [14] It is distinctive, it is irresistible, and like MacDiarmid's wild white rose of Scotland, it "breaks the heart."

In both these poems, as it happens, the metrical base is a simple three-stress line, and in both this line performs a double function: it permits what is certainly one, at least, of the secrets here of that "particular sweetness," and it gives form to the theme each poem proclaims: the miraculous reconciliation of the irreconcilable. For both poems, as we have said, accept everything. They are built on a pattern made up of the tension and the resolution of opposites, and the extreme compression of the trimeter line serves on the one hand to accentuate the tension, the contrast, the pull apart, and on the other, to effect the convergence and the harmony. Within the brief three stresses of a single line in "A Birthday," for example, the two extremes of a man's lifetime, "The first look and the last" (157), face each other in immediate, effective contrast, while the seamless whole from which both spring and into which both merge, "Acceptance, gratitude," fills the six syllables of another line with unbroken accord. Or in "In Love for Long," the succeeding lines balance against each other. "This happy happy love" is set against "Is sieged with crying sorrows"; "A little paradise," against "Held in the world's vice" (159); and the quick return of the short lines brings the opposites into a juxtaposition that at first emphasizes their polarity and then dissolves it in the act of their concurrence.

In the strict compass of these lines, moreover, the shortest, simplest words, the Anglo-Saxon monosyllables of familiar speech, seem most appropriate, and it is on such words that Muir chiefly relies, as in the opening passage of "A Birthday," with its easy, colloquial rhythm, its cherishing of the humble, whether word or plant or sensation:

> I never felt so much
> Since I have felt at all
> The tingling smell and touch
> Of dogrose and sweet briar,
> Nettles against the wall,
> All sours and sweets that grow
> Together or apart
> In hedge or marsh or ditch. (157)

Yet when these homely terms are varied, as Muir varies them from time to time, with the sudden richness of some polysyllabic word of Latin derivation still held within the same narrow trimeter limits, the effect is literally a transfiguration, both of sound and of meaning, as in these two lines, so often quoted in this book:

> Before I took the road
> Direction ravished my soul.

For here the plain, colloquial diction and rhythm of the first line are utterly changed by the multiple connotations and the fine Roman resonance of "Direction" and "ravished" in the second, while these in turn are intensified in force by the compression in which they are held, and their Latin music provides a counterpoint to the preceding simpler melody. No wonder that this "direction" towards which Muir's style has been tending from the start, a combination of simplicity with power, ease and directness with enormous reverberation of meaning, literally "ravished" his soul before he took the road, drew him to his particular true north before he had so much as decided on setting out.

Finally, there is the consummately managed conclusion of "In Love for Long," which praises the love that

> Is like the happy doe
> That keeps its perfect laws
> Between the tiger's paws
> And vindicates its cause, (160)

where a host of forces play against each other to tighten the tension and increase the power of the passage. The "happy doe" of course opposes the "tiger," with all the cosmic connotations that derive from Blake. The perfection of the doe's laws contrasts with the idea of play contained in "happy"; the idea of play itself, with the danger inherent in the "tiger's paws," while the magnificent "vindicates" at once contrasts with the simplicity of the context and raises the whole stanza, the whole poem, to a new and dizzy level. The doe that "vindicates its cause" within the tiger's dangerous grasp reflects the eternal justice that preserves the stars from harm.

And thus once more out of paradox Muir shapes unity. Out of the play of opposites he weaves a reconciliation of opposites, and does it, moreover, with a simplicity, an ease, and a force that overwhelm all rational objections to the contrary. The combination here of utter, childlike acceptance with acute awareness of the dangers so delicately held in equilibrium disarms argument or question or denial. This is imaginative vision which must be granted its authority. It speaks of those mysteries not accessible to science, nor to most of us, but which we need to know of if we are to live as human beings in an increasingly dehumanized world.

VII

" Dark on the highway, groping in the light"

After these two hymns of pure delight that conclude *The Voyage*, Muir's next volume, *The Labyrinth* (1949), opens again on a lower key, which remains dominant, although not finally controlling, throughout the whole book. Yet this is a key for which two groups of poems in *The Voyage* which have not yet been discussed have already prepared us. The four fine sonnets in the earlier volume, "Epitaph," "Comfort in Self-Despite," "The Transmutation," and "Time Held in Time's Despite," for example, heralded not only the technique but the thematic coloring of the still finer sonnet, "Too Much," which is the first poem in *The Labyrinth*. For although all four of these sonnets were more or less statements of affirmation, that affirmation was not, like "In Love for Long," an expression of immediate, sensuous experience of cosmic order and reconciliation. Rather, it was a balancing of yea against nay, light against dark, and if the yea and the light sent the scale down, the dark and the nay still exerted considerable counterpoise.

In "Epitaph," in fact, the only affirmation was in the resolution to have done with the narrow, the incomplete, the neutral, to which even death, in its "absolute honesty" (153), was preferable. "Comfort in Self-Despite" salvaged "that good I scarcely dreamt I had" (154) from a Shakespearean "waste of shame" and self-disgust. The "silent immortality" (153) offered in "The Transmutation" was a "phantom ground" of "ghost and glance and gleam," a shadow existence like that of Homer's unhappy shades. And even the wealth of love stored up in time in "Time Held in Time's Despite" was impervious to time only when stripped bare of the personal in spirit, the corruptible in body: a love as shadowy as the immortality in "The Transmutation." In comparison with these meager assertions of faith, indeed, "Too Much" is a ringing declaration: everything *is* wrong in this world, "huddled awry, at random teased and tossed" (163); nothing is as it was promised; and yet some inner vision gives assurance of the right. The light is there, illuminating the road we seek, but we are blind.

It is particularly revealing to compare this figure of a blind man threading his "dazzling way" through his night with an almost identical figure in Muir's novel, *The Three Brothers*, published almost twenty years before. For there, near the end of the book, the elder Blackadder tries to restore his son David's lost belief in some underlying moral principle in the world; and to indicate what he thinks is the instinctive human feeling that such a principle does exist, he uses the analogy of the blind man and his sense of the road. We're all like blind folk, Blackadder tells his son, "convinced for some reason— and that may mean something gey essential too, it shouldna be left out of account—that there's a road somewhere. . . ." [1] But since he himself is none too sure of his own belief, he hardly puts the case very forcefully. In his mouth the analogy diminishes into uncertainty. When Muir uses essentially the same analogy in "Too Much," on the other hand, it does not diminish. It increases in strength to become the culminating point of the entire sonnet, the conclusive proof, vouchsafed by an inward revelation, that a road, a highway, does exist. And not only so; in the process the analogy itself is transformed. For as its power develops, it carries the sonnet along with it, lifts the sestet from the broken, fretful rhythms, the casual diction of the opening two quatrains, to an altogether new level of simple, dignified language and long, sustained rhythmic phrases:

Then suddenly again I watch the old
Worn saga write across my years and find,
Scene after scene, the tale my fathers told,
But I in the middle blind, as Homer blind,

Dark on the highway, groping in the light,
Threading my dazzling way within my night. (163)

And on this new level the introduction of the name that transforms the analogy becomes possible: the name of Homer. What Muir is invoking here, it is now evident, is far more than the proverbial sixth sense of the blind. It is the insight of the imagination, of the "greatest poets and mystics at their greatest moments," as he wrote in that article for *The Scots Magazine* cited in the preceding chapter; and it is this insight which permits the recognition of the "worn saga," the everlasting fable beneath the random confusion of the years. It is this which assured Homer and assures all visionary poets their intuition of the "dazzling way" their physical eyes cannot always see.

That the truth is in the light, human understanding in the dark, except when visited by flashes of intuitive perception, is, however, not a very comforting conclusion. "Too Much" is an affirmation of good cheer, as we have already noted, only in comparison with the still less comforting conclusions of the sonnets in the preceding volume. In the same way, "The Labyrinth," the title poem of this volume, which immediately follows "Too Much," offers a vision of peace so hedged with contrary visions, so remote from the fears and troubles of ordinary experience, that its consolations would seem small were it not for the poems in *The Voyage* which set the mood for it, the five poems of dejection and sorrow either specifically or by implication connected with the war that was then devastating Europe. For while "Reading in Wartime," (148) by opposing to the impersonal destruction of the battlefield the personal image of man safeguarded in books, avoids complete surrender to horror, the other four poems, "The Lullaby," "Dejection," "Song of Patience," and "Sorrow," seem to have no force for resistance. Lacking, too, the power to make such uncompromising statements of despair as that of "The Gate," they exemplify rather an exhaustion of the spirit, an immersion in melancholy that "Folds [the mind] . . . beyond the reach of care" (150) and blunts the force of imagination; and it is of course just such an imprisonment in a meaningless shadow world, a world of error and illusion, that is the subject of "The Labyrinth." The difference, aside from the fact that "The Labyrinth" is a far more successful and exciting poem, is that "The Labyrinth" also provides at least a brief view, whether valid or not, of a "lovely world," and of gods in whose dialogue of peace "this our life" is "as a chord" (165).

Writing in a B.B.C. "Chapbook" in 1952, Muir made a few comments of his own on the origin and meaning of "The Labyrinth." It "started itself," he recalled, while he was vacationing at the Writers' House in Dobřiš from his post-war work as Director of the British Council Institute in Prague. "Thinking there of the old story of the labyrinth of Cnossos and the journey of Theseus through it and out of it, I felt that this was an image of human life with its errors and ignorance and endless intricacy. In the poem I made the labyrinth stand for all this. But I wanted also to give an image of the life of the gods, to whom all that is confusion down here is clear and harmonious as seen eternally. The poem begins with a very long sentence, deliberately labyrinthine, to give the mood." [2] Yet even when all this is said, much more remains. For this is not the first time Muir has devised such an image of human life, and as a result, "The Labyrinth" not only echoes but effectively restates and sums up many of the themes which have persisted in Muir's poetry from the beginning.

The confusing passages of the maze, for example, the paths without exit, are another version, more clearly defined, more thoroughly explored, of the Kafka-like theme of frustration, of roads that do not lead to the Castle, which Muir treated extensively as early as *Variations on a Time Theme*. The "deceiving streets/ That meet and part and meet, and rooms that open/ Into each other—and never a final room—" (165) are still another metaphor for the blurring of illusion and reality which likewise occurred in *Variations* and continues as a motif, clothed in differing forms, through such poems as "Tristram's Journey," "Troy," "The Enchanted Knight," "To J. F. H.," "The Grove," and "the Voyage." Since, moreover the blurring of the line between illusion and reality is characteristic of mental disturbance; since many of the images here, particularly these of the deceiving streets and the "Stairways and corridors and antechambers/ That vacantly wait for some great audience" are almost identical to images Muir used in his novel, *The Marionette*, to indicate the hallucinations suffered by his protagonist, the disturbed boy Hans, clearly the familiar Muir themes of madness and alienation are present in this poem too. Although Theseus lost in the labyrinth, haunted by these illusions, is more fully realized, he is essentially very like the Hero of *Chorus of the Newly Dead*. His journey through the "wild-wood waste of falsehood" is a repetition of Tristram's and Hölderlin's journeys, and of course, like theirs, it is at once a metaphor for the situation of modern man, trapped in a world he never made, and a variant of Muir's own years enclosed in the "crystalline globe" that shut him off from contact with the "still fields swift with flowers, the trees/ All bright with blossom, the little green hills, the sea" (164).

It is a very significant point, too, that the rejection of these illusions, the movement towards affirming faith in the world of green hills and flowering fields comes precisely after the forty-fifth line when Theseus is told he is "Deep in the centre of the endless maze." That is, he stands at the "burning centre and axle" of cruelty and betrayal, at the heart of the universe ruled by an "iron law," where Muir himself has been before, in "The Gate." And just as the upward movement of *The Narrow Place* and of all Muir's succeeding volumes took its start from that central depth, so here Theseus' firm, "I could not live if this [the maze] were not illusion" (165), comes only after he has reached the nadir of that illusion. Only then can he return to the upper air; only then can he experience rebirth. For what is involved here, as it was involved in the sequence of poems before and after "The Gate," and as it is involved, although always in Muir's own characteristic terms, in so many individual poems, from the early "Ballad of Rebirth" to the late "Milton," "One Foot in Eden," and "The Horses," is clearly the motif of rebirth. Here, indeed, and for that reason this passage is of particular importance, Muir makes his clues plainer than usual. After Theseus has killed the bull, he himself is "blood-splashed"; he cannot tell if he is "dead or alive" in the "twilight nothingness"; he "might have been/ A spirit seeking his body through the roads/ Of intricate Hades" (163-64). But even without these specific references to death and the underworld, the dynamics of the poem illustrates the theme: a theme which is not only, once more, one that has concerned Muir continually, but one which has affected the whole course of his poetry. It is, in fact, the theme which makes possible the acceptance of paradox, the perception of a reconciliation of contraries, which since *The Narrow Place* has represented for Muir the way out of the Labyrinth.

Equally, then, since symbolic rebirth implies symbolic new life, the concept of some promised land, of some restored harmony of man and animal in a fresher Eden, has long been an intrinsic part of Muir's metaphysics, and this concept is present here as well. Above the blooming, green landscape that awaits Theseus when he first escapes from the labyrinth, the gods sit on their mountain-isles and converse in an "eternal dialogue" that weaves all things together in peace. Yet although this vision is more Olympian than ever before, although the lucid language and the slow, stately cadences more than ever recall the utterance of the early gods in Keats's *Hyperion*, vision, language and cadences all have their precursors in earlier poems. The landscape of the lower world here is obviously another of Muir's many transformations of the Orkneys, those distant islands where the "myth" of his childhood was "enacted." The gods on their hills have already appeared in "The Mythical Journey," where they "reclined and conversed with each other/ From summit to summit" (63); and the deep serenity, the Hölderlin-like "vastness" [3] and translucency of both these manifestations of the divine, shine out of Muir's first, unorthodox sonnet, with its majestic movement and its noble diction—"The Old Gods" in *The Narrow Place*. Clearly, whatever its variations, the deep dream of peace that Muir so tirelessly evokes has an essential unity.

Yet however closely related to so many of his other poems "The Labyrinth" may be, it still has an identity and an impact of its own. Despite the fact that it is based on the Theseus myth, it not only departs from the original *donnée*, as Muir's myth poems always do; it departs farthest of all. So far, indeed, that almost all traces of the original are lost. Only the dead bull on the straw and the image of the labyrinth itself remain to point to Theseus as the subject here. His name is never mentioned in the poem. Instead, the protagonist and narrator is an anonymous "I," whose concerns are entirely unlike those of the legendary Theseus, as the maze in which he wanders is unlike the maze that Daedalus built. For this maze, although Muir may have intended it as a picture of all human life, is far more certainly a specific picture of the tormented human mind today; and although the tormented mind is a province Muir has often explored before, as we have said, he has rarely achieved all together the fullness, the immediacy, and the verisimilitude that he achieves here. All the images of entrapment, of wrong roads, deceiving streets, and indecipherable tracks that he has previously used as symbols of the apparent meaninglessness of life, the impossibility of escaping from confusion and illusion, now reappear and like converging electric currents breaking into flame, they break into dramatic dialogue between the "Theseus-I" and his "bad spirit," who of course is still another manifestation of the old "demon" Indifference from *Variations on a Time Theme*. That this "bad spirit" so nearly anticipates, too, the "ill spirit" in Robert Lowell's dialogue with himself in "Skunk Hour" is of course a coincidence; but it is also an indication, however fortuitous, of the closeness in feeling between these two poems. Both are expressions of today's intense spiritual sickness, of alienation, disgust, and despair.

While Lowell can turn for hope, however, only to the indomitable mother skunk at his back steps, Muir has that transcendent vision of the gods on their mountains; and in this difference in the degree of hope the two poets allow themselves lies the key to the difference in the final success of the two poems. W. S. Merwin, in discussing "The Labyrinth" in a review of Muir's first *Collected Poems*, gets to the root of the matter when he complains of "a distrust of the metaphor, of the terms of the poem." He goes on then to say that he discerns "a need felt to explain rather than expand and deepen the possibilities of representing . . ."; the central image of the poem, he feels, is "weakened by a passage which steps out of the illusion and comments at length on its relevance—the relevance is not made in the illusion itself." [4] And it is true that the "Theseus-I" who is protagonist here does abandon his strong dramatic role to point out what everything means. But that "distrust of the metaphor, of the terms of the poem," shows even more clearly in the fact that the peaceful sequence of the gods above their little island world does not grow out of the initial metaphor of the labyrinth; is not, indeed, really connected with it. Where Lowell's encounter with the skunk remains strictly within the confines of the scene set for his poem from the beginning, and develops logically out of elements already implicit in that scene, Muir's view of the reconciling gods derives from outside. It came "once in a dream or trance"; there is no intrinsic relation between that dream and the struggle of the "Theseus-I" to escape the "wild-wood waste of falsehood" where he has been trapped. As a dramatic representation of this entrapment, with all its frustration and anguish, the first forty-five lines of "The Labyrinth" are superb. Critics have uniformly admired what Muir called the "deliberately labyrinthine" first sentence, which spins its intricate system of dependent clauses and parentheses through thirty-five lines of freely handled blank verse. The "remarkable, sustained syntax" here "winds and turns upon itself . . . ," notes Harvey Gross in *Sound and Form in Modern Poetry*. "The syntax *acts out* the journey of Theseus." [5] But as a representation of escape from the trap, "The Labyrinth" is not so convincing. The escape is essentially contrived, and however beautiful it may be, however it may exemplify the theme of rebirth so important to Muir's poetry, it does not, as the structure Muir has given to the poem demands, counteract the powerful nightmare effect of the first part of the poem. No wonder Muir, in truth to the original terms of the poem, concludes with a return of the labyrinth:

> Last night I dreamt I was in the labyrinth,
> And woke far on. I did not know the place. (165)

A similar failure to trust the basic metaphor and follow its implications to the end flaws the seven-part sequence, "The Journey Back." For although, as a sequence, like *Variations on a Time Theme*, "The Journey Back" is of course free to shift scene, point of view, mood, and manner, from section to section, nevertheless a central theme or mood must control the whole, and each section must have its own unity of development. But this simply does not happen here. While a central theme does for the most part control the entire poem, several of the separate sections fall apart. Even the first section, despite its powerful beginning, falters towards the end, loses impetus, and concludes without ever reaching the point for which it seemed headed. After the direct, firm statement of where the poem is going in the opening lines:

> I take my journey back to seek my kindred,
> Old founts dried up whose rivers run far on
> Through you and me, (168)

with their tantalizing parallels to some of Rilke's imagery from the third Duino Elegy: "sondern die Väter, die wie Trümmer Gebirgs/ uns im Grunde Beruhn; sondern das trockene Fluss-bett/ einstiger Mutters"/ (but the fathers, who like the wreckage of mountains/ rest in our depths; but the dry river bed/ of mothers who once existed),[6] comes an equally firm statement of purpose:

> Seek the beginnings, learn from whence you came,
> And know the various earth of which you are made. (169)

And we know, it seems, where we are going and why.

Taking up again the question that continually haunted him

—that has haunted all men, and that obsesses us today—of where we come from in this life, Muir intends to "journey back" as he did briefly in "The Fathers," through the bones and blood of his kindred, to discover the forces that have, shaped his own identity. This is exactly what he proceeds to do. In the straightforward syntax, the natural rhythms, the familiar vocabulary of ordinary speech, he describes his setting out "on this calm summer evening/ From this my home and my father's," and his assumption first of his "father's farmer hands," then of the bodies and minds of a host of ancestors who went before. But as he proceeds, he seems to lose track of his purpose. Instead of seeking sources and causes, he merely goes on, from one body to another, until he is weary, "avid for the end"; until, lost in a confusion of numbers, he cannot distinguish his own personality any more, but merges into the "Many in One," the faceless multitude of "humanity in its historical development" which so overwhelmed him with loneliness in "The Solitary Place" of *Journeys and Places*. In the effort to escape from this predicament, he then abandons his purpose altogether, and in the last lines of the section seeks first for a complete release in some pre-bodily state of "sweet and vacant ease," next for what seems a moral release in the "Image of man from whom all have diverged" (Adam? Christ?), and finally, submitting to the inevitable, turns back to his "sole starting-point," his "random self/That in these rags and tatters clothes the soul" (171). But the search for his own beginnings, which was the original metaphor of this section, he has put aside. He has not explored those "old founts dried up" to their limits, nor sifted all the grains of the "various earth" of which he was made.

To a greater or lesser degree, some similar flaw affects most of the remaining sections. They may open, like the third, or close, like the fifth, with a thrust of power, but the power lapses, the thrust is diverted, and the poem disintegrates. Only in the second section is the illusion established in the beginning never broken. For here the strongly stressed trimeter and dimeter lines (3, 3, 2, 3, 3, 2), with their intricately varied feet and their insistent rhymes (*a, a, b, c, c, b*), at once suggest the "sleepwandering pace" (171) of the spirit seeking his original home who is the speaker in this section; and this pace is maintained through the whole poem. The dreamlike images, too, which half evoke and half obscure what seems to be that forgotten, fabulous time of our prelapsarian heredity, never sharpen into the clarity of waking vision, never lose the vagueness and the mystery of sleep. The mystery, in fact, is perhaps a little too easily achieved and sustained here, as if it were the result more of technical devices than of imaginative insight, but in any event, the metaphor on which the poem rests is never forgotten. The terms of the poem are consistently preserved, and the unity is intact.

In that terrifying and haunting poem, "The Combat," on the other hand, not only is the unity kept intact, the original metaphor marvelously sustained, but the imaginative insight which somehow failed to give the final touch of authority to the second section of "The Journey Back" here informs and transforms every word. For once again, as in the "Ballad of Hector in Hades," Muir has written a dream-poem that is not, like "Ballad of Eternal Life," a scattering of brilliant images, nor, like "The Narrow Place," a single brilliant image set in surrounding material of inferior luster, but a dream-poem that is, on the contrary, a coherent whole, shaped by an act of the imagination from a number of related dreams and memories. And the result is a vision so strange, so alien to all our usual experience, and yet so compelling, so inexplicably a reflection of some deep current in our experience we would prefer not to recognize, that it seems to drain the words which utter it of any other quality or meaning. They are absorbed into this strangeness, as are rhyme and meter, simile and syntax. All exist together, for the duration of the poem, in a separate, visionary world where things "not meant for human eyes" live and move and have their being. It is a world that is analogous to Kafka's, as Michael Hamburger agrees when he calls "The Combat" one "of the closest approximations in poetry to Kafka's world of absolute fiction—so subjective in origin, so inexhaustible and universal in effect." [7]

But however analogous to Kafka's, it is still a world of its own, entirely Muir's, in final effect and statement, in origin, and in manner. The image of everlasting combat which the poem presents, for example, between something which seems to represent brute force and pride and something which seems to be meekness and endurance, fuses Muir's old and never really forsaken attachment to Nietzsche's idea of eternal recurrence—an attachment that Hamburger argues persisted in Muir's thinking, along with Christian and Platonic tendencies, to the very end—together with his more recently achieved recognition of an eternal polarity of opposites: opposites that on another plane of reality, in the timeless rather than the temporal, meet in reconciliation. For although here there is little more evidence of this reconciling reality than there was in the total darkness of "Then" and "The Gate," nevertheless that little is present. The indomitable resistance of the soft round beast, at once "so helpless and so brave," and the final near despair of the "killing beast that cannot kill" (180) amount, as Muir himself suggested in a rather disjointed comment on the poem tape-recorded while he was at Harvard in 1955, to "an expression of hope . . . at the end." [8] In every other respect, the poem is, as Muir also admitted, "rather horrible"; indeed, it is very horrible; but in this horror at least a single grain of hope endures that in "Then" and "The Gate" did not exist at all. However minimal, however far from any affirmation of joy, the acceptance of paradox characteristic of Muir ever since "The Gate" is still evident even here.

Evident too are traces of Muir's own experience in dreams and memories as he recounted them in *An Autobiography*. And although, as John Holloway, in a review of the *Autobiography*, observed, such "specific links between Muir's experience and the poem" might be considered primarily of interest to "the researcher," [9] nevertheless the study of these "links" does offer certain insights, not to be overlooked, into the genesis and meaning of the poem. Helen Gardner, in her sensitive discussion of Muir's work delivered as the W. D. Thomas Memorial Lecture at Cardiff in 1961, found by comparing Muir's prose account of the dreams and memories which went into the poem with the poem itself, that in the prose a very important element of "The Combat" was missing. And that "particular horror," that "awful and nightmarish element in the poem . . . was the idea of endlessness." [10] The Nietzschean pattern of recurring cycles, in other words, which is so essential to the ultimate form and impact of the poem, was not simply given to Muir either by his conscious memories or by his subconscious as revealed in sleep. It was suggested there, to a greater extent than Miss Gardner allowed, but the suggestion was developed to its present proportions in the conscious construction of the poem, and a comparison of poem with source shows the magnitude of that development.

Similarly, neither in the dream which was the actual nucleus of "The Combat," nor in any of the related dreams and memories, is there any intimation of the eerie, inhuman character of the landscape in which the poem is set. When Muir saw in his dream the "shining bird" which, by a transmutation of a childhood memory, was to change into the "bright, fierce animal," half bird, half leopard, of the latter part of the dream and of the poem, the bird was "in a field," and Muir himself, he wrote in *An Autobiography*, "was walking with some people in the country." [11] The bird, with its antagonist—the whole drama, in fact—was located in an ordinary, rural scene, in the presence of at least "some" people. But in the poem, all possibility of the ordinary, the familiar, the human, is eliminated in the first stanza:

> It was not meant for human eyes,
> That combat in the shabby patch
> Of clods and trampled turf that lies
> Somewhere beneath the sodden skies
> For eye of toad or adder to catch. (179)

This is an inhuman struggle, clearly, in an inhuman place, a damp, desolate other world populated by those traditional representatives, in folklore and fairy tale, of all that is inhuman among living creatures—the cold-blooded amphibians and reptiles. Furthermore, in this other world with its chilly inhabitants, the very air is different. It is an "air that kills"; it breathes an immediate terror that in the prose account materialized only faintly and gradually toward the end. But both the force of this terror and the art which so economically establishes it are all the more apparent when the poem is set by the prose, where art and force have not yet been wrought to their uttermost.

Or, once more, a comparison of poem with prose indicates the degree to which Muir amalgamated various dreams and memories, in order to flesh out and carry to their logical conclusion the actions and implications that are only partially presented in the original dream, the dream of the two opposed beasts. For there, the fight which occurs in the poem did not actually take place. Muir knew from the look of the animals that they would fight again and again, and that "the dark, patient animal would always be defeated, and the bright, fierce animal would always win." [12] But he "did not see the fight," nor did he fathom its meaning. He simply "knew it would be ruthless and shameful, with a meaning of some kind, perhaps, but no comfort." The look of the appalling encounter itself, together with further clarification of its possible meaning, he gathered from other sources: from memories of brutal, one-sided battles seen in Glasgow slums; from the recollection of his brother Johnnie's "slow and painful death, during which, without being able to return a single blow, he had been battered so pitilessly"; [13] and from another dream of a boxing match between a "big, strong man and a little wizened man," [14] where the little man in the end, after being knocked down over and over, at last forced the big man helplessly to the floor.

For in this dream and in these memories Muir recognized the fully realized images of what in the first dream was still undefined. Here, he now saw, was the very "quality of Scottish Calvinism" [15] which like his fellow Scot and poet, John Davidson, he so abominated. Here, in these sickening, cruelly unequal battles, these merciless pummelings of helpless victims, was the "unanswerable, arbitrary logic of predestination." These images, weighted with these recognitions, that is, were the very material Muir required to complete the initial image of victim and aggressor, and to round out the poem; to make it, inhuman as the combat is, and waged in an inhuman landscape, nevertheless essentially a vision of "human fate as Calvin saw it." Yet, because the poem is, as Michael Hamburger says, "so inexhaustible and universal in effect," it is also, of course, much more. It is also that frightening vision of Nietzschean recurrence we have already noticed, and it is that small grain of hope that grows as the victim continues to resist and the aggressor reaches despair. It is that polarity of Pity and Indifference first defined in *Variations on a Time Theme*; and as the description of the aggressor as a "crested animal in his pride" indicates, it is likewise that polarity of two political systems which underlies both "The Ring" and *King Lear*. For the "crested animal" is surely allied both to the "Lion and fox, all dressed by fancy fine" who overturned the old order of society, based on human kindness and "natural piety" in "The Ring," and to proud, curled Edmund, the embodiment of inhumanity and impiety in *Lear*. Even to see here a reference to Lucifer, whose pride was the origin of all evil, and of the ceaseless cosmic strife between right and wrong, is by no means to go beyond what the text justifies. But just what the poem is, how much it refers to, every reader must decide for himself.

Finally, the poem could not be so "universal in its effect," so open to innumerable interpretations, if it were not written, as it is, in a style of such transparent simplicity. Like everything else about the poem, the manner is distinctively Muir's, since simplicity of statement, ever since *Journeys and Places*, has become increasingly one of Muir's characteristics when he writes at his best. But the simplicity here has a special quality, different from the spontaneous, graceful ease of "In Love for Long," for example, or the Biblical serenity of "Moses." The modified ballad stanza of five four-stress lines that Muir uses here, with its tight *a, b, a, a, b* rhyme scheme, has some of the monotony, some of the hypnotic uniformity, the apparent artlessness, of many children's nonsense rhymes; and because it is therefore so completely unlikely a vehicle for the terror it conveys, it seems almost separate from that terror. The vision it expresses shines through apparently unencumbered, unshaped by poetic or technical devices, while the vehicle eliminates itself from attention by its manifest discrepancy. In actuality, of course, the hypnotically insistent rhymes and the continually repeated four-beat measure function to intensify the terror, to focus the vision to the point of unbearable clarity, while the carefully disposed patterns of alliteration and assonance imperceptibly reinforce the same effect. So too, the occasional details of witnessing trees, of chirping cricket and grating thorn that break the silence of the intervals between bouts, serve to frame and thus again to accentuate the central combat, while the frequent colloquial turns of phrase, oddly juxtaposed with the heraldic terms and colors used to describe the aggressor beast, the proud "crested animal," similarly emphasize, by sheer contrast, the strange, unearthly nature of this unending struggle. But the primary effect, the one that matters in determining the impression of the poem on the reader, is the effect of artlessness. Because the story seems to tell itself, it is all the more convincing as vision, not art; as a universal insight, not a rendering of the limited perceptions of an individual mind.

The same vision, furthermore, is continued in another form in "The Interrogation" and in still another in "The Usurpers." To turn from "The Combat" to "The Interrogation," indeed, is almost to turn to another sphere of existence; to leave the unearthly scene where two legendary beasts act out a ritual of eternal struggle, for a setting so timely and so specific that it can be located on the map and dated in time—the Czechoslovakian border a short interval after the last World War—or today. But this disparity exists only on the surface. That central European border, as Muir well knew, has been the focus of international rivalries for centuries; the scene of human bloodshed since history began. Just as underneath "The Combat," accordingly, a very contemporary conflict is going on, so underneath "The Interrogation," that eternal ritual is continuing, as endlessly returning, it seems, as the Nietzschean wheel. The last line of the poem, in fact, says precisely that: "And still the interrogation is going on." What is more, however "modern" the poem may seem, however painfully timely the drama of questioning guard and hopeless prisoner, the actors here are basically the actors of "The Combat"—aggressor and victim—and the interrogation is another version of the endless struggle between these two. "The Interrogation," in sum, is still "The Combat," in twentieth century dress, and like "The Combat" it is an image of human fate as Calvin, perhaps rightly, saw it.

But where everything in "The Combat," as we have seen, was subordinated to the single image of unending conflict, "The Interrogation" is a poem of multiple images and implications, woven into a dense texture, and controlled by a clear line of movement. The crucial development in the movement occurs immediately in the first two lines of the poem:

> We could have crossed the road but hesitated,
> And then came the patrol; (182)

And it occurs so rapidly that it is ended almost before it is begun, which is precisely the effect intended. The opportunity to escape is lost forever in that split-second of hesitation, so skillfully suggested in the lingering last syllable of "hesitated," the eleventh in an otherwise perfect iambic pentameter line. The pattern of fate is now inexorably determined, as it was when Agamemnon waited a moment too long before despatching his message to bid Iphigenia stay at home, and only the working out of the pattern, it seems, remains to be told.

That working out of the pattern is the pounding, pitiless questioning which goes on for the next eight lines. "Who, what, where, with what purpose," the interrogatives follow each other like blows of a hammer, demolishing the victims' privacy and individuality, "question on question," time without end. But although this is what destiny determined in that fatal moment of delay, there is also the other world of what might have been, a world that actually exists on the other side of the road that was never crossed; and as this world now becomes visible in the eleventh and twelfth lines of the poem, it assumes enormous significance. The road that cuts it off becomes unexpectedly significant too. Like the road that cuts off the "country of Again," like those dangerous boundaries of ballad and romance, that divide the living from the dead, elfland from the community of mortals, this road irrevocably divides the country of oppression and depersonalization from the land of the free and the humane, where "careless lovers" pass, "wandering another star." And this free land, so maddeningly near, while at the same time as far beyond reach as "another star," magnifies to an intolerable degree the hopelessness, the inhumanity, the nightmare quality of the country on this side of the road, where there is no choice of "answer or action," and where the unlucky "we" who were caught by the patrol have been compelled to stand and answer those ceaseless questions "through the standing day." For it is not only the merciless interrogation itself, and all the brutality it signifies, but also the contrasting presence of the lovers "beyond the hedge," exacerbating that brutality, that finally brings the "we" to the "very edge," to the limits of human endurance. The way of life that fate foreclosed functions together with the way that fate elected to complete the prescribed tragedy.

But in this completed tragedy, the world of what might have been is not erased. It is integral, as we have seen, to the development of the theme, and as an interlude of a different melody it has a place within the total musical structure of the poem. For after the brusque tones, the pounding stresses of the lines describing the patrol and their questions, suddenly come lines like these:

> The careless lovers in pairs go by,
> Hand linked in hand, wandering another star,

and again:

> Though still the careless lovers saunter by
> And the thoughtless field is near. (182)

where the hovering accents of "Hand linked in hand," the grouped short syllables of "lovers in pairs" or "wandering another star," the liquid *r*'s and *l*'s, the internal rhyming and assonance of "careless," "pairs," "star," "careless" again, and "near" all create a sound pattern that is totally at variance both with the preceding harshness and with the laconic, lifeless measures that follow. Just as the sight of the lovers beyond the hedge, precisely because it contrasts so sharply with the plight of the trapped victims, intensifies their agony and moves the whole poem towards its conclusion, so the variance of this interlude from the prevailing sound pattern of the poem provides a counterpoint that deepens and enriches the harmony of the whole and clarifies its meaning. For if musically and thematically, the world beyond the hedge is part of the organic unity of the poem, not cut off from it, then it is never completely lost. It remains "becalmed in time forever." It is a vision of love that like the mutely waiting "grey-haired wives" of "The Return of the Greeks" offers a minimal yet unfailing defense against the too familiar terror of the rest of the poem.

To that terror, moreover, the final lines of the poem add a further dimension. For one thing, the fact that the last two lines form a rhyming couplet in a poem of otherwise under-stated, generally irregular rhymes, indicates a tightening of tension, a closing in of the fatal pattern. For another, the pat-tern, as we suggested before, is now seen as continuing in-definitely, even after these particular victims are over "the edge." The interrogation goes on, regardless, like the diaboli-cal machine in Kafka's "Penal Colony," for this is one of Muir's poems which is both particularly European and particu-larly Kafka-like in vision. And just as Kafka makes the most fantastic fictions at once credible and all the more horrible by simply stating them laconically as facts, so Muir at once estab-lishes here both the undoubted accuracy and the ultimate hor-ror of his conclusion merely by his level, unemotional style of utterance: "And still the interrogation is going on." The Nie-tzschean wheel revolves forever; the combat of aggressor and victim never ends; and in the process all humanity, all individ-uality, is drained away until the essentially unspeakable horror can be reduced to a sentence as cut and dried, as dead, as a statement in an official report.

What happens when all humanity is drained away, then, is precisely the theme of "The Usurpers," which is set in a fu-ture world as strange and legendary, with its dreams and darkness, its threatening waves and prophesying winds, as the primordial world of "The Combat." These usurpers, who are the spokesmen, the "we" of the poem, live in the center of a nothingness that parallels Hemingway's universal *nada*: "All round us stretches nothing; we move through nothing,/ Nothing but nothing world without end." (187). Around them is only silence, without any "answer," without any "ancestral voices," and in the night they obliterate even themselves: they "hide in the very heart of night from night,/ Black in its blackness." They are literally the embodiment of a vacuum, a lack, a hiatus; and with this word, "hiatus," a number of motifs in Muir's earlier writings suddenly reappear and fall into a connected sequence that leads directly to this poem.

"Hiatus" is, of course, the word Muir uses in his essay, "The Politics of *King Lear*," to define the evil in Lear's two daughters and their allies. They are evil, he says, because there is a "craving blank" [16] in them, a lack of that necessary component of the human soul known as memory, a recognition of loyalties and duties. Without memory, they are "mere animals furnished with human faculties," [17] and in this shape, as we have seen, they are the counterparts of a series of characters in Muir's own work, all embodying a "craving blank," all representing evil. The Indifference of *Variations*, who is "all offence," is clearly, we saw, the bestial half of the human soul, opposed to and lacking Pity, the redeeming half. Archie Blackadder of *The Three Brothers*, that personification of inner vacuum, of "brute insensibility," is a "wee beast" himself, totally unconscious of any distinction between right and wrong; and the "Lion and fox, all dressed by fancy fine/ In human flesh" and armed with human weapons, who break down the citadel and "nose the shrine" in "The Ring," do so in "bestial wonder," in sheer ignorance of what they are doing. They have "haughtily put aside the sorrowful years" (113); they have no memory of the tradition and the rituals that made the shrine sacred. As representatives, like Goneril and Regan, Edmund and Oswald, not only of the evil in every man but particularly of the pitiless, amoral new society which was beginning even during the Renaissance, according to Muir, to replace the older moral order, with its system of mutal rights and responsibilities, they have no comprehension of any realities except "interest and force." [18] All else is sunk in that "hiatus," that "craving blank" that wipes out their humanity.

But however strong the forces of animal indifference in man or in society, once again according to Muir, they are never, except at the lowest point of *The Narrow Place*, completely successful. A perpetual though one-sided battle goes on between aggressor and victim. It is "The Combat," in fact, that goes on; and when "The Combat" is viewed from this angle, the significance briefly attributed to a small detail in that poem becomes justified, while the possibility of still another level of meaning in the poem as a whole becomes plain. The "crested animal in his pride" bears a resemblance, as was suggested earlier, not only to the haughty marauding animals of "The Ring," but also to proud, curled, animal Edmund, the partner of Goneril and Regan, as described by his brother Edgar. Thus whatever else may be involved in "The Combat," whether Nietzschean recurrence or grim Calvinist fate, the continual conflict between two concepts of society, two ways of life, and ultimately between right and wrong, is involved here too. The same conflict, of course, is involved in "The Interrogation" as well, where both the character and the pattern of events and particularly the single word, "indifferent" in the fourth line: "the men surly, indifferent," link this poem to Muir's persistent animal versus man, indifference versus compassion, emptiness versus wholeness dichotomy. Indifference, emptiness, and evil, furthermore, are in control here. The endurance of the resisting human forces is "almost done." And in "The Usurpers" that resistance seems to have been eliminated. Only emptiness and evil, apparently, are left.

If only emptiness is left, however, then the "we" who are the protagonists in this dramatic monologue must necessarily be the empty ones; and in writing this poem Muir therefore faced a difficult twofold problem. He had to express convincingly a point of view totally opposed to his own, while at the same time he had to indicate, through these alien spokesmen, that his own way of thinking still persisted, suppressed, ignored, and half forgotten, but invincible. Yet his solution is very simple. The "we," the "Usurpers"—their name alone suggests the falsity of their position—merely protest too much. They begin by protesting, using a rigid declarative sentence pattern that betrays their insecurity:

> There is no answer. We do here what we will
> And there is no answer. (187)

and their insistence that "there is no answer" at once suggests that there probably is. "It was not hard," they continue, "to still the ancestral voices:/ A careless thought, less than a thought could do it"; and again the arrogance of the assertion makes it suspect. But the Usurpers do not stop there. In their need to compensate for their obvious uneasiness, they not only go on to praise, with unconscious irony, the nothingness where alone they feel safe, but they also confirm, by their repeated denials, the existence of something else, some opposing and, in the end, unconquerable force, which constantly surrounds and assaults their nothingness. There are the dreams they make light of, that live on the dangerous frontiers of their territory, where night meets day; there are the images, the ghosts, the muttering voices. There are the strange words, spoken in one of Muir's own dreams, used earlier in "The Narrow Place," and reiterated here: "I lean my face far out from eternity." Then too, there are the judgments uttered, although the Usurpers maintain that they are all lies, by the rocks, the trees, the waves, and the wind. "These are imaginations. We are free" (188), the Usurpers are still protesting at the end, but they have already proved beyond doubt that they are not free, that the ancestral voices are still potent, and that no matter how absolute the triumphs of the impersonal, the brutal, the evil may seem, the forces of uncorrupted nature and of uncorrupted man persevere in steadfast opposition. The paradox persists. The good still flourishes beside the ill, planted together in the same field.

Once again, as in "The Combat" and "The Interrogation," Muir has found at the last this narrow margin between him and the abyss. But the good that flourishes beside the ill in all three of these poems is hardly sufficient to provide much comfort, and in "The Bargain," the sonnet following "The Usurpers," Muir for once allows himself a wry complaint:

> I strike the bargain, since time's hand is there;
> But having done, this clause I here declare. (189)

He declares, that is, that the bargain man must strike with time —that other face of evil—is unfair. Creatures of time that we are, we cannot help but accept time's terms, but those terms take away far more than they give. They give life, indeed— "And life is quick and warm and death is cold"—but they take away that sense of a harmony and a whole which gives meaning to life. They take away ". . . the story that can never be told,/ The unfading light and the unbreaking wave," and leave us, "forlorn and strange," in a divided world where the cruel beast of "The Combat," the surly, indifferent guards of "The Interrogation," and the empty "Usurpers," who outlaw memory and imagination, can assume control. In what court of law would such a contract be upheld?

In what court of law could such a contract be challenged? The complaint is futile, of course, and although the three quatrains of this sonnet are intensely serious, the concluding couplet clearly strikes an ironic note. But the irony is transient. The seriousness returns again in the next poem, "Oedipus," where Muir takes up the same problem from another angle. For however frequently, since *The Narrow Place*, he has succeeded in reaching a faith in a final harmony, a reconciliation of irreconcilables, he has just as often found himself compelled to question this faith; and in this volume, particularly, where he seems to feel the oppression of the contemporary world, with all its appalling past and its new, unprecedented horrors, to an unusual degree, he is compelled to question once more. How, in the twentieth century, can any man accept the human condition, the bargain forced on him by time? How, especially, can a man accept it who has so accurately recorded its hopelessness in so much of his poetry? Yet Oedipus, Sophocles tells us, learned to accept an even worse bargain, perhaps the unfairest any man except Job ever suffered. If he could find some justification in his fate, then surely there must be justification for others too; and accordingly, what Muir does here, in this dramatic monologue, is to assume the mask of Oedipus and examine his tragic story once more in an effort to discover, through his way out to final peace, a way for modern man as well. Oedipus' case thus becomes a paradigm for today; and Oedipus' affirmation of ultimate good, yet another answer to Muir's persistent questions, another barrier against the despair which seems to wait at every turn of *The Labyrinth*.

Since the Oedipus through whom Muir speaks, however, is the blind, aged wanderer, not the young king in his passion and torment, it is a backward look that he casts over his life. Like Muir in "A Birthday," he can now "discern" the pattern of his experience "whole or almost whole." Further, because he is blind, he can look not only backward, but inward. Like Homer in the sonnet "Too Much," or the mystic who could peer into the third glass, he is gifted with the inner eye of the imagination. But although this eye, in so many of Muir's previous poems, has infallibly perceived beneath time's wrongs the eternal weaving together of all polarities into a single whole, Oedipus is slow to come to such a vision. Because Muir is insisting that the vision, if it is achieved, must be fully earned, here Oedipus in the beginning can see only paradox, and the paradox perplexes him. Admitting in the first line of the poem that it was his destiny to err, that both his name and his physical deformity signaled he was "made to stumble" (189), he nevertheless insists on questioning and probing deeper into the causes of his fate, and the more he probes, the more inescapable the paradoxes become. Recalling his innocent-guilty love for Jocasta, his sinful yet sanctioned murder of his father at the crossroads, his punishment and his purification, in line after line he weighs one opposite with another—innocence with guilt, dark with light, evil with good—for this balancing of antagonistic elements is actually the structural principle of the entire poem—until he comes to the point where he can probe and struggle no more. There is nowhere else to turn. He must face the fact that paradox itself is the only unity, that innocence and guilt are indissolubly joined, and that he himself is the walking emblem of that "riddle" (191).

This is, of course, the pivotal point of the whole poem. As so often in Muir, some extreme limit must be reached before the movement of a poem can be reversed; and here Oedipus' realization that evil is inseparable from good suddenly transforms his exhausted surrender into affirmation. For if evil and good are inseparable, then evil must be built into the universe. But this insight, far from terrifying Oedipus, gives him a glimpse of an undreamed-of dignity and significance in man's role in the world; and in the final lines of the poem, which achieve a new serenity, a new spaciousness of rhythm and vision, he acknowledges that it is man's duty to bear his share of evil, to ease

> The immortal burden of the gods who keep
> Our natural steps and the earth and skies from harm. (191)

For man, by sinning and suffering for it, by incurring guilt and cleansing himself to win new innocence, perpetually performs the rituals which ward off chaos and maintain that equilibrium of opposites that, from the point of view of the gods, is harmony. But not only this. In struggling against his natural imperfection, man also helps in the working out of the law that moves the stars. There is, in other words, an echo of Dante here, an echo Muir was to make still more explicit in a later poem, "The Church," where he uses Dante's very words: "The Love that moves the sun and the other stars" (264); and in this invocation, however muted, of the principle of universal love, even more than in the noble assertion of man's function in the cosmos, there is that affirmation of transcendent good that Muir was seeking. Still another time, love has intervened, to redeem the bargain imposed by time.

Undeniably, then, "Oedipus" is restrained in statement and attitude. Undeniably, too, it is very close in feeling as well as in theme and conclusion to the opening sonnet in this volume —"Too Much"—with its similar reliance on the strange insight of the blind, its play on the paradoxical relationship of dark and light, and its acceptance of man's limitations. But closely as it relates to this poem and to the low key thus set for the entire volume, "Oedipus" is also, and this is equally undeniable, a declaration of belief. Where the assurance granted in "The Combat," "The Interrogation," and "The Usurpers" was minimal, as we have seen, "Oedipus" offers not only a stoic magnanimity but the possibility of love. And in offering this possibility, it prepares the way for another poem, "The Transfiguration," where Muir finds a principle of radiant good not in eternity, not among the stars, but here on earth. Momentarily, perhaps, the transition is startling, but it is valid; and thus "Oedipus," with its interdependence of opposites, its fusion of dark and light, acts as a bridge between the predominantly dark poems which take up most of this volume and the vision of light which "The Transfiguration" gives us.

This vision was, indeed, implicit in the verdict that "The Usurpers" brought against themselves. Those forces of the imagination that would not be silenced, that source of dreams that would not be extinguished, are simply given a body and a name in "The Transfiguration"; they are the "clear unfallen world," the "radiant kingdom" of Eden, that can never be destroyed. It "lies forlorn,"

> . . . no human voice
> Is heard among its meadows, but it speaks
> To itself alone, alone it flowers and shines
> And blossoms for itself while time runs on. (200)

The essential, eternal good, that is, lies still unspoiled, still undefeated, at the heart of life. It waits only for new human voices, repeating "out of their dream the long-forgotten word" (113), to summon it back. For in this poem, which is based on several dreams, and particularly one that Muir retold long before in the "Ballad of the Nightingale" of his *First Poems*, the transfiguration which takes place is not the transfiguration of Christ as Matthew described it, but rather a transfiguration of the whole world and its inhabitants, which Muir imagines as occurring at the same time. Or more accurately yet, it is the momentary revelation of "the unseeable/ One glory of the everlasting world" which remains "Perpetually at work" in the universe, "Though never seen" under the accumulated dust and debris of the years.

Because Christ—presumably it is Christ; the figure is introduced so casually, and without capitalization of the pronoun, that, until later on in the poem, it is hard to tell—walked "into the town" that day with the speakers of the poem, who again presumably are the disciples; and because "he had said, 'To the pure all things are pure,'" suddenly all the underlying purity in man and beast, houses and clothing, even the refuse heaps, was made manifest:

> The shepherds' hovels shone, for underneath
> The soot we saw the stone clean at the heart
> As on the starting-day. The refuse heaps
> Were grained with that fine dust that made the world. (199)

And although the glory visible then did not last, although "the world/ Rolled back into its place" and left things as they had been before, still the disciples had seen this other, deeper, all-inclusive reality once, and they knew it could come again. When "all things,/ Beasts of the field, and woods, and rocks, and seas [those same spokesmen of nature that bore witness against the Usurpers],/ And all mankind from end to end of the earth" (200) were ready to "call him with one voice," then, "it's said," Christ would return and restore the lost "radiant kingdom." And not only so. With the restoration of the "clear unfallen world," all the consequences of the Fall would be undone: Christ's death and crucifixion, undone; the cross, dismantled and regenerated into "a tree/ In a green springing corner of young Eden"; and Judas himself, the figure of deepest damnation, the symbol of what for Muir was always the inmost core of evil, betrayal, would be not only forgiven but made innocent again, "a child"

> Beside his mother's knee, and the betrayal
> Be quite undone and never more be done. (200)

That the betrayal could be so annulled, the results of the Fall wiped out forever, was not, indeed, one of the constant tenets of Muir's beliefs. It was a devout wish, which he had already expressed many times, in *Variations*, in "Judas," but his more settled faith, as we have seen, had come to accept both Eden and the Fall, king and rebel, "the corn and tares compactly grown"; and the concept in this poem, of a cancellation rather than a reconciliation of sin and its aftermath, is more a natural development of the particular vision here, of a universal cleansing, a world-wide renewal of original purity, than it is of Muir's customary thinking. Much more integral to his deepest convictions is the concept on which the earlier, and undoubtedly more effective part of the poem is based, the idea of a residual glory surviving still in every part even of the fallen world, and waiting only for some moment of transfiguration, the glance of some pure eye to which all things are pure, to reveal itself once more. For this was something which Muir himself had actually experienced, not only in dreams but in the flesh while wide awake. Once or twice in the excitement of so-called religious "conversions" while he was still a lad, he had felt a sense of being lifted out of himself into a general stream of love and righteousness; and later in Glasgow, after a conversion in a different direction, to Socialism, he had witnessed what seemed to him a revelation of "a fable which was always there, invisibly waiting for anyone who wished to enter it." [19] At the first May Day demonstration he attended, "all mankind" appeared "made of some incorruptible substance." There were all kinds of people in the crowd—handsome, misshapen, well-to-do and ragged, grown-ups and children, but no matter: "all distinctions had fallen away like a burden carried in some other place, and . . . all substance had been transmuted."

As time passed, Muir came to see that the transmutation of substance and the realization of an ideal world would not come about, as he had believed in his first enthusiasm for Socialism, almost of itself, "by little change after little change" after "an almost infinite peaceful expanse" [20] of years. He "had been made a Socialist by the degradation of the poor and the hope for an eventual reign of freedom, justice and brotherhood," and that deeply humane concern and hope he never abandoned. But he had to recognize that the *Realpolitik* of the twentieth century hardly portended any transition to a millennium. The universal purification he had participated in, however; the direct contact he had made, in time, with the timeless fable which is always there, waiting for our entry—this was still real too, and the problem—again a matter of accepting paradox, of reconciling opposites—was how to fit the two realities together in some acceptable, constant pattern. "I feel," he wrote in his *Autobiography*, that these experiences, of contact with the fable, "should 'go into' life; yet there seems to be no technique by which one can accomplish the work of their inclusion." [21]

From his reading of Hölderlin he had, it is true, derived a pattern, an image which expressed the intersection of time and the timeless on a cosmic scale. The sign of God is quiet in the thundering sky, Hölderlin wrote near the end of *Patmos*,

> Und Einer steht Darunter
> Sein Leben lang.[22]

> (And One stands thereunder
> His life long.)

But Muir, who was not yet ready to acknowledge, like Hölderlin, that "Christ was the one symbol which united . . . the two truths which he perceived in existence: a truth transcending time, and a truth immanent in time . . . ," [23] had to amend this magnificent emblem to fit his own purposes. For him the image of "timeless human life" was "the intersection and interpenetration of a stationary beam falling from heaven and the craving, aspiring dust [cf "The suppliant Dust, the moving Hand" of "The Fall" (69)] rising for ever to meet it, in denial or submission, in ignorance or comprehension." [24] He had not yet, however, found the way to fit individual experiences of contact with the timeless, such as his, into the ordinary course of events in time, to make them " 'go into' life," as it is lived from day to day. He could only recount them, as he does in "The Transfiguration," as momentary but valid visions.

That the source of the transfiguration in the poem is some unextinguished glory in the world of time, responding to the timeless, rather than any imposition from that timelessness, the first line at once makes clear: "So from the ground we felt that virtue branch" (189). The purifying virtue is not sent down from above. It springs from the "ground," the earth, and branches up like a sturdy tree, restoring veins, wrists, and hands, our common flesh and blood, to their original sanctity. As it mounts and branches in this organic growth, furthermore, the seven-line-long opening statement grows and branches with it. From the initial emphatic inversions and the prolonged "So," with its connotations of amazement and awe, this periodic sentence progresses clause by clause, from wonder to wonder, all earth-rooted, until, when the "source of all our seeing" has been "rinsed and cleansed," what the pure eye sees in the final completing predicate in the seventh line, is the indestructible pattern of the fable—the "clear unfallen world." In a single, closely knit syntactic unit, the "unseeable/ One glory of the everlasting world" has been made visible. And not only visible. A carefully varied selection of words and images, all suggesting purification and illumination, gives the effect at last of a pervasive radiance, while the slow, stately cadences of the blank verse lines, the elevated though still simple diction, the rich interplay of alliteration and assonance, together produce a grave, hymnlike music, radiant too in its quality of exalted joy. When, later in the poem, Muir elaborates on the brightness of his initial vision, he somewhat dims its luster; but the first half of "The Transfiguration" remains a testimony to the presence of the underlying eternal fable, the "pure and touching good" within time itself. It is a reiteration, in transfigured form, of the love that has endured as a last defense against despair in so many of the poems in both *The Voyage* and *The Labyrinth*; it is another, more human version of the conclusion of "Oedipus," which invoked the love that moves the stars; and it is the positive way of putting what "The Usurpers" proved by negation: the "imaginations" that the

Usurpers claimed were nothing are really everything. They are the voices of that "radiant Kingdom" that lies "forlorn" but undying and invincible despite all the assaults of the "crested animal," empty Usurper, or brutal, dehumanized twentieth century economic or political system.

In maintaining this defense against despair, moreover; in affirming the unconquerable force of the imagination in opposition to animal indifference, "The Transfiguration" once again asserts that vision of a reconciliation of irreconcilables, a coexistence and interdependence of contraries which since *The Narrow Place* Muir has come to see as the only exit from the Labyrinth, the only way of coming to terms with the paradox inherent in the human condition. Yet "The Transfiguration" is not merely a repetition of what Muir has already said in other forms, in other poems, such as "The Ring" or "The Trophy," "In Love for Long," or even "Oedipus." There is in "The Transfiguration" a more explicit realization than ever before of a quality necessarily intrinsic to Muir's acceptance of paradox: a broad, all-encompassing humanity. By shifting the focus of the myth in this poem from the glorified Christ to the glorified earth; by finding immortal substance in the travel-stained garments of the disciples; the clean stone under the soot of the shepherds' hovels; and grains of "that fine dust that made the world" even in the refuse heaps; and by gathering into the worshipping multitudes the lonely, the lost, the liars, even the murderers, "with rags tied round their feet for silence," who appeared originally in the "Ballad of the Nightingale," Muir brings everyone and everything of this world into his transfiguring vision. Nothing is too corrupt, nothing too ugly or mean, to be included in this infinite mercy. And in at last making manifest this compassion, which hitherto has informed Muir's poetry only silently, by implication, "The Transfiguration" not only makes a statement important in itself, but serves as prologue for the most compassionate, the most reconciling, of all Muir's books, his last volume, *One Foot in Eden*.

VIII

"Standing on earth, looking at heaven"

Just before Muir was taken to the hospital in his last illness, Mrs. Muir recalls in *Belonging*, he said to her very urgently, although in reference to nothing in particular: "There are no absolutes, no absolutes." [1] She does not speculate on what he meant by this, but surely, whatever the personal implications may have been, there was a summing up, in these few words, of an attitude that Muir had firmly held to ever since he renounced his allegiance to Nietzsche: an intellectual honesty and integrity that refused to be tied to any preconceptions, accepted no doctrines not "proved on the pulses," and remained open, always, to new possibilities of feeling and seeing. Nor could there be a better summing up of both the attitude and the content in Muir's last volume of poems, *One Foot in Eden* (1956), as well as in the few poems he wrote thereafter until his death in 1959.

As the increasing evidence of a thematic pattern in his work suggested would be the case, these final poems are primarily, of course, the direct, inevitable outgrowth of all that has gone before. In them are the themes Muir recognized as his own from the beginning, now refined, clarified, and to a large degree brought together into a coherent whole. That "direction" which "ravished" his soul before he "took the road" has now brought him where he was going. "Like travellers" returning home, his original promptings and insights now "return/ And stand where first they stood." Yet at the same time, there are excursions in still untried directions. Old themes are reconsidered in new parables. New themes are introduced. In the context of the whole *One Foot in Eden* volume and the nearly two score poems not previously collected, it is true, this fresh subject matter, this experimental approach, is of relatively limited extent. Yet it is there, indicating both a stubborn refusal on Muir's part to accept even his own hard-won conclusions as absolute, and a willingness, even at almost seventy, to try out different subjects and techniques. He was still ready to "make it new." Moreover, in the process of making it new, he necessarily gained a new inventiveness, a new vigor, that infused itself as well into his more familiar material and pushed that material beyond its old limits. It broadened even further, for instance, the scope of his compassion, so that although a good deal of what Muir says in *One Foot in Eden* he has certainly said before, he has never said it so consistently in quite this way, with this assurance, this strength, this pervasive warmth, and this down-to-earth solidity.

The most obvious sign of this coexistence of fresh matter with the tried and true, now brought nearer perfection, is Muir's own division of *One Foot in Eden* into two parts. The parts are unequal both in length and in quality, but the fact that the division exists at all suggests Muir's awareness that he was moving in two different directions, towards the past and towards the future; that he was abstaining, once more, from taking an absolute position. Thus in the far longer and on the whole more successful Part I, which is introduced by a sonnet to Milton, are grouped poems which deal for the most part with themes long familiar to Muir: Eden and its loss, Scotland and its sad history, stories from Greek and Biblical myth. In Part II, on the other hand, where the introductory sonnet is addressed to Franz Kafka, whose name the Muirs, by their translations of his work, helped to make synonymous with contemporary frustrations and fears, there are such new ventures as the series of penetrating character studies called "Effigies," allied indeed to earlier studies of estrangement and disorientation, but more compact, more presentative, and still more sympathetic to the "frustrate and the half."

Indeed, even within Part I there is much new matter. There are, for example, several poems based specifically on the Christian myth, which Muir had hitherto, except in "The Transfiguration," touched only obliquely; and in the cluster of Greek poems, a number either comment on the meaning of the Christ figure or provide parallel images of reconciliation and acceptance. In Part II, on the contrary, there is still a preponderance of Muir's more customary style and subjects. "Day and Night," although new in its basic stance, represents everything typical of Muir in the way of theme, imagery, language, rhyme, and meter, all handled now with easy mastery. "The Horses" projects the familiar animal-man relationship and the loss and restoration of Eden themes into the future that awaits us after nuclear war. But by and large, in essential feeling each of the two sections of *One Foot in Eden* performs a different function. Part I looks back over the years and gathers scattered strands of meaning into a satisfying unity. Part II, in its smaller way, together with many of the hitherto uncollected poems, looks more dubiously to present and future. Each prevents the other from advocating any absolute.

The sonnet, "Milton," which opens Part I, in fact, acts as a magnet to draw together into a more clearly recognizable pattern many of those strands of meaning distributed through earlier volumes. For at Milton's name, some of Muir's most persistent motifs suddenly appear in a new light, acquire a new identity. What has Muir's preoccupation with lost childhood and innocence been but another, more modest variant of Milton's great theme of Paradise Lost? And that ceaseless conflict of animal aggressor and pitying or pitiful victim, which we have followed through Muir's poetry from *Variations* to its most forceful image in "The Combat" and its contemporary and future images in "The Interrogation" and "The Usurpers," is certainly another version of the Miltonic warfare between good and evil, between the powers of light and of darkness. The "crested animal" of "The Combat," after all, resembles Lucifer in his pride. This conflict is too, of course, a statement in Muir's terms, just as the warfare in Heaven was a statement in Milton's terms, of what Muir once described as the "fundamental moral struggle within the individual [which] was for many centuries accepted as the essential character of man"; and it is this sort of man, as Muir continued, a "being suspended between good and evil by a law inherent in his nature [that] is the man of Dante and Shakespeare, and of Balzac and Tolstoy." [2] By repeatedly choosing symbols of this moral struggle within each individual as his subjects, therefore, Muir allied himself, however humbly, with the grand tradition of Dante and Shakespeare, Balzac and Tolstoy, so that they, as well as Milton, are his patterns and his patrons; their seriousness of theme is likewise his.

It is with Milton, however, that the relationship is closest, and this closeness gives to Muir's sonnet to Milton its special quality of human warmth and sympathy. This sonnet is not addressed, like Wordsworth's, to a distant, godlike Milton, whose "soul was like a Star, and dwelt apart," but to a man like any other. A man, indeed, so much like Muir himself, that in writing of him Muir could blend his own experience, in perfect propriety, with that of the greater poet. In the first quatrain, for instance:

> Milton, his face set fair for Paradise,
> And knowing that he and Paradise were lost
> In separate desolation, bravely crossed
> Into his second night and paid his price. (207)

the repeated "Paradise" clearly has several meanings. It is of course the Paradise of *Paradise Lost*. It is the future Heaven, the house of many mansions, promised to Christian believers. It is the Kingdom of Saints on earth, the society of prophets, which Milton once, at the beginning of the Commonwealth, fondly hoped to see established in England. It is also, surely, the Paradise of early childhood, that "myth/ Enacted in a distant isle," which Muir recognized with particular clarity in the pattern of his own life, but which he also believed to be a stage in the universal fable underlying the life story of every man.

Furthermore, because all of these symbols of past felicity or future hope have this in common, that they are to a greater or less degree "lost," that they have suffered some eclipse, from sin or time or doubt or sheer human weakness, here too there is a parallel between Milton's and Muir's experience. Just as Milton's Paradise and he himself, "On evil days . . . fall'n, and evil tongues;/ In darkness, and with dangers compast round," were each "lost/ In separate desolation," so Muir too in Glasgow was "lost" in a world of squalid slums and senseless suffering, where an "iron law" was the principle of life. This was, in fact, Muir's Hell, and it is precisely this Hell which provides the imagery here for the nether regions that Milton must journey through on his way to rebirth. The scene described in the next eight lines of the sonnet is not the distant dungeon of burning sulphur to which Milton assigned fallen Satan and his legions. Rather, it is a very real, very much of this earth and this age, industrial Glasgow, blackened by the smoke and flames pouring from the funnels of a hundred factories, and filled with the uproar of brutalized workers and slum dwellers "enjoying" their Saturday night off:

> There towards the end he to the dark tower came
> Set square in the gate, a mass of blackened stone
> Crowned with vermilion fiends like streamers blown
> From a great funnel filled with roaring flame.
>
> Shut in his darkness, these he could not see,
> But heard the steely clamour known too well
> On Saturday nights in every street in Hell.
> Where, past the devilish din, could Paradise be? (207)

Moreover, because the symbol for Muir of the cruelty at the core of life which inevitably betrays man into pain and degradation, was a gate, there is a gate here as well: the entrance, it seems, to the inmost citadel of Hell, the door, like "The Gate," to the heart of darkness. Nor is that all; "set square" in that gate is the mysterious "dark tower" to which Childe Roland came, emblem of all the fearful unknown attending death.

Taken all together, these details add up to an inferno as agonizing to the human spirit as Milton's own.

There is still another important aspect of this Glasgow interlude, however: between the opening and closing lines of the poem, with their essentially conventional evocation of the radiance of Paradise, these eight lines compose a solid block of the specific details of Hell. It is visual detail that is dominant in the first four: the "dark tower" is "Set square," with merciless precision, in the "mass of blackened stone" that is the gate. From its top, as if from the "great funnel" of a Glasgow ironworks, stream out "vermilion fiends" like flames, and the effect of that word "vermilion" is literally electric. Hell is visible for the split second that the red flash endures. Since for Milton in his blindness, however, not even lightning could make things visible, it is the sounds of Hell, which told Milton where he was, that dominate the next four lines: the metallic, dehumanized, "devilish din" of the workers in those black Satanic mills trying to forget themselves in one night of drink and noisy quarrels. But here something else happens too. As John Holloway points out in his excellent discussion of "The Poetry of Edwin Muir" in *The Hudson Review*, the "concrete common-language quality" of those phrases about "the steely clamour known too well/ On Saturday nights in every street in Hell" tell us, too, "where we are." Through them, with their simultaneous familiarity and strangeness, we "re-enter our own real landscape by an unexpected and revelatory gate." [3] What is more, the sudden intrusion in the next line of what seems an actual speaking voice, questioning in exasperation more than fear, brings us still closer to our own private Hells. Where, we all ask, when the questions of an "Interrogation," for instance, have brought us "to the very edge," have almost completely distracted us, "Where, past the devilish din, . . . [can] Paradise be?" (207).

At this point we become aware of the dynamics of the poem. These eight lines of concrete detail have taken us deeper and deeper into Hell, until it is impossible to go farther. As this intimately human outcry indicates, the limits of endurance have been reached. A change must come; and precisely now, when it is inevitable, it does come. The tone alters abruptly, the level shifts, and the simple grandeur of the first few lines returns, far more welcome now after the intervening "devilish din." But not only more welcome. To the original simplicity and grandeur has been added a new serenity, a new vision, because the protagonist here (whether Milton or Muir or ourselves) has risen from the depths. The darkness of "The Gate" has been passed, Hell left behind, and what Milton, with eyes made whole to see it, now beholds, is Paradise regained after his passage through Experience:

> One footstep more, and his unblinded eyes
> Saw far and near the fields of Paradise.

Since Muir too, as we have seen, regained his Paradise, however altered by time's destructive "deluge," it is altogether appropriate that these last two lines from his sonnet to Milton should be inscribed on his grave at Swaffham Prior.

But "Milton" not only serves to indicate the parallels between Muir and Milton, to give a Miltonic identity to some of Muir's major themes, and to link Muir with the great tradition of those writers whose subject has been "the fundamental moral struggle within the individual." By invoking Milton, who told the story of Creation and Eden, of the Fall and the fate of Adam's sons, and finally, in *Paradise Regained*, of the triumph of a second Adam, Muir sets the stage for his own retelling of parts of that story in the first section of *One Foot in Eden*. For although the twenty-seven poems which make up this first section fall only roughly into a sequence, and although Prometheus, Oedipus, Orpheus, Helen, and Penelope, as we shall see, mingle here with Abraham and Isaac, to enrich and extend the meaning of the story, still the over-all chronicle approximately matches Milton's. There, of course, since it was never Muir's intent to imitate Milton, the similarity ends. What Muir is interested in here, as always when he is handling myth, is in reshaping the mythic story to fit his own purposes, to provide a foundation for his own peculiar vision. The Miltonic presence in the background, however, like the even remoter presence of Genesis, provides both a norm against which to measure Muir's departures and an orderly whole where the *disjecta membra* Muir presents have a place.

Actually, as his previous treatment of myth has already proved, and as the poem immediately following the Milton sonnet, "The Animals," proves again, what Muir does with these stories is not so much to depart from them as to shift their emphasis. In the twenty-three lines of "The Animals," which takes as its subject the Genesis account of the fifth day of Creation, when the fowl of the air and the fish of the sea were made, Muir does make one small change in the given facts. He implies that all the animals, beasts as well as birds and fish, were created on this one day, whereas both Genesis and Milton make clear that the beasts of the field came on the sixth day, the same day as man. But by this slight alteration Muir does not affect either the essential content or the significance of the Bible story; on the other hand he does succeed effectively in what he particularly wants to do: he widens the gulf between animal and man.

This, in fact, is the point of the whole poem, which is a restatement, plainer and more compendious than any he has made before, of the precise nature of the animal-man relationship as he understood it. Through all his previous work, as we have so often noticed, there have been two divergent strains: in "Horses," in the novel *Poor Tom*, in Section Ten of *Variations*, in "The Covenant," animals appeared as fabulous creatures of unspoiled innocence, while quite conversely, in *The Three Brothers*, in Section Nine of *Variations*, in "The Grove," "The Combat," "The Interrogation," and "The Usurpers," either animals or the animal quality of a lack of memory, a "hiatus," a "craving blank," represented utmost evil. In "The Ring," it is true, innocent and evil animals were brought together at the end in a new harmony, closed in a new circle: nevertheless it is still not until now, in "The Animals," that the paradox is at last clarified and resolved—and resolved, paradoxically again, by being sharpened. For the difference between animal and man, it now becomes clear, in the world of time at least, is forever impassable. It was ordered from the beginning and shall continue forever, while time endures, because animals were made on the fifth day, man on the sixth, and between the creatures of different days there can be no communication.

There can be no communication for the simple reason that the animals cannot speak. "No word do they have, not one" (207); and having no words, they have no memories. Because they recognize neither past nor future, furthermore, but live in an eternal present, an "unchanging Here," which is still the same "fifth great day of God" on which they were created, they are eternally innocent; and thus they qualify for the role of "golden lion and lamb," of mysterious creatures breathing the air of some unspoiled world, which they play in some of Muir's poems. They cannot, indeed, forsake that role. But man, as the only one of God's creatures with the power of speech, and thus of fiction, can of course play any part he chooses; and it is when man abjures the memory with which his speech endows him; when he crosses the forbidden gulf to the fifth day and assumes the mark of the animal, the "hiatus" where word and recollection and immortal spirit should be, that what was innocent in the animal becomes evil in the man. Then man as animal becomes the symbol of the indifference, the brute insensibility, the callous betrayal that wars unendingly with good. It is man as animal (not the innocent beasts of the fifth day) who noses the shrine in "The Ring," batters the poor brown rag of a creature in "The Combat," and at last, in "The Usurpers," denies himself all that once made him human: significantly, the voices, the dreams, the memories, the answers.

In "The Animals," however, man does not appear until the very last line. Ominously isolated as it is from the body of the poem: "On the sixth day we came" (208), this one line is sufficient to indicate the unbridgeable gap between the days of Creation, and at the same time to carry the threat of some future contagion. But until this point, the poem, like the world, belongs, to the animals; and Muir's effort is all to show what they have and what they have not. And they have not, it is important to notice, even a name. Throughout the poem they are called simply "they." From the title and from the context it is of course obvious who "they" are. There is no obscurity, no ambiguity here at all. Instead, there is an "acting out," a representation of the fact, that because they have no words, because words have not as yet been created, they therefore have nothing to call themselves. They must remain anonymous, as the first stanza shows they must remain placeless, timeless, and homeless. For where words do not exist, everything is evanescent. There is no fixed foundation under foot, nor any solid earth around. There is only utter deprivation, in which the animals, by their nature, are condemned to live.

In contrast is the world which the animals can never know, the world built by names—the subject of the second stanza:

> For with names the world was called
> Out of the empty air,
> With names was built and walled,
> Line and circle and square,
> Dust and emerald;
> Snatched from deceiving death
> By the articulate breath. (201)

And although, as Janet Emig has observed in her excellent analysis of this poem in *English Journal*, almost every word here is "a familiar Anglo-Saxon monosyllable," [4] there is one particularly outstanding exception which occurs in the last line of this stanza: the word "articulate." After the long succession of monosyllables, which again "act out" the completely disjointed character of the environment in which the animals must live, this Latinate word of four connected syllables by its very structure effectively conjures up the coherent, comprehensible, enduring world that only language makes possible. By its inner core of meaning, furthermore: "having parts or distinct areas organized into a coherent or meaningful whole" [5] it reinforces and substantiates what the interlocking sequence of its syllables has already suggested: the power of "the articulate breath." Placed at this precise point in the poem, too, with this precise function and significance, it indicates the touch of a master.

But however completely beasts and birds and fish may be deprived of everything language gives, of memory, tradition, and meaning, there is one thing of inestimable virtue that they possess. And this, the subject of the third stanza, as we said before is innocence. The freshness of Creation still shines on all the animals. They seem to have issued only now from the hand of God, since the day when they were made still remains "the same,/ Never shall pass away." Thus they preserve intact into our corrupted present the uncorrupted good of Eden. They are living witnesses of that residual glory of the unfallen world which was momentarily revealed in "The Transfiguration." As representatives and envoys of that unfallen world, moreover, they bear the promise of a redemption man himself has forfeited; and in the later poem, "The Horses," we shall see that after man has brought on himself the ultimate disaster of nuclear war, it is the animals, the horses, some of them colts, "new as if they had come from their own Eden," (247) which offer to the few human survivors the possibility of new life.

"The Horses" is thus in a way the final chapter of a story, to which "the Animals" contributed part of a first chapter. The rest of that first chapter is contained in "The Days." For where "The Animals" gives an account of only one day in the making of the world, with a hint of the very different and ominous day to come, "The Days" narrates the entire history of the Creation from the first through the seventh days. Beginning "practically in a whisper," according to Louise Bogan, who calls it "surely one of the great lyrics of our time," [6] "The Days" like "The Animals" acts out its meaning. From the brief three or even two stresses of the opening lines, the verse grows as the world grows from nothing, until it reaches a full pentameter measure. Then decreasing to two stresses once more and increasing again, decreasing and increasing, it mimics the coming and going of the successive days with all their new wonders. But although at first, as this process goes on, the miracle of the process itself dominates the poem; although Muir's consistent use of the imagery of water and reflections in water to indicate the apparition of each day's works inevitably lends a consistency, a homogeneity, to the whole sequence of days—they all seem to flow onward like a single river—nevertheless, once the seventh day has been called forth, and the world we all know, with its familiar landmarks and activities, stands completed, it is again the separateness of the days of creation that becomes the theme of the poem. True, there is little of the foreboding here which was suggested by the separate final line of "The Animals," but the facts of division and the sadness of it are clear. The mountains stand "in the third day/ (Where they shall always stay)" (209); and although a life-giving river runs, "Threading, clear cord of water, all to all," still the "fish in the billow's heart," the "man with the net," and the "animals watching man and bird go by" (210) are all divided from each other in their distinct and different days. Since the longing of all life is for unity and wholeness, the poem ends, indeed, with a magnificent prayer for the wholeness that only eternity can bring:

> For the passing of this fragmentary day
> Into the day where all are gathered together,
> Things and their names, in the storm's and the lightning's nest,
> The seventh great day and the clear eternal weather. (210)

but the problem which "The Days" as a whole presents is the problem of division: the division which is inherent in time and all its works; the division which in fact is another face of time, and thus of pain, death, and evil.

Each in its own way, accordingly, both "The Animals" and "The Days" introduce the idea of evil into the very genesis of things; and thus the question of evil and its relation to good which has been one of Muir's most constant as well as most Miltonic themes, once more becomes a dominant theme in the first section of *One Foot in Eden*. But now there is a difference. Because in exploring the nature of evil over the years Muir has already plumbed its depths in "The Gate"; has already seen its most appalling image in "The Combat"; and because he has been able to turn from those depths and that image to find the love of "The Commemoration," the joy of "In Love for Long," and the light of the "clear unfallen world" in "The Transfiguration," he has no need to descend again into the absolute darkness of the pit. He knows it is there, knows that the "happy happy love" he has found is "sieged with crying sorrows." If love or joy "Flourishes sweet and wild," he is well aware that it still flourishes "in imprisonment," still "keeps its perfect laws/ Between the tiger's paws" (159-60); and this precisely, of course, is the miracle he has come to accept: that light and dark, good and evil, are woven together in a "knot intrinsicate," that they coexist in inexplicable confederacy. It was this belief that operated with more or less force, as we have seen, in all the poems after "The Gate," keeping most of them from touching that extreme brink of despair, and illuminating a few with radiant acceptance. And it is this belief that now more than ever informs and illuminates the poems of *One Foot in Eden*, particularly of Part I. Opposites join here in accord; irreconcilables meet in reconciliation; the "famished field and blackened tree/ Bear flowers in Eden never known" (227).

Irreconcilables meet in reconciliation, for example, in the concluding line of "Adam's Dream," a poem surely suggested, as J. R. Watson believes, by the vision of the future granted to Adam in *Paradise Lost*.[7] Although the major part of the poem records, in irregularly moving, troubled blank verse, Adam's bewilderment at the meaningless, disorderly world of time where his descendants live and multiply; and although Muir relies initially, to a degree unusual for him, on the orthodox doctrine of the Fortunate Fall to restore Adam's peace of mind, the lovely last line of the poem suddenly presents the true agreement of opposites, the coexistence of all contraries, which was Muir's own, strictly personal image of the underlying harmony of things—the "peace of the humming looms." When Adam's dream of the future is ended and he turns again to sleep, he finds his rest, it is important to notice, "In love and grief in Eve's encircling arms" (212). For here grief is not superseded, as in the concept of the Fortunate Fall, where sin and grief give way to greater good and joy; nor is Eve, the temptress, in any way derogated from her position as archetypal wife and mother. Rather, grief lies in the embrace of love, as Adam lies in the warmth and protection of "Eve's encircling arms." Both grief, the price of Eden's loss, and Eve, who caused that price to be paid, are welcomed in the final gathering together, which Muir's acceptance of paradox implied, of all earth's children and their joys and sorrows.

Warm and compassionate as this vision may be, however, it is still, in "Adam's Dream," only a flash from a single line. In the following poem, "Outside Eden," on the other hand, it pervades the whole. For "Outside Eden" is a parable of simple, uncomplaining acceptance, told appropriately in the simple ballad style so natural to Muir from the first. It is not, of course, a true ballad. The stanzas, after the first, vary in length, and the rhymes vary in occurrence. The opening six-line stanza, however, composed of an alternately rhymed tetrameter quatrain followed by a refrain-like rhyming couplet, sets a ballad pattern which echoes through the rest of the poem, and the four-stress lines continue to enforce a characteristic ballad compression and directness. Like a ballad, furthermore, the poem enters abruptly into the middle of the action; without introduction or explanation, it presents the bare outlines of a scene which dramatizes the act of acceptance:

> A few lead in their harvest still
> By the ruined wall and broken gate.
> Far inland shines the radiant hill.
> Inviolable the empty gate,
> Impassable the gaping wall;
> And the mountain over all. (212)

This handful of folk who are the protagonists here do not grumble or lament the inheritance they have so plainly lost. Instead, they humbly continue the necessary life-giving rituals of seed-time and harvest in the very shadow of the gate they were forbidden to re-enter so long ago that the bars have long since fallen. When they lift their eyes, they still see and rejoice in the "radiant hill." Thus although they are barred from Eden, they remain so close to it that their "Guilt is next door to innocence"; like Oedipus, they are innocent even in their guilt; like him, they are emblems of that reconciliation of opposites which Muir has so often celebrated and now, in *One Foot in Eden*, celebrates more persistently than ever. As this particular poem continues, it is true, he lapses momentarily from his theme to "browse in sin's great library," but in the end he returns triumphantly to the power and objectivity of the sharp initial image. The final lines are austerely unadorned, solidly concrete, and deeply moving. Even more than the opening stanza, they take us straight to the heart of what acceptance and reconciliation truly mean:

> Their griefs are all in memory grown
> As natural as a weathered stone.
> Their troubles are a tribute given
> Freely while gazing at the hill.
> Such is their simplicity,
> Standing on earth, looking at heaven. (214)

From acceptance, furthermore, it is only a few steps to joy, as *The Narrow Place* testified, where from the resolution of paradox achieved in "The Ring," Muir moved easily to the praise of love in "The Annunciation" and "The Commemoration," and at last, in *The Voyage*, to the pure joy of "A Birthday" and "In Love for Long." But in *One Foot in Eden*, before he takes these steps, he prolongs his exploration of the meaning of acceptance. Two variations of the legend of Prometheus precede the "felicity" of "Orpheus' Dream," and another picture of Oedipus "on the Peloponnesian roads," another version of faithful Penelope's story, together with accounts of the wanderings of Abraham and Isaac and the simple intrepidity of unnamed men in "The Heroes," all serve as prologue to the equally intense vision of beatitude in "The Annunciation." For the most part, these prologue poems are less highly charged than those they introduce, but they are nevertheless important in effect. By extending the range and complicating the significance of what the actual experience of acceptance can involve; by bringing in a variety of symbols of reconciliation from Greek myth, Old Testament, and Muir's own fable-making mind, these poems at one and the same time indicate again Muir's refusal to take any absolute position, and provide an environment, a soil, in which not only the more powerful poems of reconciliation can be firmly rooted, but the poems of felicity as well.

Thus the first "Prometheus," which follows "Outside Eden," is logically structured as a series of questions about what constitutes reconciliation. It also suggests, in the imagery, the earth-bound quality of the initial and by far the most successful section of the poem, something about the particular kind of reconciliation Muir will celebrate in his most explicit statements on that theme in this volume, "The Annunciation" and "One Foot in Eden." Overtly, however, it pursues a different course. For instance, in the opening blank verse lines, deliberately muted in tone, Prometheus seems almost to have achieved a reconciliation that is merely resignation. He has been lying chained to his rock so long that the changes which mark the passing of time for man have faded into a meaningless sequence, a dream, for him:

> The careless seasons pass and leave me here.
> The forests rise like ghosts and fade like dreams.
> All has its term; flowers flicker on the ground
> A summer moment, and the rock is bare. (214)

Yet a faint hope for something more positive survives. What the old Titan hopes for is the end of time, when the race of man to whom he once gave fire will have been consumed by fire, will lie "strewn in ashes on the ashen hills" (215). For then, when the reason for the "feud" is over, the "heedless gods" who punished him so long ago may forgive him and bid him "come/ Again among them." But would this forgiveness be any more of a reconciliation than mere resignation? What would Prometheus find to say to these gods? He is not, like Shelley's Titan, unwilling to accept any terms with the tyrant Zeus, nor does he contemplate the sort of bargain Aeschylus' Prometheus is supposed to have made to gain his freedom. He is willing simply to resume his old relationship with these deities, but he sees at once that between him and them there is a gulf not even gods can cross. He has suffered and they have not. They have no answer for "earth's dark story."

A further question occurs to Prometheus. What if Olympus should be vacant? What if man, because the gods had no answer for his story, lost his faith in them, neglected their shrines, forgot the mystery of earth and air? In this empty world, reconciliation would be not only meaningless but impossible. On the other hand, there might be other heavens and other gods, and this possibility finally gives Prometheus the consolation he has been seeking. He has heard that from such a heaven another god came down, "Not in rebellion but in pity and love": a god who was born in mortal flesh, lived and died as mortals do, but rose again "with all the spoils of time" —that is, with the experience and memory of suffering. "If I could find that god," Prometheus concludes, "he would hear and answer" (216).

Muir himself, however, was not satisfied with the poem. He wrote to T. S. Eliot, who had requested a poem of about this length—fifty-nine lines—for publication in pamphlet form as one of Faber's series of Ariel poems, that although he was sending the piece because he had promised it, he was "not pleased with it," and could "scarcely think it adequate or suitable." [8] When Eliot suggested that a line or two might be added to clarify the fact that Prometheus has survived in the poem "into our own epoch," [9] Muir obligingly inserted the material about the disappearance of the gods from Olympus, but this addition merely compounded the problem. For the problem lies neither in obscurity nor in lack of adequate transitions, but in diffuseness. There is no single inner, organizing vision in the poem.

There is, as we indicated earlier, a logical organization which carries the poem along on the surface through a series of meditations on the nature of reconciliation, and this series leads to two conclusions: that true reconciliation comes only through suffering, and that the Christian revelation, which recognizes suffering, offers a more satisfactory faith than the "heedless gods" of Olympus. But this logical argument does not make an imaginative whole. The first twenty-nine lines, which remain within the framework of the natural universe; which begin with the hush of time reduced to a dream and end with the hush in heaven and earth when time is over, do indeed form a unity, but the rest of the poem falls apart. When the thirty-third line, "Zeus with the ponderous glory of the bull," came to Muir in a dream, as he recalls in *An Autobiography*, he admitted that it was "quite unlike any poetry that I write" (46); and it remains alien, unassimilated here. Equally unassimilated are the final lines of the paragraph Muir added to the poem to please Eliot. They are based on a strange image of eddying, malevolently animate dust Muir used in his first novel, *The Marionette*; and there they belonged, not here. Nor does the Christ-like god who is introduced at the end, the god who "Was born a son of woman, lived and died,/ And rose again" really belong here, either. He is a *deus ex machina*, arbitrarily brought in to give Prometheus an answer; he does not derive from Prometheus' own world, the natural world of earth and animal, man and stars, so quietly and on the whole convincingly evoked in the first part of the poem. Yet this is the world, the setting, where a Prometheus who is so manifestly at one with the seasons, the forests, and the flowers, must find his reconciliation or not at all.

It is, therefore, more as another variation of Muir's insistence on the place of suffering in any final harmony than as a valid poetic statement, that this "Prometheus" has interest for the reader and fulfills its function in *One Foot in Eden*. But with the next, and closely related poem, "The Grave of Prometheus," the case is quite different. For although these sixteen blank verse lines do not have the weight or the intensity of some of Muir's major poems, they do have that imaginative unity which the earlier poem lacked. They begin with the same isolated yet earthly setting, and they do not depart from that setting. They attempt to answer essentially the same question: what happened to Prometheus when the gods to whose company he belonged ceased to have meaning in the modern world? But they introduce no inappropriate image of Zeus, no god from another heaven. Instead, as if the "heavenly thief" (216) of fire had been tormented by his kindred gods with the fire he stole, Prometheus simply burns out, like an extinct volcano, when those gods forsake Olympus. He turns to "common earth," he becomes "his barrow," and in this reunion with the sweet and life-giving soil, the ancient benefactor of man at last finds his fulfillment and his rest. In a final touch that is exactly right, his agony is transmuted to a field of flowers. And yet the whole poem has been just as "right." The sustained dignity and simplicity of the language, the concrete details that give credibility to the vast bulk of the Titan's body, the accurate notation of geological change, all function together with that image of fire metamorphosed into daisies, to create a coherent, freshly imagined parable of reconciliation totally within the natural world. Through that parable, moreover, they point explicitly to what was only implicit in the first "Prometheus": the concept of reconciliation already suggested in the miracle of "The Transfiguration" and in the acceptance of "Outside Eden," and now to be enunciated most clearly in "The Annunciation" and "One Foot in Eden"—the concept that time and the timeless, evil and good, suffering and joy somehow meet in harmony here and now. Here and now, in the world we all live in, as Wordsworth knew, "there is a dark/ Inscrutable workmanship that reconciles/ Discordant elements," whether in the human psyche whose growth he was describing, or in that natural world with its interaction and equilibrium of warring substances Muir describes in the superb concluding lines of "The Grave of Prometheus":

> A mineral change made cool his fiery bed,
> And made his burning body a quiet mound,
> And his great face a vacant ring of daisies. (216)

Again, however, as if exploring every other possibility before homing in at last to his appointed place, Muir does not go directly where these lines seem to lead. Instead he takes up the theme of joy heralded in the simple acceptance of "Outside Eden" and shows us "felicity"—but a felicity still a little removed from the natural, the ordinary. It is a felicity experienced in dream and framed, once more, in Greek myth. In its own terms, however, it carries absolute conviction. Where in "Outside Eden" there was a momentary falling off from the strict objectivity, the clean directness of the whole; where "Prometheus" was diffuse and "The Grave of Prometheus" lacking some degree of intensity, in "Orpheus' Dream" there are no aberrations; nothing is diffuse; everything is intense. Every detail in the three six-line stanzas of this poem is perfectly adjusted to every other, because it is, to repeat a phrase of Muir's, a poem on which "fate . . . [has] put its palm."

Not only so. It is also a poem of enormous resonance. Because Muir, like Milton too on several occasions, has taken the legend of Orpheus and Eurydice for a theme, he has necessarily invoked all the meanings clustered around that myth: the heartbreak of irrevocable loss, the implacability of fate, the remorselessness of death, the power of song, and the strength of love, that almost "made Hell grant what Love did seek." But at the same time, as in his handling of the Prometheus myth and of so many others, he has reshaped his material. Here, specifically, he has changed the ending. His Eurydice returns intact, it seems, from the underworld, so completely freed from the dominion of death that both she and Orpheus can safely ignore the taboo once laid on Orpheus by Hades' king: they can turn their heads and see

> The poor ghost of Eurydice
> Still sitting in her silver chair
> Alone in Hades' empty hall. (217)

And by this drastic alteration in the original, Muir of course introduces a set of meanings into his poem which completely oppose the implications of the ancient myth. The love that made Hell grant, conditionally, what it sought, now unconditionally gains what it seeks. Fate is not unvaryingly implacable, loss not always irrevocable. Where there was death, there is rebirth. Yet none of these implications—and this of course is the case whenever Muir recasts mythical materials—really cancels any of the old. Rather, the old remain along with the new, in simultaneous opposition and conjunction, so that here the tragic fate of the Greek Eurydice still echoes in the happiness she now possesses. The traditional associations of sorrow still persist, side by side with the freshly discovered possibilities of joy, and each enriches the other.

Muir builds directly, in fact, on this simultaneity of opposition and conjunction. Instead of rearranging or omitting any of the familiar version, he relies on it. "And she was there," the poem begins, clearly indicating by the initial co-ordinating conjunction that it is carrying on a story already partly told, a story which is the legend that ends with Eurydice's return to Hell. Because that dark half of the tale is so close—immediately on the other side of the "and"—not only do the general associations of the past reverberate in the present and intensify it, as we have seen; more particularly, Eurydice's sudden appearance in the "little boat" of Orpheus' dream is all the more dazzling set directly against that darkness. It is all the more unexpected, too, since nothing in the earlier story prepares us for this development. Precisely because it is so unexpected, furthermore, it is all the more convincing. It happens without warning, without explanation, as a miracle happens and this is exactly what it is.

How miraculous, every detail of the first stanza works to testify. That breathless opening sentence, "And she was there," for example, which announces the astonishing event, does not even bother to say who "she" is. It is not until the fourth line of the poem that Eurydice's name is mentioned, because until then, in the first surprise, it is taken for granted: who else could it be? The overwhelmingly important thing at this point is "her" presence "there," wherever Orpheus is; and in token of the virtue contained in that word, "there," it is taken up as a rhyme in the third line, where it is paired with the "despair" that it wipes out, while in the fourth line it is repeated. It is repeated, furthermore, in a restatement of the original announcement that is almost identical with the first, except that now Eurydice is named; and in both cases, significantly, the statement brings the whole movement of the stanza temporarily to a halt. There is a strong caesura after the initial sentence ("And she was there./ The little boat"), as if the speaker had to regain his breath before he could even begin to describe where "there" was or who "she" might be, while both before and after the second statement come two more long pauses: one after "Stopped" ("Stopped,/ for Eurydice was there.") and the other after "there" at the end of the line. And these three prolonged breaks in the otherwise uninterrupted flow of the stanza, with its beautifully interchanging iambs, trochees, and dactyls, prove extraordinarily moving. They are like the catches that come in the breath when some sensation is too sweet to bear, and they signal that in this poem, similarly, the limits of bearable "felicity" have been reached.

Once Eurydice's presence is unquestionably recognized, however, although the wonder does not cease, the movement of the poem changes. In the second stanza there are no more pauses. Instead there is a sweeping, flowing measure that parallels the sweep of an interior tide of the mind, a tide that carries the "little boat," once dangerously coasting those "Zones of oblivion and despair" so often visited in previous volumes, on to a complete recovery of original good. For not only does Orpheus gain back Eurydice here. Eurydice gains back Orpheus. Each, in this mutual fulfillment, is given back to each, until both are "Swept" on, "Past every choice to boundless good" (217); until, in the third stanza, they reach such a wholeness of love, such a healing of all division, that when they turn back to look at Hell from the vantage point of their completeness, they perceive a startling fact: in contrast with their fullness, Hell is empty.

And here, mid-way through the third and last stanza, the movement of the poem shifts again. Volume and tempo both abate, as if drawing towards a conclusion. The brimming flood of the lovers' beatitude, represented by the full, varied vowels of these two lines: "Forgiveness, truth, atonement, all/ Our love at once—till we could dare," dwindles away into the thinner tones of such lines as these, dominated by [I]: "The poor ghost of Eurydice/ Still sitting in her silver chair." The imagery of wholeness is replaced by the image of a single insubstantial shade, abandoned and "Alone in Hades' empty hall."

Everything dies away into the appropriate "dying fall" by which music sinks into silence. But not only is this diminuendo formally appropriate; it is also thematically right. It is the final, perfecting touch which makes the vision of reconciliation in "Orpheus' Dream" complete. For how could reconciliation be complete if anything were left out? If Hades were still thronged with other souls, less fortunate than Eurydice, denied rebirth? Hades must be empty, the harmony must be universal, or it is not true harmony. And at once we remember that emptiness, a "hiatus," a "craving blank," is precisely what always represented evil in Muir's eyes. No wonder his Hell is vacant. It has to be, because Hell is vacancy, while Heaven is fullness, and in the fullness of joy which Orpheus and Eurydice reach is the consummate symbol of the "boundless good," the limitless peace and concord towards which, miraculously, Muir saw all contraries converging.

Closely related to "Orpheus' Dream" in perfection of form, in overflowing delight, and in the central image of two souls brought together in fulfillment from opposite poles, whether of life and death or of earth and heaven, is another important poem, "The Annunciation." But just as "Orpheus' Dream" follows an interlude of several minor but thematically related pieces, so too "The Annunciation" follows a group of related, but less powerful poems. Thus "The Charm" and "The Other Oedipus" are both studies of reconciliation turned to indifference through loss of the memory of sorrow. In "The Other Oedipus," the blessedness of the blind king on his way to Colonus is no longer human, it lacks the touch of reality, because unlike Muir's earlier Oedipus, this old man has forgotten the guilt and the suffering that true reconciliation must contain and yet transcend. Other poems ask questions about the nature of human destiny: a grown-up Telemachos, for example, in "Telemachos Remembers," recalls how as a child he could not understand the part Penelope's love and loyalty played in bringing Odysseus home to the destined end of his wanderings. Similarly, "Abraham" and "The Succession," in Biblical terms, and "The Road" and "The Heroes" in Kafka-like fables, all seek in their different ways an answer to the same problem: how can a human being find the road he must take? How can he recognize his destiny and reach the consummation he instinctively believes is his? Some of these poems offer possible answers; but since in none of them is there any really satisfactory solution to the problem—since nowhere is there any immediately convincing image of reconciliation—the image, the solution that Muir presents at last in the almost flawless shape of "The Annunciation" become by contrast not merely convincing, but irrefutable.

But there is another, even more essential difference between "The Annunciation" and these poems which precede it and set it off. Where they are all derived, like "Orpheus' Dream," from Greek myth, or from the Old Testament, or from that universal storehouse of images Muir so often drew upon, "The Annunciation" belongs at least partially to the Christian story, and herein lies the particular relevance of this poem to Muir's slowly developing answer to the question of how to find fulfillment in this world; how to "fit that world to this"; how to make intimations of the timeless "go into" time. For although paradox and the acceptance of paradox have been implicit, as we have seen, in all Muir's thinking almost from the beginning, one persistent difficulty has been finding an adequate way to bring the opposite terms of paradox together into an enduring unity. Love, itself compounded of paradox, "gathers all," he knew. In the third of "The Three Mirrors," although he did not claim that he himself had ever looked there, he had faith that evil and good, growing side by side, at last composed a whole. In dreams, which still reach back into Eden, into the lost world of natural good, he found the long-forgotten word which in "The Ring" restored the broken concord between animal and man, rounded a new circle including innocence and experience. And in "The Transfiguration," he recorded a momentary insight, a transient purity of vision that revealed the light of the "clear unfallen world" still shining under the corruption of the fallen one, the eternal fable still underlying the world of time. All these images were scattered, however; all these moments of insight, disconnected. There was no single principle binding them all together, no key which explained their common meaning, and this was the key Muir sought.

It was not until he came to Rome in 1948, as director of the British Institute there, that he found what he had been seeking. He found it in the images of the Incarnation "to be seen everywhere, not only in churches, but on the walls of houses, at crossroads in the suburbs, in wayside shrines in the park, and in private rooms" [10]: images which told him, for the first time, that Christ "was born in the flesh and had lived on earth," and that the flesh could be good. When, as a boy, he had attended "Calvin's kirk crowning the barren brae" (228), he had never been aware that Christ was flesh. Christ was the Word, cold and abstract, totally alien to warm and suffering humanity. The flesh was by definition evil. As early as 1939, indeed, Muir had found himself one night involuntarily reciting the Lord's Prayer, and had vaguely sensed that "Christ was the turning-point of time and the meaning of life to everyone, no matter what his conscious beliefs";[11] but he had no real evidence to support or clarify this feeling. In Rome, on the other hand, in the carvings and paintings where the mystery of the Word was visibly embodied in the shape of man, Christ was manifestly human, not alien. He was God, but a God who had assumed both "the burden of our flesh" [12] and its glory; in Him the eternal intersected with and transfigured the world of time. There was in these images, in other words, a representation of the intersection of the timeless with time comparable to Hölderlin's great image of Christ standing "Sein Leben lang" under God's sign in the thundering sky. And now, because the face of incarnate deity proved to him from every wall that Christ was mortal flesh and blood as well as immortal spirit, Muir could accept both Hölderlin's image and Hölderlin's interpretation, that "Christ was the one symbol which united . . . the two truths . . . in existence: a truth transcending time, and a truth immanent in time. . . ." [13] For Muir, as for Hölderlin, Christ thus became the key which explained and the emblem which incarnated all paradox and all reconciliation.

Yet for Muir, as for Hölderlin, Christ remained a figure very different from the figure of the New Testament, or of orthodox Christianity, or of Milton. Even in such avowedly Christian poems as "The Son" and "The Christmas," which later, along with the more Herbertian "The Lord," he omitted from the *One Foot in Eden* group in his final *Collected Poems*, as if still in doubt that he meant to avow so much—even here the Christ that he pictures is more a symbol of opposites mystically resolved, of flesh transfused with spirit, than an exponent of any particular theology. Similarly, the meeting of Christ's mother Mary with the angel Gabriel, which is the basis of "The Annunciation," becomes in Muir's treatment simply a meeting of an "angel" and a "girl." Through them opposites meet, through them heaven and earth, eternity and time mingle; through them mortal clay is impregnated in the union which resulted in the Incarnation, in that turning-point in time when momentarily divine and human law were reconciled. But while Muir clearly insists on the metaphysical significance of this encounter, he carefully avoids all sectarian associations and interpretations.

In the title, it is true, he gives the reader a clue to the place of this event in the Christian story. In the poem, however, he concentrates on as objective as possible a rendering of the mystery he saw represented on "a little plaque on the wall of a house in the Via degli Artisti. . . ." For there he saw "an angel and a young girl, their bodies inclined towards each other, their knees bent as if they were overcome by love, 'tutto tremante,'" who "gazed upon each other like Dante's pair"; and that "representation of a human love so intense that it could not reach farther" seemed to him the "Perfect earthly symbol of the love that passes understanding." [14] It is, accordingly, on the human love, the outward and visible sign of the inner mystery, that Muir focuses so marvelously in the poem: on the "Immediacy/ Of strangest strangeness" in the bliss that paralyzes the limbs of both angel and girl; on the wonder that makes "each feather tremble in his wings" (224). And in this rendering of so intense a fleshly love between mortal and eternal spirit, Muir finds an image for that reconciliation of opposites, that communion of time with eternity, of which Christ, he believed, was the universal symbol. But neither here, in dealing with the Annunciation, nor elsewhere in dealing with the figure of Christ, does he speak in conventional religious terms. In that kirk of Calvin's on the barren brae, particularly, as he well knew, his picture of the Annunciation "would have seemed a sort of blasphemy." [15]

Yet it was the barren braes of Orkney, after all, which were home, and he remained incorrigibly northern, incorrigibly Scottish. Much as he learned to love the light and color of Italy on his second visit there, on his first, shortly after his marriage, he was "repelled by the violence of the colours, the sea like a solid lake of blue paint, the purple sky, the bright brown earth"; to his "unaccustomed eyes the contrast seemed crude and without mystery." [16] And thus it is only fitting that in this volume, which in so many ways is a summing up of his whole life's work, and which still shows, in poems such as "Scotland's Winter" and "The Incarnate One," his continuing concern with Scottish problems, the poem which most of all stands as a summary—the title poem, "One Foot in Eden"—should be not only a poem of reconciliation, but one which finds its symbols of reconciliation in the gray Scottish landscape and in the harvest imagery of Muir's Orkney boyhood.

For the "darkened fields" and "beclouded skies" of "One Foot in Eden" are surely Scottish, not Italian; and the "famished field and blackened tree" denote once more, as Butter suggests in his shorter study, *Edwin Muir*,[17] the sooty, ravaged wasteland around industrial Glasgow, which provided the initial background, so long ago, for *Variations on a Time Theme*. Similarly, the planting and harvest rituals here, the corn and tares, the foliage and the fruit, all derive at least partially from Muir's childhood on an Orkney farm. But at this point, it is important to notice, something extraordinary has happened. For the first time, in statements such as the opening "One foot in Eden still, I stand" (227), and the couplet which introduces the second stanza: "Yet still from Eden springs the root/ As clean as on the starting day," Muir acknowledges that he never really left Eden, that it is not possible really to leave it. As "The Transfiguration" suggested, "One Foot in Eden" now unequivocally asserts: the "clear unfallen world" remains forever at the heart of the fallen one. Even in Glasgow, the Orkneys were not lost, and now the "distant [Orkney] isle" where the "myth" of Muir's childhood was "enacted" merges in reconciliation with the city of squalor and slums where life was ruled by an "iron law." When the angel from "far beyond the farthest star" and the earthly girl who was Mary came together in "The Annunciation," the discord which they resolved in harmony was not so extreme.

It is obviously not only from Muir's own experience, however, that the planting and harvest motifs through which this poem develops are derived. In this harvest imagery there may well be an echo of the millennial harvests in Hölderlin's *Patmos*, which Muir lovingly interprets in his *Essays on Literature and Society*.[18] Further, as J. R. Watson, in "Edwin Muir and the Problem of Evil," points out, although the particular phrase, "corn and tares" is of course Biblical, the image of a field where good and evil grow together is also unmistakably Miltonic.[19] "Good and evil in the field of this world grow up together almost inseparably," Milton wrote in *Areopagitica*,[20] and since the influence of Milton has been so pronounced throughout the first section in this volume, it is not unrealistic to see a parallel with his words in these lines:

> Evil and good stand thick around
> In the fields of charity and sin
> Where we shall lead our harvest in. (227)

Yet there is more than a parallel. There is also a change. Whether Muir has taken his images from his own boyhood, from Hölderlin, from the Bible, or from Milton, he has changed them all. As two of his earlier poems of reconciliation, "The Trophy" and "The Three Mirrors," indicated in their treatment of essentially the same image, the important point for Muir is not that corn and tares, good and evil, king and rebel, stand side by side in the field of this world, to be separated in the next, when the tares, the evil, and the rebel will be cast into the everlasting fire. The point is that in this world both good and evil, corn and tares, king and rebel are the apparent signs of a division that in the underlying fable is made whole. They are the terms of a paradox that in "the third glass" is resolved into unity, the "peace of the humming looms." Whereas in "The Trophy," however, that fundamental agreement of good and evil happened in "deep confederacy far from the air," in "One Foot in Eden" it happens here and now. As "The Transfiguration," "The Grave of Prometheus" and "The Annunciation" had each in a different way anticipated, and as "The Island" in the second section of this volume confirms, the agreement in "One Foot in Eden" takes place in the natural world, in everyday life. In the simple language, the compact, uncluttered tetrameter lines of Muir's familiar ballad style, the poem states plainly that even on our polluted earth, in our disastrous times, still:

> . . . Famished field and blackened tree
> Bear flowers in Eden never known.
> Blossoms of grief and charity
> Bloom in these darkened fields alone. (227)

Out of evil, as in *Paradise Lost*, as in the orthodox doctrine of the Fortunate Fall, good has come at last. But unlike the orthodox doctrine, unlike Milton, Muir has not called on divine intervention to bring this about, nor does he postpone it to some future in a new Jerusalem. For him the good has been latent in the scheme of things from the beginning. For him "evil and good" and "charity and sin" are all part of the harvest, and for him the harvest is now, in this world. "Had we but eyes to lift up, the fields are white already."

Because the reconciliation in this culminating poem of the first, Miltonic section of *One Foot in Eden* so clearly involves the things of this world, moreover, the transition from here to the present- and future-directed second section and to many of the uncollected poems, all presided over by Kafka, is easy and natural. There is even a relationship between the Scottishness of "One Foot in Eden" and the inverted Calvinism of the sonnet "To Franz Kafka." For here, with a tough satirical humor familiar in his prose but new in his poetry, Muir mocks the Calvinist tenets of election and non-election he had already dealt with mercilessly so long before in his biography of John Knox. He makes light of that grim image of fate as Calvin saw it that so appalled him in "The Combat." By a manipulation of the multisyllabic, formidably abstract language of the Calvinist creed, he produces lines like this, the first in the sonnet, "If we, the proximate damned, presumptive blest" (233), or this, the sixth, "Equivocal ignominy of non-election," which are at once masterpieces of compression and wit and deadly parodies of doctrinaire jargon. Yet parody is of course not the aim of the sonnet. The intention, a very serious one, is to contrast with the cold rhetoric of this rigid creed the warmth and compassion of Kafka—and Muir, with unusual tenderness on his part, addresses him as "dear Franz"—who welcomed and forgave the very souls that in the strict divisions of Calvinism were condemned neither to bliss nor to damnation. In these in-betweens, the "drab and half," whom Knox's ministers would have scorned, and with whom Muir himself, in some of his earlier poems, such as "Epitaph" and "Scotland 1941," showed impatience, Kafka found not only "meaning," but that meaning of meanings for which Muir searched all his life. It is a meaning he now describes in a line which gives to the sonnet its final surge of power: "Eternity's secret script, the saving proof"; and thus what Muir is acknowledging here is not only the broadness of Kafka's welcome compared with Calvin's, but the fact that his own had not been broad enough: that not only good and evil, charity and sin, belong together in ultimate reconciliation, but the non-authentic, the "flickering souls" (153), belong there too.

As if in token of this new expansion of scope and interest, Muir in the following five poems, called "Effigies," explores the minds and motives of some of these "flickering," frustrated, and unfulfilled souls. But although these pieces are sensitively handled; although Muir shows again the psychological insight and understanding, honed now to a keener edge, which went into his earlier studies of madness and alienation, the portrait genre itself, even when treated in depth, apparently never caught his imagination. It might have in time, as the probably unfinished sketch of his cousin Sutherland, found among his papers after his death and printed in the *Collected Poems* as "There's Nothing Here" (294) so tantalizingly indicates. For here the long dead, incorrigible rake comes to life again, speaking very nearly the authentic Orkney he used to speak, to express a natural dismay at finding himself—of all places—in heaven. But in this second section of *One Foot in Eden*, it is clearly not so much Kafka the portraitist of the "drab and half" who strikes fire in Muir's mind as it is that other Kafka with whom, as we have seen, he has shown a kinship ever since *Variations on a Time Theme*: Kafka the maker of myth, and here, particularly, of contemporary myth.

There is thus only one of the five "Effigies" which has the vividness of that later Sutherland fragment; and this, the fourth, is not really a character study at all, but a fiction such as Kafka might have created: a complete and self-sufficient story. In only twelve alternately rhyming lines of irregular length, Muir has devised an image of stark horror which we recognize immediately as an image of our age, although how or of what we cannot say. It is an image of blood and war, of some incomprehensibly broken machine, and of dead who will not die. Like "The Combat," which it resembles in its implications of endlessness, it is a pure fantasy risen from the unconscious. But unlike "The Combat," it has no known antecedents in any of Muir's dreams. It stands by itself, powerful and haunting, a reminder that even in this volume where the major trend is towards reconciliation of opposites, Muir was still aware that on another level the everlasting conflict of opposites continues.

It is precisely this awareness of continuing conflict, moreover, this sense of the fact that reconciliation is never stable but always in need of renewal, that gives to most of the poems in this section their particularly contemporary tone, and in several instances provides singularly arresting images of the contemporary condition. Even the poem following "Effigies," for example—"The Difficult Land"—although couched in too rural terms and set at too leisurely a pace for our agonizing pressures, is nevertheless an expression of these pressures. It manages to convey by simple insistence and by recourse to archetypal symbols of cloud and bird and dream that still move us, both the feel of a world grown barren, a frustrating world where inevitably "things miscarry" (237), and the realization that this is also the world to which we must somehow accommodate ourselves, a world which is both "a difficult country, and our home" (238). Much more effective, however, as a type of our present predicament is the uncompromisingly bare wasteland sketched in a few lines of reiterated negatives—no, no, nothing was there, "Nothing, it seemed, between them and the grave"—in the stark sonnet, "Nothing There But Faith" (238). For although here there is faith; although out of nothing faith makes for the "them" who inhabit this desolation a whole "great world" that rolls "between them and death," this faith by its very nature is strictly of the present, of our age. It has nothing, as the first lines of the sonnet so emphatically state, nothing to justify it, no traditions on which to rely, no rock on which to rest; nothing but man's own indomitable will to believe, to make order out of chaos, a whole out of emptiness. Essentially, of course, this is no more irrational a resolution of paradox than the "blossoms of grief and charity" of "One Foot in Eden," but stripped of the familiar trappings of the Eden story and the suggestion, if not the actual presence of the Christian myth, this particular resolution stands revealed in the nakedness which is at once the hallmark of its times and the source of its strength—it can lose nothing more.

"Dream and Thing," with its virtuoso play on only three end-rhymes in the course of sixteen lines, comes to a similarly harsh conclusion: there is no faith except in faith itself. "There is no trust but in the miracle" (242). And the two delicate miniatures which conclude the volume, except for Muir's renewed pledge of love to his wife in the little "Song," reaffirm the same proposition once again. For in both "The Late Wasp" and "The Late Swallow" two of summer's creatures face the end of summer, when all that has warmed and nourished them until now suddenly fails them. But where the one, in this extremity, is reduced to hopelessness, the other feels the call to fly south; and out of this instinctive urge to migrate to warmer, life-renewing regions, Muir makes another parable of the creation of faith out of faith alone.

Surprisingly—and refreshingly—Muir begins "The Late Wasp" on a note of dry humor that permits him to address the insect as "A lonely bachelor mummer" (253), and to record its struggles to free itself from the marmalade. As he continues, however, his mood rapidly changes, and he observes with increasing seriousness and sympathy the meaning of winter's approach for this inhabitant of the air. The wasp's "blue thoroughfares have felt a change," he notes, in a brilliant phrase, where the word "thoroughfares," at once so strange and so accurate, transforms the "lonely . . . mummer" into one of an endless horde in transit from summer to winter, from life to death. There is even, in the suggestion of a great throng of travelers implied by "thoroughfares," a distant echo of Dante's line: "I had not thought death had undone so many." But Muir does not develop the echo; he returns at once to the simple insect image with which he began; and in the chill that deepens about the poor marmalade thief, he sees, there is no comfort left, nothing but "despair." For the bird in "The Late Swallow," on the other hand, the same chill that brought despair to the wasp brings a summons to new hope. The "swiftly aging narrowing day" (253) does drive the bird from its "well-loved nest," but it also serves as a signal to the swallow to try those "avenues of the air" that now are becoming treacherous, to adventure "Through all the heavens of ice" in search of the miracle the wasp could not imagine: a "southern paradise/ Across the great earth's downward sloping side." And there, once again, Muir asserts, there will be "homing air" to bear the swallow's wings; there the bird will "light and perch upon the radiant tree."

Inevitably, it is Muir himself, now almost seventy, who seems to stand behind both wasp and swallow here; and this personal dimension, although so well concealed, adds an unbearably touching note to images already sufficiently touching as universal symbols of the passing of life and time. But the aim here is not to catch at the heart; it is rather, once more, to affirm faith in the face of despair, to insist that, in a world where all the old values have crumbled, where nothing is left for sustenance or support, "eternity's secret script" somehow remains, that on the southern half of the globe, while winter closes in on the north, the "radiant tree" still shines.

Yet this, after all, is really Muir's final position, in both sections of this volume and throughout all his poetry since *The Narrow Place*. This is really what acceptance of paradox involves, whether arrived at through a reappraisal of old myths or invention of new ones; whether through restating Milton's eternal theme of the struggle of good and evil or looking at the contemporary scene with Kafka-like vision. Either way, such acceptance means not only the gathering together of all extremes into reconciliation, but the recognition that the process is unending; that out of each new agreement of opposites there is a genesis of new and sharper paradox; that at the same time paradox is perpetually resolved, it is perpetually reborn. There are, in other words, no absolutes. There is no final resting point, except the fact of continual conflict itself, and this conflict, if our own century is any indication, is forever intensifying.

As the world became bleaker around him, consequently—though it had been bleak enough from the beginning—Muir's affirmation of faith in the hidden, underlying rightness of things necessarily had to grow stronger. He could not dismiss the prevailing wrongness; he recognized it with too painful clarity. But his conviction that the timeless could and must be fitted into time, the fable made to "go into" the story, simultaneously intensified; and in "Day and Night," one of his loveliest lyrics, he proves his case by doing just this: he fits "that world to this" (240). Instead of merely affirming faith where all the evidence counsels despair, as he does in so many of the poems in this section, here he makes his faith transform the evidence. Without denying that he is an old man in a world that grows colder, without resorting to philosophical or religious props, he nevertheless reaches, and reaches legitimately, the triumphant assurance that he achieved in the earlier part of the volume in "Orpheus' Dream" and "The Annunciation."

At the same time, momentarily at least, he fits the two parts of *One Foot in Eden* together into the whole that they actually are, if paradox makes a whole, since in order to come to terms with the contemporary world, which has been the over-all setting of the second section of the volume, Muir uses both the manner and the matter of much of his earlier poetry, the source of the first section. He uses, that is, the balladlike, octosyllabic, irregularly rhyming lines in which he has moved so naturally and surely, from Section Ten of *Variations on a Time Theme* to "One Foot in Eden"; and with a skill made beautifully precise by years of practice, he invokes once more the familiar image of his Orkney childhood, the memory of an unspoiled world where man, animal, and gods lived together in original harmony. But now, in "Day and Night," once he has invoked this image, he requires of it something unfamiliar, something different and urgent. He demands that the voices of the night, which spoke to him as a child, speak to him again now that he and the world are older. He asks that the lesson they taught him in their special language—the "Archaic dialogue of a few/ Upon the sixth and the seventh day"—be repeated for him today, in the twentieth century, to assure him that the purpose and direction underlying creation when it was new are still there.

In "The Transfiguration," "The Annunciation," and "One Foot in Eden," of course, Muir has already found such assurance. He has already seen the "clear unfallen world" at the heart of this fallen one; already perceived that "still from Eden springs the root/ As clean as on the starting day." In each of these poems, however, this vision of intrinsic good has been *given* to him. He has not had to ask for it, whereas in "Day and Night" he not only must ask, as we have seen; he must exert his will even to catch a glimpse of such a vision. He must *"try,"* he says—and the use of this verb here is emphatic—"to fit that world to this,/ The hidden to the visible play." He *"Would"*—again a significant word that receives particular emphasis—"have them both, would nothing miss," so that clearly, in this poem, although the hands are the hands of Esau, the voice is Jacob's. Although language and line, image and intimation belong to the Muir of previous volumes and of the first half of this, the situation belongs to the Muir who was Kafka's kin and who speaks in the second half of this volume: the Muir who believes because for modern man there is nothing left except belief, because there is no "trust but in the miracle." But precisely because there is no reason for it, the faith of this second, more contemporary Muir is all the stronger. He is able, therefore, without any incongruity, to merge with his earlier self in the magnificent conclusion of this poem, which is half prayer, half sheer determination, and all affirmation. Speaking with one voice, both Muirs together tell us here what all of us must do to find the direction that in "this," the visible world, where roads run wrong and the mountain summits are sealed in wrath, has been all but lost. We must:

> Learn from the shepherd of the dark,
> Here in the light, the paths to know
> That thread the labyrinthine park,
> And the great Roman roads that go
> Striding across the untrodden day. (240)

Futhermore, in "The Horses," which T. S. Eliot called "that great, that terrifying poem of the 'atomic age,'" [22] Muir finds that Roman road, that direction, for us, even after the madness of the contemporary world has resulted in the final catastrophe of nuclear war. For "The Horses," too, like "Day and Night," is a poem which binds both sections of *One Foot in Eden* together. As we indicated previously, in discussing "The Animals" and "The Days," it is really the conclusion of the story begun in those two earlier poems, the story of Creation. Just as in those poems the world was made in seven days, here in seven days it is unmade. Just as the making then was detailed day by day, here the unmaking is detailed, until at last nothing is left of all God's original work except for the planet itself and a few human survivors who live on, in some remote area, in silence. In the fields, a few tractors are left rusting, symbols of the technological hubris that destroyed everything else. "That old bad world" (246) which had gone irremediably astray, has like Uranus, swallowed its children. But those nations "lying asleep" in the belly of this Uranus-world are "curled blindly," it is important to notice, in a foetal position. They are waiting for rebirth; and in an assertion of belief in continuing good, despite the utmost horror, that outdoes all of his earlier, similarly desperate assertions, Muir makes that rebirth happen. It comes when the horses come; when suddenly and miraculously, like Eurydice, like grace, the horses arrive out of their original world of innocence, the great fifth day of God, to restore the "long-lost archaic companionship" of the early world that spoke to the child in "Day and Night," and that the grown man insisted must speak to him again.

That it is Eden the horses are bringing back, that they are rounding again "The Ring" so long broken by the prevailing forces of evil, the "half-a-dozen colts" among them make clear, since those colts are "new as if they had come from their own Eden" (247). But that is not all. The horses come not only to restore innocence. They come to serve, to work, to set going again another world of time which from the first will be irradiated with eternity. For that "free servitude" they offer, that bearing of man's burdens, evokes the figure of Christ, as C. B. Cox points out in an explication of this poem in *Critical Survey*.[23] And because Christ had come eventually for Muir to represent the turning-point of time for everyone, the point where the timeless intersected with time and transformed it, the implied presence of Christ here, at the start of a new world, implies as well the start of a better world. "Our life is changed," conclude the speakers in the poem; "their coming our beginning." In the life that begins now for these survivors, that is, the world of day will fit the world of night and dream; the light of the "clear unfallen world" of Orkney will be visible in Glasgow.

For this new beginning to be made, however, the holocaust had first to be endured. Once again, accordingly, Muir affirms the simultaneous attraction and opposition of paradox, the impossible reconciliation of the irreconcilable. End and beginning here are one. Death and life, good and evil, are here woven together into a vision at once breathtaking in its promise and chilling in its terror. Yet the terror must be accepted, the whole body of Muir's poetry maintains, if the promise is to be realized. For only through immersion in darkness, a knowledge of suffering and evil, can man experience rebirth into light and joy. We would prefer not to have the light and joy on these terms, but Muir, who was a realist as well as a visionary, knew that there are no other terms for us to choose. As a realist, furthermore, he would not turn aside from the cruelty, the violence, the barbarity of life as it has been and as it is today. By the dispensation of that mystery that still haunts us in our supposedly rational, computerized times, however, it is the miraculous fact that even in this brutal world the "blossoms of grief and charity" still flourish. Even in the polluted wasteland of the twentieth century, a man may see "a little tree/ Put out in pain a single bud/ That . . . does not fear the ultimate fire" (270); and this single bud justifies fire and terror and wrong.

To sustain such a vision in an increasingly spoiled world is not easy. As we have seen, Muir found himself through all his work again and again lapsing backward down the slope into the depths he had touched in "The Gate." Even in his last poems, not included in *One Foot in Eden* and published only in his final *Collected Poems*, there is the same division between light and dark, hope and desperation, joy and sorrow. "Ballad of Everyman" (290) and "Nightmare of Peace" (291), for example, which are probably different versions of the same, never-completed poem, transfer that image of endless conflict which Muir saw in "The Combat" to the human scene, with the important difference that decent, honest Everyman seems to have less staying power than the poor brown rag of an animal in the earlier poem. In the radiant "The Brothers" (272), on the other hand, Muir sees his two brothers, who died so long ago in torment and frustration, playing again on the green where they used to play, with all "The beauty and the buried grace" that was invisible then, now made manifest. In still other poems, such as "After 1984" (267), or "The Voices" (279), or even "The Last War" (282), in one way or another Muir seeks again to bring opposites together, as in that strange dream-story, "The Song" (257), he makes a song out of the pain of a great mythical wounded beast. For still, even in these latest poems, Muir is refusing to take a final position. He still resists any absolute. Yet always in the end it is the vision of reconciliation that remains dominant. However he many deny any absolute, Muir accepts paradox, at last, in an affirmation which includes everything that breathes, all that is, even the stones of our hovels and the dust of our refuse heaps, in an all-embracing warmth and compassion.

What is most important, that affirmation constitutes as well a major poetic statement. Quiet as Muir's voice may have been, his work as a whole is strong, serious, and humane, and charged moreover with overtones of that "vast area of life which science leaves in its original mystery." It speaks significantly of the things that matter most to us as human beings: of where we have come from, where we are going, and how we should deal with one another while we are here.

Notes

INTRODUCTION

1. "Notes," *Modern Poetry*, eds. Kimon Friar and John Malcolm Brinnin (New York, 1951), p. 524.

2. Cambridge, Mass., 1965, p. 21.

3. "Preface," *Collected Poems* of Edwin Muir (New York, 1965), p. 4.

4. *Essays on Literature and Society*, p. 95.

5. *Ibid.*, p. 121.

6. "The Poetry of Edwin Muir," *Hudson Review*, XIII (Winter 1960), 563.

7. "The True Legendary Sound: The Poetry and Criticism of Edwin Muir," *The Sewanee Review*, LXXV (April-June 1967), 318.

8. "The Circular Route," *Poetry*, LXXXIV (April 1954), 32.

9. "Edwin Muir," British Council Series, *Writers and Their Work*, No. 71 (London, 1956), p. 33.

10. New York, 1962, p. 117.

11. "In the Major Grain," *The New Republic*, CXXVII (July 21, 1952), 18.

12. *Barbarous Knowledge* (New York, 1967), p. 227.

13. LXXXVIII (September 1956), 395.

14. "Review of *Collected Poems* of Edwin Muir," *The Listener*, LXIII (May 26, 1960), 941.

15. Baltimore, Md., 1966, p. 469.
16. XLVII (December 1957), 286.
17. II (Spring 1965), 18.
18. Cambridge, Mass., 1962, p. 69.

CHAPTER ONE

1. *An Autobiography* (London, 1954), p. 14. In this chapter, the numbers in parentheses following quotations refer to pages of this book.
2. *Collected Poems*, p. 113.
3. *Ibid.*, p. 118.
4. *Belonging* (London, 1968), p. 54.
5. *Collected Poems*, p. 199.
6. T. S. Eliot, *The Complete Poems and Plays 1909-1950* (New York, 1962), p. 122.
7. *Collected Poems*, pp. 157-58.

CHAPTER TWO

1. *An Autobiography*, p. 208.
2. P. 193.
3. *First Poems* (New York, 1925), p. 9. In this chapter the numbers in parentheses following quoted material refer to pages of this book.
4. P. 33.
5. P. 224.
6. London, 1940, p. 263.
7. *An Autobiography*, p. 93.
8. *Ibid.*, p. 22.
9. *Ibid.*, p. 22.
10. London, 1932, p. 172.
11. *Ibid.*, pp. 173-75.
12. *An Autobiography*, p. 36.
13. *Ibid.*, p. 47.
14. *Ibid.*, p. 48.
15. *Ibid.*, p. 54.
16. *Ibid.*, p. 54.
17. P. 164.
18. *Ibid.*, p. 166.
19. P. 165.

20. *Ibid.*, p. 43.
21. *Ibid.*, p. 206.
22. "Introduction," *Golden Treasury of Scottish Poetry* (New York, 1941), p. xxiv.
23. New York, 1924, p. 15.
24. Edwin Muir, *Scott and Scotland* (London, 1936), p. 178.
25. Edwin Muir, *Scottish Journey* (London, 1935), p. 227.
26. *Scott and Scotland*, pp. 60-71.
27. *Scottish Journey*, p. 232.
28. *Scott and Scotland*, p. 181.
29. London, 1940, p. 260.
30. *An Autobiography*, p. 62.
31. *Collected Poems*, p. 36.

CHAPTER THREE

1. P. 223.
2. *Chorus of the Newly Dead* (London, 1926), p. 6. In this discussion, the numbers in parentheses after quoted material refer to pages of this book.
3. *An Autobiography*, p. 223.
4. New York, 1967, p. 101.
5. *An Autobiography*, p. 149.
6. Muir to Sydney Schiff, as quoted in Butter, p. 100.
7. *An Autobiography*, p. 201.
8. Muir to Schiff, as quoted in Butter, p. 104.
9. *An Autobiography*, p. 206.
10. *Ibid.* p. 205.
11. *Ibid.* p. 231.
12. *Ibid.* p. 222.
13. Butter, pp. 171-72.
14. *An Autobiography*, p. 240.
15. *Ibid.* p. 240.
16. *Essays on Literature and Society*, p. 122.
17. New York, 1929, p. 22.
18. *Scott and Scotland*, p. 74.
19. *Collected Poems*, p. 39. In this and the following chapters, numbers in parentheses following quoted material refer to pages of this book.
20. *An Autobiography*, p. 92.
21. *Ibid.* p. 205.

22. *The Modern Poet* (London, 1938), pp. 168-70.
23. *An Autobiography*, p. 150.
24. Muir, "Note," as quoted in Butter, p. 125.
25. *The Three Brothers* (New York, 1931), p. 270.
26. *Ibid.* p. 266.
27. *Ibid.* p. 240.
28. *Essays on Literature and Society*, p. 49.
29. *The Estate of Poetry*, p. 9.
30. *Transition* (New York, 1926), p. 186.
31. P. 46.
32. *Ibid.* p. 47.

CHAPTER FOUR

1. "Edwin Muir," *Encounter*, XV (December 1960), 49.
2. *Latitudes* (New York, 1924), p. 101.
3. Muir to Spender, as quoted in Butter, p. 196.
4. Muir, "Author's Note," *Journeys and Places* (London, 1937), p. viii.
5. London, 1935, pp. 212-13.
6. P. 121.
7. "Author's Note," *Journeys and Places*, p. vii.
8. *Essays on Literature and Society*, p. 90.
9. *An Autobiography*, p. 55.
10. *Essays on Literature and Society*, p. 95.
11. *Ibid.* p. 88.
12. *Barbarous Knowledge*, p. 228.
13. London, 1966, p. 211.
14. *Ibid.* p. 212.
15. *The Estate of Poetry*, p. 31.
16. V (February 1963), 6.
17. As quoted in Butter, p. 141.
18. *Ibid.* p. 141.
19. *Essays on Literature and Society*, p. 122.
20. *First Poems*, p. 21.
21. "Between the Tiger's Paws," *Kenyon Review*, XXI (Summer 1959), 430.

CHAPTER FIVE

1. "Symbolic Action in a Poem by Keats," *Accent*, IV (Autumn 1943), 31.

2. *An Autobiography*, p. 180.

3. *Ibid.* p. 181.

4. *New Poems*, ed. J. B. Leishman (New York, 1964), p. 108.

5. As quoted in Butter, p. 200.

6. Edinburgh, 1958, p. 337.

7. *An Autobiography*, p. 56.

8. *The Present Age* (New York, 1940), p. 84.

9. "Between the Tiger's Paws," *Kenyon Review*, XXI (Summer 1959), 428.

10. London, 1949, p. 27.

11. P. 33.

12. "Alice in Wonderland: The Child as Swain," *English Pastoral Poetry* (London, 1938), p. 264.

13. *First Poems*, p. 9.

14. New York, 1962, pp. 85-87.

15. *The Three Brothers*, p. 266.

16. *Ibid.* pp. 12-13.

17. *Ibid.* pp. 15-16.

18. *Ibid.* p. 272.

19. Butter, p. 155.

20. Edwin Muir, *The Story and the Fable* (London, 1940), p. 240.

21. *An Autobiography*, p. 64.

22. "The Achievement of Edwin Muir," *The Massachusetts Review*, II (Winter 1961), 254.

23. As quoted in Butter, p. 198.

24. *Essays on Literature and Society*, p. 49.

25. *Ibid.* p. 43.

26. *An Autobiography*, p. 52.

27. *Ibid.* p. 52.

28. *Ibid.* p. 53.

29. *Ibid.* p. 53.

30. *Ibid.* p. 53.

31. *Essays on Literature and Society*, p. 154.

32. *An Autobiography*, p. 179.

33. March 27, 1943, 154.

CHAPTER SIX

1. *An Autobiography*, p. 206.

2. *Ibid.* p. 36.

3. *Ibid.* p. 46.
4. *Ibid.* p. 47.
5. *Op. Cit.* pp. 204-5.
6. P. 56.
7. P. 49.
8. Ann Arbor, Mich., 1964.
9. New York, 1924, p. 143.
10. As quoted in Butter, pp. 186-87.
11. Butter, pp. 187-88.
12. *An Autobiography*, p. 18.
13. *Ibid.* p. 46.
14. "Edwin Muir," *Review*, V (February 1963), 8.

CHAPTER SEVEN

1. New York, 1931, p. 231.
2. As quoted in Butter, pp. 215-16.
3. *Essays on Literature and Society*, p. 94.
4. "Four British Poets," *Kenyon Review*, XV (Summer 1953), 469-70.
5. Ann Arbor, Mich., p. 69.
6. *Duino Elegies*, eds. J. B. Leishman and Stephen Spender (New York, 1939), p. 38.
7. "Edwin Muir," *Encounter*, XV (December 1960), 51.
8. As quoted in Butter, *Edwin Muir* (New York, 1962), p. 84.
9. "Enacted in a Distant Isle," *Hudson Review*, VIII (Summer 1955), 309.
10. *Edwin Muir* (Cardiff, 1961), p. 22.
11. P. 65.
12. *Ibid.* p. 65.
13. *Ibid.* p. 107.
14. *Ibid.* p. 108.
15. *Ibid.* p. 107.
16. *Essays on Literature and Society*, p. 43.
17. *Ibid.* p. 45.
18. *Ibid.* p. 49.
19. *An Autobiography*, p. 114.
20. *Ibid.* p. 234.
21. *Ibid.* p. 114.
22. As quoted in *Essays on Literature and Society*, p. 102.

23. *Ibid.* p. 102.
24. *An Autobiography*, p. 166.

CHAPTER EIGHT

1. P. 315.
2. *Essays on Literature and Society*, p. 151.
3. XIII (Winter 1960), 553-54.
4. LII (October 1963), 540.
5. *Random House Dictionary*, Unabridged.
6. "Verse," *The New Yorker*, XXXII (October 6, 1956), 179.
7. "Edwin Muir and the Problem of Evil," *Critical Quarterly*, VI (Autumn 1964), 246.
8. Muir to Eliot, as quoted in Butter, *Edwin Muir: Man and Poet*, p. 252.
9. Eliot to Muir, as quoted in Butter, p. 252.
10. *An Autobiography*, p. 278.
11. *Ibid.* p. 247.
12. *Ibid.* p. 248.
13. *Essays on Literature and Society*, p. 102.
14. *An Autobiography*, p. 278.
15. *Ibid.* p. 278.
16. *Ibid.* p. 210.
17. New York, 1962, p. 89.
18. P. 101.
19. *Critical Quarterly*, VI (Autumn 1964), 246.
20. *The Student's Milton*, ed. Frank Patterson (New York, 1934), p. 738.
21. *Ibid.* p. 749.
22. "Preface," Muir's *Collected Poems*, p. 5.
23. I (1962), 21.

Bibliography

Works by Edwin Muir

Verse
  First Poems. New York, 1925.
  Chorus of the Newly Dead. London, 1926.
  Variations on a Time Theme. London, 1934.
  Journeys and Places. London, 1937.
  The Narrow Place. London, 1943.
  The Voyage. London, 1946.
  The Labyrinth. London, 1949.
  Collected Poems, 1921-1951, ed. J. C. Hall. London, 1952; New York, 1957.
  One Foot in Eden. New York, 1956.
  Collected Poems, 2nd ed., with preface by T. S. Eliot. New York, 1965.

Prose
  We Moderns: Enigmas and Guesses. New York, 1920.
  Latitudes. New York, 1924.
  Transition. New York, 1926.
  The Marionette. London, 1927.
  The Structure of the Novel. London, 1928.
  John-Knox—Portrait of a Calvinist. New York, 1929.

The Three Brothers. New York, 1931.

Poor Tom. London, 1932.

Scottish Journey. London, 1935.

Scott and Scotland. London, 1936.

The Present Age. (*Introductions to English Literature,* ed. Bonamy Dobrée, Vol. V) New York, 1940.

The Story and the Fable. London, 1940.

An Autobiography. London, 1954.

Essays on Literature and Society, 2nd ed. Cambridge, Mass., 1965.

The Estate of Poetry. Cambridge, Mass., 1962.

Prose by Muir Published in Other Books or Periodicals

"Introductory Note," *The Great Wall of China,* by Franz Kafka, trans. Willa and Edwin Muir. London, 1933.

"Franz Kafka," in *A Franz Kafka Miscellany.* New York, 1940.

"Introductory Note," *The Castle,* by Franz Kafka, trans. Willa and Edwin Muir. New York, 1947.

"Translating from the German," in *On Translation,* ed. Reuben A. Brower. Cambridge, Mass., 1959.

"Some Letters of Edwin Muir," *Encounter,* XXVI (January 1966), 3-11.

Works about Edwin Muir and related works

Blackmur, R. P. "Edwin Muir: Between the Tiger's Paws," *Kenyon Review,* XXI (1959), 419-36.

Bogan, Louise. "Verse," *New Yorker,* XXXII (October 1956), 178-79.

Brown, George Mackay. "Edwin Muir," *Gambit* (Spring 1959), 12-14.

———. *An Orkney Tapestry,* London, 1969.

Bruce, George. "Edwin Muir: Poet," *Saltire Review,* VI (1959), 12-16.

Burke, Kenneth. "Symbolic Action in a Poem by Keats," *Accent,* IV (Autumn 1943), 30-42.

Butter, P. H. *Edwin Muir.* New York, 1962.

———. *Edwin Muir: Man and Poet.* New York, 1967.

Carruth, Hayden. "An Appreciation of Muir," *Prairie Schooner,* XXXII (1958), 148-53.

————. "Edwin Muir's *Autobiography*," *Poetry*, LXXXVII (October 1955), 50-52.

————. "The Separate Splendours: Homage to Edwin Muir," *Poetry*, LXXXVIII (September 1956), 389-93.

Cazamian, Louis. "Edwin Muir et le Temps," *Etudes Anglaises*, V (August 1952), 236-38.

Cecil, Lord David and Allen Tate, eds. *Modern Verse in English 1900-1950*. New York, 1958.

Cohen, J. M. *Poetry of This Age: 1908-1958*. London, 1959.

Cox, C. B. "Edwin Muir's 'The Horses,'" *Critical Survey*, I (1962), 19-21.

Craig, David. *Scottish Literature and the Scottish People*. London, 1961.

Daiches, David. *The Present Age in British Literature*. Bloomington, Ind., 1958.

Drake, Leah Bodine. "New Voices in Poetry," *Atlantic Monthly*, CXCIX (June 1957), 75-76.

Duval, K. D. and Sydney Goodsir Smith, eds. *Hugh MacDiarmid, A Festschrift*. Edinburgh, 1962.

Eberhart, Richard. "The Middle Way," *Poetry*, LXXV (January 1950), 239-42.

Eliot, T. S. "Edwin Muir," *The Listener*, 1835, May 28, 1964, 872. Reprinted as Preface to *Collected Poems*, New York, 1965.

Eliot, T. S. "Mr. Edwin Muir," *The Times* (London), January 7, 1959, 14b.

Emig, Janet. "The Articulate Breath," *English Journal*, LII (October 1963), 540-41.

Empson, William. *English Pastoral Poetry*. London, 1938.

Fowler, Helen. "To Be in Time: the Experience of Edwin Muir," *Approach*, VIII (1961), 11-18.

Fraser, G. S. "The Inward Transformation," *New Statesman and Nation*, XXXVIII (July 16, 1949), 75-76.

Fraser, G. S. "Poetry," *The Year's Work in Literature, 1949*, ed. John Lehmann. London. 1950.

Friar, Kimon. "The Circular Route," *Poetry*, LXXXIV (April 1954), 27-32.

Friar, Kimon and Malcolm Brinnin. *Modern Poetry*. New York, 1951.

Fulton, Robin. "The Reputation of Edwin Muir," *Glasgow Review*, II (1965), 17-19.

Gabriel, Marcel. "Edwin Muir," *Etudes Anglaises*, XIII (January 1960), 10-25.

Galler, David. "Edwin Muir," *Poetry*, XCIV (August 1959), 330-33.

Garber, Fred. "Edwin Muir's Heraldic Mode," *Twentieth Century Literature*, XII (1966), 96-103.

Gardner, Helen. *Edwin Muir*. (W. D. Thomas Memorial Lecture) Cardiff, 1961.

Gill, Bernard. "Sunset Light: A Poet's Last Days," *The Western Humanities Review*, XIV (1960), 283-88.

Glicksberg, Charles. "Edwin Muir: Zarathustra in Scotch Dress," *Arizona Quarterly*, XII (Autumn 1956), 225-39.

"Good Man, Good Poet?" Anon. rev., *Times Literary Supplement*, July 6, 1967, 601.

Goodwin, K. L. *The Influence of Ezra Pound*. London, 1966.

———. "Muir's 'The Toy Horse,'" *The Explicator*, XXIII (September 1964), Item 6.

Graves, Robert. "Piping Peter and Others," *The Nation and Athenaeum*, XXXIX (August 28, 1926), 617.

———. "Review of *First Poems*," *The Nation and Athenaeum*, XXXVII (May 2, 1925), 142.

Gregory, Horace. "The Excitement that Wells from Edwin Muir's Poems," *New York Times Book Review*, April 5, 1952, 1, 17.

———. "Speaking of Books: Edwin Muir," *New York Times Book Review*, February 27, 1966, 2, 40.

———. "To Explain is Not to Understand," *New York Times Book Review*, March 11, 1962, 5, 24.

Grice, Fred. "The Poetry of Edwin Muir," *Essays in Criticism*, V (July 1955), 243-52.

Grieve, Christopher. "Contemporary Scottish Poetry," *The Nineteenth Century and After*, CVI (October 1929), 534-44.

Gross, Harvey. *Sound and Form in Modern Poetry*. Ann Arbor, Mich., 1964.

Hall, J. C. *Edwin Muir*. British Council Series, Writers and Their Work: No. 71. London, 1956.

Hamburger, Michael. "Edwin Muir," *Encounter*, XV (December 1960), 46-53.

Hassan, Ihab H. "Of Time and Emblematic Reconciliation. Notes on the Poetry of Edwin Muir," *South Atlantic Quarterly*, LVIII (Summer 1959), 427-39.

Hoffman, Daniel. *Barbarous Knowledge*. New York, 1967.

Hollander, Robert. A Textual and Bibliographical Study of the Poems of Edwin Muir. Unpublished Ph.D. thesis, Columbia, 1962.

Holloway, John. "Enacted in a Distant Isle," *Hudson Review*, VIII (Summer 1955), 308-13.

———. "The Poetry of Edwin Muir," *Hudson Review*, XIII (1960), 550-67.

Hough, Graham. "Review of *Collected Poems* of Edwin Muir," *The Listener*, LXIII (May 26, 1960), 941.

Howard, Richard. "British Chronicle," *Poetry*, CVIII (September 1966), 399-400.

Jennings, Elizabeth. "The Living Dead—VII: Edwin Muir as Poet and Allegorist," *London Magazine*, VII (March 1960), 43-56.

———. "Review of *Edwin Muir* by P. H. Butter," *The Listener*, LXVIII (November 22, 1962), 871.

Joselyn, Sister M. "Herbert and Muir: Pilgrims of their Age," *Renascence*, XV (1963), 127-32.

Kazin, Alfred. "Review of *An Autobiography*," *New York Times Book Review*, March 13, 1955, 4.

Kinsley, James, ed. *Scottish Poetry: A Critical Survey*. London, 1955.

"The Listener's Book Chronicle, *One Foot in Eden*." Anon. rev., *The Listener*, LVI (July 26, 1956), 135.

MacCaig, Norman. "Review of Edwin Muir's *Collected Poems*," *The Spectator*, CCIV (April 22, 1960), 582.

MacDiarmid, Hugh, ed. *The Golden Treasury of Scottish Poetry*. New York, 1941.

"Man's Conflicts," Anon. rev., *Times Literary Supplement*, XLV (May 11, 1946), 225.

Mellown, Elgin W. *Bibliography of the Writings of Edwin Muir*. University, Alabama, 1964.

———. "The Development of a Criticism: Edwin Muir and Franz Kafka," *Comparative Literature*, XVI (1964), 310-21.

Merton, Thomas. "The True Legendary Sound: The Poetry and Criticism of Edwin Muir," *The Sewanee Review*, LXXV (April–June 1967), 317-24.

Merwin, W. S. "Four British Poets," *Kenyon Review*, XV (1953), 461-76.

"A Metaphysical Poet." Anon. rev., *Times Literary Supplement*, XL (March 27, 1943), 154.

Mills, R. J., Jr. "Eden's Gate: The Later Poetry of Edwin Muir," *The Personalist*, XLIV (1963), 58-78.

Mills, R. J., Jr. "Edwin Muir: A Speech from Darkness Grown, *Accent*, XIX (1959), 50-70.

Moore, Geoffrey. *Poetry To-Day*. London, 1958.

Morgan, Edwin. "Edwin Muir," *The Review*, V (February 1963), 3-10.

Muir, Willa. *Living With Ballads*. London, 1967.

———. *Belonging*. London, 1968.

Murphy, Gwendolen, ed. *The Modern Poet*. London, 1938.

Peschmann, Hermann. "Edwin Muir: A Return to Radical Innocence," *English*, XII (1959), 168-71.

Porteous, Alexandra. "The Status of Edwin Muir," *Quadrant*, VII (1963), 80-82.

Raine, Kathleen. "Edwin Muir: An Appreciation," *The Texas Quarterly*, IV (1961), 233-45.

———. "In the Major Grain," *New Republic*, CXXVII (June 21, 1952), 17-18.

———. "The Journey from Eden," *New Statesman and Nation*, LIX (June, 1960), 595-96.

———. "A Poet of the Northern Isles," *New Statesman and Nation*, XLIV (July 1952), 48-49.

———. "Poetry," *The Year's Work in Literature, 1950*. London, 1951.

Read, Herbert. "Edwin Muir," *Encounter*, XII (April 1959), 71-73.

Richart, Bette. "A Kind of Grief," *Commonweal*, LXIV (August 3, 1966), 449.

Riggs, Thomas, Jr. "Recent Poetry—A Miscellany," *The Nation*, CLXXVI (May 2, 1953), 376-78.

Rosenthal, M. L. "Edwin Muir: 1887-1959," *The Nation*, CLXXXVIII (April 25, 1959), 392-93.

———. "Tradition and Transition," *The Nation*, CLXXXIII (November 3, 1956), 372-74.

Ross, Alan. *Poetry 1945-1950*. London, 1951.

Sanders, Gerald, John H. Nelson, and M. L. Rosenthal. *Chief Modern Poets of England and America*, 4th edn. New York, 1962.

Scholten, Martin. "The Humanism of Edwin Muir," *College English*, XXI (March 1960), 322-26.

Scott, Alexander. "Scots in English," *Glasgow Review*, II (1965), 12-16.

Scott-Craig, T. S. K. "The Toy Horse," *The Explicator*, XXIV (1966), Item 62.

Silkin, Jon. "The Fields Far and Near," *Poetry*, LXXXVIII (September 1956), 393-95.

Spender, Stephen. *Poetry Since 1939*. London, 1946.

Stanford, Derek. "Edwin Muir (1887-1959), *Contemporary Review*, CXIX (March 1959), 145-47.

———. "A Study of the Work of Edwin Muir," *The Month*, V (April 1951), 237-44.

Summers, Joseph H. "The Achievement of Edwin Muir," *The Massachusetts Review*, II (Winter 1961), 240-61.

———. "Edwin Muir," *Books Abroad*, XXXIV (1960), 123.

Tindall, William York. *Forces in Modern British Literature*. New York, 1956.

Tomlinson, Charles. "Poetry Today," *The Modern Age*, ed. Boris Ford. (Pelican Guide to English Literature 7) Baltimore, Md., 1966.

Tschumi, Raymond. *Thought in Twentieth Century Poetry*. London, 1951.

Van Doren, Mark. "First Glances," *The Nation*, CXX (June 24, 1925), 719.

Watson, J. R. "Edwin Muir and the Problem of Evil," *Critical Quarterly*, VI (1964), 231-49.

Whittemore, Reed. "Five Old Masters and their Sensibilities," *Yale Review*, XLVII (December 1957), 281-88.

Wittig, Kurt. *The Scottish Tradition in Literature*. Edinburgh, 1958.

Index